Education in the Eighties

Education in the Eighties

The Central Issues

Edited by
Brian Simon and William Taylor

BATSFORD ACADEMIC AND EDUCATIONAL LTD

Batsford Academic and Educational Ltd
4 Fitzhardinge Street
London W1H 0AH

First published 1981
© Brian Simon, William Taylor 1981

Photoset in Monophoto Plantin by
Servis Filmsetting Ltd, Manchester

Printed in Great Britain by
Billing & Son Ltd
London, Guildford & Worcester
British Library Cataloguing in Publication Data

Education in the eighties.
1. Education – Great Britain
I. Simon, Brian   II. Taylor, William, b.1930–
370'.941   LA632

ISBN 0 7134 3679 4 cased
ISBN 0 7134 3680 8 limp

Contents

The Contributors

WILLIAM TAYLOR has been Director of the University of London Institute of Education since 1973. He was previously Professor of Education in the University of Bristol and part-time Research Adviser to the Department of Education and Science. He is author and editor of a number of books on teacher education and educational administration.

HAROLD ENTWISTLE is Professor of Education at Concordia University, Montreal. He was previously on the staff of the University of Manchester Department of Education. He is the author of many books on educational issues, the most recent being concerned with the educational ideas of the Italian marxist leader, Antonio Gramsci.

ALAN LITTLE is Lewisham Professor of Social Administration in the University of London, his chair being held at Goldsmiths' College. One time Head of the Research and Statistics Unit of the Inner London Education Authority, he has also been Director of Research for the Community Relations Commission and a lecturer at the London School of Economics.

JOHN GRAY is a Lecturer in Education at the University of Sheffield. He trained and worked at the Harvard Center for Educational Policy Research and Sussex University prior to becoming a Research Fellow at the Centre for Educational Sociology, Edinburgh University. He is co-author of a forthcoming empirical study of post-war secondary education in Scotland and has particular research interests in issues relating to school and teacher effectiveness.

NIGEL GRANT is Professor of Education at the University of Glasgow, having previously been Reader in Educational Studies at Edinburgh. He is a specialist in Comparative Education and the author of a number of books and papers on education in the USSR, Eastern Europe and the British Isles, and on the problems of minority groups and multiculturalism.

DENIS LAWTON is Deputy Director of the University of London Institute of Education, having for some years prior to his appointment in 1978 been Head of the Curriculum Studies Department of the Institute. The most recent of his many books on curriculum matters is *The Politics of the Curriculum* (1980).

BRIAN SIMON recently retired from his Chair in Education at the University of Leicester. He is the author of several books on the history of education as well as in the fields of psychology and contemporary educational issues.

MICHAEL ERAUT is Reader in Education at the University of Sussex. He has recently helped to direct the studies in accountability carried out at that University with the support of the Social Science Research Council.

JOHN NISBET is Professor of Education at the University of Aberdeen. He has been Chairman of the Educational Research Board of the Social Science Research Council, and currently edits *Studies in Higher Education*.

PAT WHITE is Senior Lecturer in Philosophy of Education at the University of London Institute of Education. She has written a number of articles on political education. At present she is writing a book on the relevance of recent developments in democratic theory for issues like political education, parents' rights and equality in education.

D.A. HOWELL is Senior Lecturer in Educational Administration at the University of London Institute of Education. He worked with George Baron on a pioneering study of school governing bodies, and his current research interests are in educational decision making at both central and local levels.

GABRIEL CHANAN is editor with the National Foundation for Educational Research. He wrote *What School is For* (with Linda Gilchrist) in 1974 and has since continued to contribute to curriculum debate through various publications. He is Chairman of Windsor Arts Centre and has also published stories and novellas.

JOHN WATTS was given his first teaching appointment in 1953 at Sawston Village College by Henry Morris. In 1964 he was chosen by Jersey to open its first community school, Les Quennevais. Between headships he was a lecturer at the University of London Institute of Education and, in 1972, became Principal of Countesthorpe College in Leicestershire.

KIM TAYLOR is Head of Educational Programme Services at the Independent Broadcasting Authority. He was formerly Head of Sevenoaks School and was involved in some of the early curriculum development work of the Nuffield Foundation. He has also worked as a consultant to the Organisation for Economic Cooperation and Development.

Introduction

Collections of educational essays serve many different purposes. Some put between hard covers papers and articles that have already appeared in scattered form elsewhere, in journals or conference proceedings. Others enable a number of different authors to contribute from their distinctive viewpoints to the discussion of a single more-or-less closely focused issue. It is even alleged that some represent conspiracies between academics with a duty to publish but without the ability or the energy to prepare books of their own. The chapters that follow fall into none of these categories. Each has been written specially for this volume. Each reflects the personal interests and concerns of its author. The unifying theme is the identification and discussion of issues likely to feature in discussions·of educational policies in the 1980s. Few of these issues are completely new. The problems of contraction, work and leisure, race, equality and national identity that feature in the contributions to Part One have been around for some time. But as the various authors show, the form in which they will manifest themselves over the next decade is likely to take its colouration from economic, social and political conditions very different from those of the 1960s and 1970s.

The consequences of demographic downturn are often discussed in terms of school closures, possible contraction in curricula choice and diminishing career opportunities for teachers. All these are important, but as Taylor shows in Chapter 1, the facts and the form of contraction are not simply dictated by demography. That falling rolls constitute a problem rather than an opportunity has much to do with the context of attitudes towards education and the part it plays in the life and growth of capitalist society. The views that we hold about the relation between education and social change, and the directions that might be taken by the latter, powerfully influence the extent to which educational investment is seen as a desirable priority.

In the chapter that follows Entwistle considers how and why our expectations of the part that knowledge might play in technological development have changed, and the possible relation between education, work and leisure in the eighties. He contrasts the effects of *mechanisation* with those of *automation*; it is the latter, a process made

9

possible by the power and sophistication of computers and electronic control systems, that will influence the shape of work and leisure opportunities in the eighties. Demand for the services of the highly qualified seems unlikely to diminish. There will remain many jobs, mainly of a less-skilled and often unpleasant kind, that no conceivable computer technology is likely to replace. In between, many of the tasks on which the majority of the working population have hitherto been engaged will be eliminated or transformed by new technologies. Entwistle underlines the fatuity of the assumption that greater all-round affluence will simply free more time for education and leisure at the beginning, in the course of and at the end of a shorter and less-intensive working life. Leisure cannot be thought of sensibly except in relation to work, and the vocational education of the future will need to include political, aesthetic and moral education, not merely the acquisition of technical or professional skills.

Entwistle shows that the challenge of the micro-chip in the eighties is as much political and social as technical and economic. One critical aspect of the political and social dilemma of the period will be our ability to work towards a genuinely multi-racial society, successfully to counter the tendencies towards disaffection and alienation experienced by many members of non-white communities. Such tendencies are unlikely to be restrained by the employment trends characteristic of recession and structural change. In Chapter 3 Alan Little argues for a more positive race relations policy, one which recognises the problems for education created by ethnic concentration, newness, variety of needs, social disadvantage, the possibility of white backlash, the demands of minorities themselves, under-functioning at school and both overt and covert discrimination. Central government, local authorities, teacher-preparing institutions and specialised bodies have failed individually and collectively – the latter in part because of ineffectual co-ordination of their efforts – to devise satisfactory policies for multi-racial education. Yet without such policies the problems of the eighties in this area are likely to be even more serious than some pessimistic critics have suggested.

If success has yet to be achieved in devising and implementing policies of multi-racial education, this is even more true in respect of the press towards greater equality in educational provision and outcomes that has been one of the central pillars of educational effort for more than half a century. Given the modest nature of the gains that have been made, it is proper to question just how real these efforts have been, as does John Gray in Chapter 4. Recent surveys, on which he draws, show that the working-class handicap is as real as ever it was. Studies of educational effectiveness which take the school as their unit of description show some of the ways in which this handicap is compounded by experience of schooling between 5 and 16, and underline the limitations of positive discrimination as a policy imperative. Further attempts to improve equality of access and of outcome will need to rest upon a broader base of knowledge than was the case in the sixties and seventies, one which takes full account of the unintended and sometimes counter-productive effects of action programmes.

To the policy issues for the eighties posed by contraction, work and leisure, race and equality can be added those which arise from our position within the European Economic Community and the ways in which we deal with problems of national and regional identity within Britain. In Chapter 5 Nigel Grant argues that the model of unity as the gradual relinquishing of national peculiarities, and the eventual emergence of a common educational system is much too simple. The dimensions of difference are more numerous and complicated than is often recognised. The realities of internal cultural heterogeneity are too strong to be ignored. In Grant's words, 'we are all minorities now'. Educational and official policies which fail to take this into account are unlikely to avoid conflict. 'It is perfectly possible to be (say) human, "western" European, British, Scots and Highland simultaneously and to endow these roles with meanings that reinforce rather than contradict each other.'

Contraction, work, race, equality and nationalism all pose central questions for educational policy makers in the eighties. The issues dealt with in the chapters that make up Part Two are equally central, but they have more to do with the curriculum, the pedagogy and the means of assessment that are likely to be used in our schools. The first three chapters in this part directly address these issues.

During the seventies the curriculum came into much greater prominence than in previous decades, due in part to anxieties about the quality of educational provision and a feeling that neither individual families nor the nation as a whole were receiving a fair return on their educational investments. Such feelings and anxieties had much to do with the economic and political characteristics of the period, but by the end of the decade they had spurred central and local governments into much more explicit interventions in respect of the content and organisation of schooling than had been customary during most of the inter-war and post II World War period. Whether such interventions have a positive or negative effect is likely critically to depend on the assumptions they embody about the organisation of knowledge and the nature and sequence of learning. In Chapter 6 Denis Lawton shows how dangerously easy it will be to espouse the wrong kind of curriculum model, especially when, in the form of a core curriculum and apparently clear-cut objectives, such a model satisfies the requirements of a narrowly conceived demand for greater accountability. He recommends that instead, the idea of a *common curriculum*, based upon an adequately thought-through cultural analysis, should permeate the planning of secondary education in the eighties. Such an approach is capable of meeting criticisms of cafeteria-style elective systems that have led to the demand for a core curriculum, but avoids the narrowness and specificity that the latter would almost certainly impose.

It could be argued that a common curriculum requires a coherent pedagogy, of a kind that has so far failed to develop in Britain. Brian Simon states the case for such a pedagogy in Chapter 7, linking its absence with the lack of regard for professional training that existed among elite schools in the nineteenth century (and still to some extent today), with the stress on individualisation that characterised the progressive education movement between the wars, and the hold that psychometrists exercised for so long on the development of educational studies. He goes on to suggest that without a properly conceived science of teaching, relevant to a unified rather than a divided system of secondary education, we are unlikely to be successful in meeting the economic and technological challenges of the eighties.

Curriculum, pedagogy – and assessment. In Chapter 8 Michael Eraut examines some recent developments in evaluation and account-ability, terms that came into common currency in Britain only in the mid-seventies, but which represent movements likely to be a more-or-less permanent aspect of future policy making. The discussion of standards of attainment has been clouded by political considerations. During the next ten years evidence will be available from the periodic surveys of the Assessment of Performance Unit and more sophisti-cated analyses of public examination results. It seems doubtful, however, even if this evidence shows steady improvement, that this will satisfy those who wish to blame the schools for all the ills of society. Despite efforts to avoid undesirable back-wash effects on the curriculum and teaching styles from APU-type exercises ('teaching to the test'), any extension of regular testing at local authority level, especially where the individual school is used as a unit of analysis, is unlikely to be without consequences for what goes on in the classroom. Eraut offers a number of alternative ways of giving parents and citizens the information they legitimately require about the performance of schools, designed to minimise negative back-wash effects.

The importance of an improved knowledge base for decision-making is a recurring theme in the chapters that make up the rest of Part Two, and in Chapter 9 John Nisbet considers how educational research may in future contribute to such a base. It can only do so if we get away from naïve conceptions of the purposes and potential of educational research such as have featured so strongly in the educational debates of the seventies. The impact of research on policy and practice is real and important, but seldom direct. Instead, research findings help to shape our perceptions of educational reality and the concepts by means of which we interpret such reality. They influence aspirations, motivation, the climate of opinion and our 'vision of the achievable'. This is not to under-rate the importance of the scientific approach to educational problems, nor to deny that some research has an early and decisive effect on decision-making (not always of a kind later investigation shows to have been justified or desirable). It *is* to accept that educational research takes many different forms, and to look to it for 'answers' to value-laden problems creates expectations impossible of fulfilment.

The significance and pervasiveness of such values are brought out clearly in Pat White's discussion of the prospects for political education that constitutes Chapter 10. During the late seventies, against the background of an apparent retreat from rationality in many aspects of political life, and fears in some quarters for the future of democracy, pressure built up for more time and attention to be devoted to political education within the school curriculum. Mrs White argues such explicit political education cannot be thought of without reference to the influence that the organisation of school life itself exercises on the attitudes and behaviour of students. There are many opportunities for schools to embody in their own practice the principles of a genuinely participative democracy. During the eighties we should be 'determining in a non-arbitrary, rationally defensible way how we ought to be using the organisation of the school as part of political education'.

This is not the only question affecting government and management of schools during the eighties. The report of Lord Taylor's Committee *A New Partnership for our Schools* (1977) is still receiving active consideration, and the next few years may see substantial shifts in the extent to which parents, citizens, teachers and pupils are involved in the formal management of schooling. In Chapter 11 David Howell shows how far we have come in this respect since 1944, and indicates some of the directions that future policy making may take, particularly in reconciling such apparently conflicting objectives as autonomy and accountability.

The final trio of chapters points towards some of the ways in which the coming decade may see a redefinition of certain familiar notions of what constitutes education. In Chapter 12 Gabriel Chanan defends the case for maintaining and encouraging many alternative forms of educational provision, and disputes the possibility and desirability of reinstating (if it ever existed) a single consensual framework for curricula decision making. In his view, it 'should not be thought that a drive to centralisation in the name of standards or national needs will necessarily lead to any closer fit between education and the real needs of adult life'. Only by emphasising diversity, rather than a 'common core' are we likely to meet the diverse needs of a 'community of complementary people, not a mass of interchangeable individuals'.

The idea of community also features strongly in Chapter 13, in which John Watts looks at some of the contrasting styles by means of which community education has been approached in the past and considers the possibilities for developing the tradition of such work in conditions of the eighties. Schools, far from being dead, may yet become the instruments that will embody the otherwise somewhat nebulous notions of recurrent education, life-long education and *éducation permanente* that were featured so strongly in educational discussion in the sixties and seventies.

Finally, Kim Taylor shows how the idea of what constitutes 'educational broadcasting' is currently undergoing major review and suggests some ways in which the media may contribute to education in the years ahead. Such contributions are likely to be influenced less by technological possibilities, such as remote-controlled video-taping, as by a cultural context which stresses accessibility and understanding, fitting what is offered to the known interests and habits of the viewers rather than imposing 'high culture'. If the outlines of policy for the educational use of TV in the eighties are already emerging, those for the employment of local radio have yet to be formulated.

It would be a fallacy to claim that these fourteen chapters identify all the questions likely to be central to educational policy-making in the eighties. Even given our editorial decision largely to exclude post-secondary education, there are obviously many other issues which could have been dealt with. We would contend, however, that it is unlikely that educational policy-makers will be able to avoid questions relating to contraction, work and leisure, race, equality, national identity; curriculum, pedagogy and assessment; educational research; the internal and external government of schools, alternative choices, education and the community and the role of the media in education – and we believe that on all these matters our contributors have things to say that are new and worthy of more detailed consideration. Our thanks are due to Dudley Fiske, Chief Education Officer at Manchester, who participated in the early stages of the planning of this volume; and to Sue Morrell who held the project together for many months, typing and retyping succeeding drafts of the chapters and assisting centrally with the compilation of the bibliography.

Brian Simon
William Taylor

PART ONE

1
Contraction in Context

William Taylor

Periods of rapid educational growth were not unknown before the twentieth century. For example, there was a furious spate of school-building following the enactment of the Education Act of 1870, spurred on by the desire of voluntary bodies to offer religious education to as large a proportion of the population as possible. From a very different base line, the third quarter of the twentieth century saw a rate of growth in education greater than that of any preceding twenty-five years. During the period after 1950, the demand from a larger population for longer and better schooling produced more students, more teachers and more schools. It stimulated demand for both established and 'new technology' products – buildings, books, audio-visual aids, desks, chalk and writing paper – attracted the attention of intellectuals in describing, analysing and evaluating what was going on, raised the demands that education made on the public purse, and established a pattern of expectation, the political and social costs of which are likely to be among the most troublesome features of the slower growth and, in some respects, actual decline that will character-ise the eighties.

These expectations of growth and all that goes with them are such a ubiquitous part of our contemporary consciousness that it is important to remind ourselves how rapid and recent it has all been.

At the beginning of the century there were 5.7 million children in grant-aided elementary and secondary schools in England and Wales. Half a century later the total had risen to only 5.8 million. True, over the same period the number of teachers nearly doubled, mainly due to improvements in pupil-teacher ratios. But over half the gain, from 48.3 in 1900 to 26.9 in 1950, occurred during the century's first decade. The remaining improvement, from 36.0 to 26.9, took forty years to accomplish.

Within the twenty-five years after 1950 the school population grew much more rapidly, reaching some nine million by 1977 (Ministry of

Education 1950; DES 1979a). All the children who will be in secondary schools in the eighties are already born. We know primary numbers only to the middle of the decade. Combining what we already know about secondary numbers and a set of assumptions about primary enrolments that seem reasonable on the basis of existing trends, it looks as if by 1990 total enrolments will be down from the 9 million at which they peaked in 1977 to not much more than 7 million. Primary totals reached 6.3 million in 1973. By 1987 they may very well be down to 4.5 million. Secondary enrolments have been falling since 1978, at which point they had reached 3.6 million. By 1990 they will be down to 2.5 million. Several things need to be said before examining the direct educational consequences of falling rolls.

Economics and attitudes
There is no *necessary* relationship between a fall in numbers and contraction in educational provision. The limits to growth in education have more to do with demand and with finance than with population downturn. If it was decided to establish minimum class sizes of say, twenty, to appoint large numbers of advisers and curriculum development specialists, to re-equip schools with the latest that micro-processer technology has to offer, to replace inadequate buildings, to keep 'uneconomic' institutions open for social and community reasons, to release large numbers of teachers for in-service training and refreshment and to pay for their substitutes in the classroom, to expand adult and continuing education, to encourage staying on at school beyond the compulsory leaving age and taking up of higher education places, then expansion would continue almost indefinitely. It is true, of course, that optimistic forecasts of the proportion of young people keen to extend their schooling beyond the compulsory limits of 5–16 and the numbers that would seek places in universities and polytechnics have proved to be misplaced. What is called the 'age participation ratio' (APR) of 18 to 21 year olds has in fact fallen. The scale of unsatisfied demand for adult and continuing education, although significant, is not such as to exercise a major impact on policy-making and the determination of social priorities.

But the demand for education is not an autonomous variable. The perceived rate of return to extra years of schooling may be significant, but it is not the only factor that influences individual decisions about staying on. Governments can influence demand by helping to create attitudes favourable to higher rates of participation, as well as by direct and indirect subsidy – higher student grants, the payment of allowances to 16–19 year olds. Why have they not done these things? Does it reflect a lack of conviction concerning the likely value to the individual and to the economy of making available substantial additional resources during the period of compulsory education?

The answer is partly to be found in anxieties about the inflationary effects of increases in public expenditure. The reduction of Government borrowing has been an imperative for recent Labour and Conservative administrations alike. But there is more to it than this. During the first half of the twentieth century Britain experienced three major wars. Each gave rise to strong movements in favour of post-war reform and educational improvement. Each fuelled humanitarian feelings, writings and actions which, combined with hopes of the economic advantage that would accrue from attending to the manpower needs of a developed technological society, encouraged educational investment.

The past thirty-five years have seen relative peace and deteriorating economic performance in the face of heightened international competition. There has been no collective purging through suffering in a common cause, in relation to which education might offer fresh hope of general progress. The consensus provided by war and its aftermath has been replaced by a sharper sense of social and economic difference, of forces in society that divide rather than those that unify. A better understanding by educationists of the limitations of their influence on individual and social development has been turned against them by sections of the public, and used to underline the alleged shortcomings of the schools. The cultural needs to which successful schools might minister, not just for a section of the population but for all, have failed to develop on the scale and in the direction hoped for by many of those who placed their faith in the extension of educational provision. The latter are inclined to blame television, radio, packaged entertainment and the press for pandering to the lowest common denominators of taste and failing to accept their responsibilities as forces of cultural enrichment in the educative society.

None of this helped to build consensus on educational goals, to enhance confidence in the missions and outcomes of schooling or to foster educational growth. Disenchantment did not set in overnight. But for so long as each year saw a larger number of children demanding admission to reception classes, and more being willing to stay in school past the minimum leaving age, then more teachers had to be trained, more cash to be found. Declining numbers have given the opportunity to test the priority of education's claim on the public purse, since fewer students to teach meant either that existing standards could be maintained at lower cost, or resources freed by reductions in numbers could be retained within education in order to achieve improvements in such standards. Faced with the insistent need to reduce public spending overall, plus demands for more money from other welfare sectors, Governments have decided to take out of education much of the money 'saved' by smaller numbers. Most of the problems that will have to be faced in the eighties as a concomitant of falling rolls are a product of such political and financial decisions, rather than of declining numbers as such.

Growth and capitalism

What are the links between growth or the absence of growth in education and the contemporary 'crisis of capitalism'? It is not difficult to recognise the extent to which many of the social and economic mechanisms of our society are dependent upon continued growth for their successful operation. Full employment; the availability of an incremental margin of benefit that can be redistributed in accordance with the contemporary commitment to equality; meeting expectations for continuous increase in command over goods and services and the ability to exercise control over nature for individual purposes; the sustenance of a 'modern' identity in which growth itself becomes the touchstone of national health and welfare, and an assurance that one is not slipping behind the international productive competition are all examples of such mechanisms.

Much of the debate about growth at this level is carried on in terms of contrasts drawn between Marxist values and praxis on the one hand, and those of capitalism on the other. This simplifying rhetoric is not particularly helpful when it comes to looking at the effects of population expansion, resource depletion and pollution on the future of industrialised societies. For it is the level of industrialisation, not the particular political arrangements of a society, that is critical as far as consequences of a diminished growth are concerned. The manager in Moscow and the manager in Manchester have many tasks and problems in common.

There are, therefore, good reasons for trying to shift the terms of the debate away from a simple opposition of capitalist and socialist values, structures and processes towards an analysis of the consequences for the culture of industrialised societies of a slowing down or reversal of growth.

The direct and indirect effects of falling rolls on education not only parallel those arising from the absence of growth in the economy but interact with them in a number of significant ways. For example, some of the more broad brush and speculative social and political scenarios of a non-growth society have important implications for the values instantiated in educational processes. There are those who believe any long-term failure to meet the expectations generated by growth will inevitably result in a more repressive form of government, whether of right or of left, in order to contain the pressures generated by dissatisfaction. On this view, the relaxation of social and political constraints on individual behaviour and action, whether in the autocratic State, or by the loss of the force of custom, tradition and convention in pluralist democratic societies, is dependent upon growth, upon the ability of the economic and political system to meet a steadily rising curve of demand. Harsher restraints, whether those of an existing police state or of a pluralistic society in one of its more conservative and moralistic phases, are alike the consequences of the lack of social lubrication that is otherwise provided by growth.

The question of whether growth is essential to the survival of capitalist forms of organisation has been much debated. There is a danger that those who wish to preserve the political freedoms associated with capitalism will find themselves, explicitly or implicitly, identifying actual or potential break-downs in the social and cultural pattern of capitalist societies as steps towards an inevitable socialism. By attributing a kind of oppositional legitimacy to the Marxist critique, we are led to attach meanings to social and political events that may themselves contribute to the fulfilment of such theses. As Hussain (1977) has emphasised, a state of crisis is the 'normal' condition of capitalism as far as a Marxist critique is concerned, periods of boom and success being merely transitory and atypical.

Another focus of interaction between social change and educational values can be seen in the impact on curriculum of those who stress the physical and ecological 'limits to growth'. Ecological lobbies, by interpreting the undeniable consequences of present-day utilisation rates of expendable resources in a way that fails to give enough attention to the effects of price and possibilities of substitution, have almost certainly affected the content of curriculum in the social studies, although the impact of such influence remains to be documented. It is difficult to believe that systematic teaching about the impracticability and the moral unacceptability of continued growth does not have some kind of effect on individual values and aspirations, and thus on the extent to which such growth features in policies for and the outcomes of social and economic action.

Hitherto, most analyses of the relationships between activities in the educational domain and those in other segments of social activity have employed categories which imply largely one-way relationships, whether between the values of a capitalist elite and those of the teachers and schools (as in so-called 'correspondence theory'), or in the functional, technologically determinate formulations characteristic of the optimistic fifties and sixties. But as yet there is no really satisfactory theory or theories which do justice to the complexity of these relationships. There are a number of significant pointers in the work of, for example, Bernstein and Bourdieu, which incorporate the possibility of a measure of autonomy and initiation for education, rather than depicting the work of schools and teachers as essentially responsive to changes in the external environment.

In fact, the sheer difficulty of conceptualising the relationship between, on the one hand, the educational transmissions experienced by millions of pupils and students in thousands of classrooms, and, on the other, the institutions and processes by means of which productive activities are pursued, precludes useful description based upon detailed empirical analysis.

Instead, we have metaphors masquerading as metatheories. The so-called 'correspondence theory' is plainly an attempt to understand the educational process in terms of an industrial metaphor. Such metaphors can be useful, especially as suggestive frameworks in terms of which detailed empirical studies can be carried through. Unfortunately, most such studies are either completely bereft of theoretical orientation, or fail to make adequate connections between the analysis and interpretation of classroom and school level observations and the theoretical formulations that they are supposed to test.

Nonetheless, some useful beginnings have been made. Whilst agreeing that the 'correspondence' between the manpower and socialisation needs of a developing capitalism and the work of the school provides a plausible explanation of the motives for educational expansion during the nineteenth century, Hurn (1978) argues that its fit with twentieth-century development is less good. In his view, those who advocate correspondence ideas tend to over-emphasise the rationality and intentionality characteristic of capitalistic production relations and schooling, and to assert a better 'fit' than in fact exists. A similar point is made by O'Keefe (1979) who suggests that the frequent complaints now heard about the failure of schools to prepare children adequately for life in the work place suggest that 'correspondence' is hardly the currently dominant feature of relationships between school and society. As Hurn (p. 77) puts it, 'neo-Marxist theory . . . ignore(s) that much of what schools teach is either irrelevant to or even subverts the presumed requirements of the capitalist social order'.

The purpose of the preceding discussion has been to emphasise the element of indeterminacy in the economic, political, social and educational arrangement of society, and the dangers of assuming that what happens in schools is simply a reflection of changes in the other spheres, a set of responses to the messages of markets, to political interventions and social policies.

If the expansion of education over the past hundred years was not simply a response to demographic, industrial and political change, then there is no reason why a one-to-one relationship should exist in future between any slowing down of economic growth, changes in the political balance and the work of the school. This is not to deny, given the way in which education is supported and funded, the importance of interactions between economic, social, political change. But there is no *inevitable* set of educational developments that can, in Sahlins' words, be 'read off from' a set of determining productive relationships.*

Institutional closures

The two most obvious and dramatic consequences of falling rolls are the closure of institutions and loss of jobs. The effect of closures will in the eighties increasingly be felt by three types of educational establishments – primary schools, especially in rural areas; colleges of higher education; and secondary schools, particularly those in urban districts affected by population migration.

The closure of rural primary schools is no new thing. On grounds educational rather than economic, and in the wake of population movements from country to town, many local authorities have during the past 25 years systematically reduced the number of small village schools. B. Taylor (1978) quotes the example of Somerset, where 500 primary or First Schools that existed in 1947 had by 1974 been reduced to less than 350. In a decade characterised by falling rolls, financial stringency and a commitment to democratic consultation and participation in decision-making, the problems to which closures give rise are bound to be highlighted. It was estimated in 1978 that to maintain average enrolments in 1983 at the same level as they had been five years previously would require the closure of some 4,000 schools.

There is, of course, no intention of bringing about closures on so draconian a scale. But this figure does underline the fact that the effects of a 20 per cent or more reduction in enrolments will be felt by a very high proportion of all schools as the decade progresses. There will be exceptions. Some areas will continue to experience a substantial net increase in population, as a result of employment shifts and new housing developments. Elsewhere, the average national fall in numbers may be greatly exceeded, calling into question at an early date the continued viability of local schools.

Proposals to close schools were in the past much easier to deal with than today, when there is greater consciousness of rights and less respect for bureaucratic judgement. In the United States, superintendents who have made unpopular decisions about closures, and

---

* '. . . no cultural form can ever be read from a set of "material forces" as if the cultural were the dependent variable of an inescapable practical logic. The positive explanation of given cultural practices as necessary effects of some material circumstances – such as a particular technique of production, a degree of productivity or productive diversity, an insufficiency of protein or scarcity of manure – all such scientist propositions are false . . . it is not that the material forces and constraints are left out of account, or that they have no real effects on cultural order. It is that the nature of the effect cannot be read from the nature of the forces, for the material effects depend upon their cultural encompassment' (Sahlins 1976, p. 206).

failed to involve the local community in the process of reaching such decisions, have lost their jobs (Divorky 1979). In this country, managers and parents have begun to use the Courts in an effort to prevent local authorities from enforcing notice for closure. Referring to applications to the High Court made by Managers of an East London primary school, Spencer (1980) states:

> Counsel for the Managers will claim that the authority reached its decision *ultra vires* and that it has failed to provide the Managers with enough information on which to base their objections, failed to consult them properly, and failed to give them sufficient notice of the closure.

Muted protests at a public meeting, or letters of complaint to councillors and education officials, have been replaced by carefully orchestrated community action. Early in 1979 the Advisory Centre for Education published a handbook on closures entitled *Schools under Threat*, publicity for which included the following:

> Hundreds of schools have been closed down over the last few years. This is often without any real consultation with those most directly concerned – teachers, parents, pupils and the local community. Falling school rolls are now bringing more and more schools under the axe. Is shutting a school the only answer? What are the alternatives as we move into the empty eighties? If you want to fight a school closure how do you go about it? This new 88-page Handbook from ACE tells you how to run an effective campaign; gives many facts and figures surrounding the arguments for and against closure; suggests alternatives and tells you where to find out more information.

It has become a common experience for a proposal for closure to provide an issue that focuses many discontents – a dislike of 'faceless bureaucracy'; a desire to maintain and enhance a sense of community, for which the school serves as actual and symbolic focus; anxiety about standards of behaviour in city schools and the undesirable influences to which 'bussed' children may be subjected; a desire to maintain the social mix that is often characteristic of the small school; consciousness of the benefits of small classes and individual teaching; a desire to preserve a particular cultural or linguistic tradition – all these have played, and can be expected to continue to play a part in the argument about what constitutes a viable school (Nash *et al* 1976, Nash 1978).

In the face of what is often strenuous and well-organised opposition, councillors and officials have sought alternatives to closure. It has been argued that the savings that accrue from such action are smaller than sometimes thought, and in a few cases even exceed the high social and political costs that closure incurs.*

In some counties, experiments have been tried with 'cluster' schools, introduced split-site working at the primary stage as a deliberate act of policy. One head and administration control the work of several annexes, which individually would not be viable. It has been argued that such federations have two major advantages, apart from keeping schools open – they allow more resources to be made available, and provide a career structure for the rural teacher.

As yet, there seems to have been little attempt in this country to emulate the example of some school districts in the United States, which rather than close schools in the face of population down-turn have sought alternative educational uses in order to maintain occupancy of existing plant. So parts of buildings are leased for such purposes as 'a police aide program, a Senior Citizens' Center, a youth job training program, an adult education program, a Montessori pre-school program, an extended day program for school-aged children, a Reading Clinic and Recreational Program' as well as, in some cases, such activities as 'an Eye Clinic, an Electronic Firm's Training Program, a Telephone Solicitation operation (and) a Real Estate Office' (Divorky 1979).

Some Authorities have tried modifying their pre-secondary stage organisation, with a view to maintaining a role for the small school. But however assiduous the efforts that elected members and administrators may make to ease the pains of closure, it seems clear that schools will continue to disappear in the face of declining numbers, shortage of resources and patterns of rural/urban migration. There is no single formula that can be legitimated in relation to a decision about closing or retaining schools of a particular size. Financial pressures are not felt uniformly. Local Authority education statistics for a recent year showed a range from £385 per capita to £224 in primary schools, and from £551 to £343 in secondary (the mode for primary was £265 and for secondary £407). Generally speaking, the cost per head of small schools is considerably greater than that of large units. Nonetheless, as we have seen, authorities may very well feel that the total savings that a programme of closures might achieve are hardly worthwhile in the face of the antagonism and political unpopularity to which such a programme might give rise. The claim that a school is the focal point of its rural community can be better sustained in some places than in others. The state of the premises has to be taken into consideration, as do the possibilities of alternative use.

★ '. . . it may now be impossible to close many schools however powerful the reasons, both educational and financial, simply because the local people are overwhelmingly opposed and not persuadable. In view of the commitment of the major political parties to a direct say by local people in key educational decisions, it is likely to be more and more exceptional for elected members to fly in the face of well-managed and nationally supported campaigns' (B. Taylor 1978).

The processes by which professional staff advise administrators, and consultations with parents, community and teachers' professional organisations take place, proposals are debated, recommendations and representations made to the Secretary of State, and eventual decisions implemented, are inevitably lengthy and complicated. At every stage there are evaluations and assessments to be weighed, considerations of power and of politics to be reckoned with, benefits and losses to be assessed. In the process of supporting or opposing a recommendation for closure, there are plenty of opportunities for research evidence to be drawn upon in a partial rather than disinterested spirit, for some facts to be played up and others played down, for the heat of debate to transmute conditionals into certainties. The task of the administrator and the elected member look like being no easier in the eighties than they were in the preceding decade.

The absence of clear-cut criteria in support of a particular line of action, the inapplicability of formula solutions, has been nowhere more apparent than in the recent history of the colleges of education. The full story of how a complete sector of higher education institutions virtually disappeared between 1972 and 1981 has yet to be documented and told. The effects of diminished birth rates on the demand for teachers were clearly recognised towards the end of the sixties. But it was expected that continuing expansion of post-secondary education, plus a steady improvement in staffing standards, in-service release and other 'teacher-consuming' developments, would enable the plant and resources released from initial teacher preparation to be used for other educational purposes. It was also recognised that the frequency and amplitude of changes in the birth rate demanded a flexibility in teacher supply that was unlikely to be forthcoming from a sector of single-purpose institutions. By diversifying courses in existing colleges of education, merging smaller institutions to create larger multi-faculty institutions and absorbing colleges into established universities and polytechnics, a rapid increase in the supply of newly qualified teachers could be achieved during upswings, without maintaining expensive courses in being or producing large-scale unemployment among the newly qualified in the troughs.

The manner in which the necessary diversification, closures and mergers was achieved has been much criticised (Hencke 1978) and vigorously defended (Fowler 1976). In relation to the difficulties to which proposals for closing schools give rise, the reorganisation of teacher education took place with what will in retrospect seem comparatively little fuss. A number of factors played their part in this. Teacher education institutions have never been politically strong, and muster few powerful friends. The closures and amalgamations were set in train at a time when public and professional concern was preoccupied by larger issues of economic survival. Agreement to apply the provisions of the so-called 'Crombie Code', with its relatively generous compensation provisions, originally introduced to facilitate early retirement of administrators following local government re-organisation, lubricated necessary redundancies and premature retirements among teacher education staff. At the beginning of reorganisation in 1972 there were in excess of 150 self-standing colleges of education, concerned solely with the preparation of teachers. By the early eighties there will be no more than 10 or 15 institutions in which teacher training constitutes more than 75 per cent of the work (W. Taylor 1978a, Lynch 1979).

No single set of criteria was applied when reaching decisions about the future of particular colleges. Each case involved a complex process of negotiation between the Principal, Staff, Governors, Local Authority, HM Inspectorate and DES Administrators. A document issued by the Department of Education and Science about the considerations relevant to these decisions made it clear that although regional, physical, academic, professional and other educational criteria would all be weighed, there were in the last analysis judgments to be made which could not be reduced to a formula. (For the consequences of changes in the Colleges of Education on opportunities in higher education generally see Russell and Pratt, 1979.)

Secondary schools are the third type of institution directly hit by falling rolls. Enrolment inevitably peaked later in secondary than in primary education, and numbers will be falling throughout the eighties. Encouraged by planners in the Department of Education and Science, local administrators have been busy for some time examining ways in which the necessary reductions can be brought about with minimum damage to the educational fabric and to opportunities available to the secondary age pupils of the eighties.

Nearly all secondary schools will feel the impact of declining numbers. The Secondary Heads Association have modelled an 11–16 secondary school based upon national average rates of reduction, and show that from having 571 pupils in the first to fifth years in 1976, producing a Burnham unit total of 1,727 and a staff of 31, by 1991 such a school will have an enrolment of 402, a unit total of 1,239 and a staff of 22 (Secondary Heads Association 1979a). Close attention has had to be given to the size of sixth forms, particularly in relation to the subjects that can reasonably be offered. In the early post-war years, one of the strongest arguments for very large comprehensive schools was the necessity to ensure an adequate range of sixth form subject choice. A large number of Authorities, unable or unwilling to create schools with 1,500 or 2,000 on roll, divided the secondary stage between Junior and Senior High Schools (11–16, 16–18), or planned Middle Schools which took upper primary pupils and the first two or three years of what had traditionally been regarded as the secondary age range.

Even in Authorities which have preserved the principle of all-through 11–18 schools, there has been a shift of opinion in favour of somewhat smaller units, the social and community advantages of which have in some cases been felt to outweigh the smaller range of courses that can be offered. In some cases, however, such schools will inevitably be truncated as a consequence of falling rolls, with students of sixth form age being concentrated on a single site.

A variety of co-operative arrangements are being worked out and implemented, especially in respect of subjects where sixth form groups are normally small and 'uneconomic'. Such arrangements are being forced on some schools that have lost specialist members of staff whose replacement cannot be justified on existing and likely future totals. It has been argued that an adequate range of education can be offered to a 150-strong sixth form staffed at a ratio of 12:1. Such a school could reasonably expect to offer 17 different A-level subjects without encountering too much difficulty, or working with grossly uneconomic groups. On the basis of these calculations, it seems doubtful if fewer than 50 students in a sixth form can produce a viable curriculum, no matter how generous the staffing ratios concerned (Deale 1979).

Detailed calculations apart, there are two important issues that will characterise discussions about secondary school futures during the eighties. One has to do with the future of the sixth form, the other with the relations of parental choice and successful planning for contraction. In the words of Briault and Smith (1980) 'are parents to choose the school they prefer or is contraction to be planned, controlled and managed at the expense of parents' freedom of choice?' (p. 52).

There are many educationists, particularly of a radical persuasion, who feel the time has come for unifying all the forms of education provided for 16–19 year olds. Traditional sixth forms are seen as not only uneconomic in size and composition, but restrictive in the range of options that can be offered, elitist in their values and assumptions, and unsuited to the needs of many students of post-compulsory age. By combining the resources of sixth forms and further education, not only would a more economic use of resources be achieved, but higher education opportunities might be made available to a broader cross-section of the population, and greater understanding achieved between future managers and administrators, and those more likely to find a future on the shop floor. Those ideologically opposed to the values and principles they see embodied in the traditional sixth are likely to employ the facts of falling rolls to support their proposals for reform. Whether or not such proposals are embodied in policies turns on the balance of political advantage, not only between the major parties, but also within the Labour Party itself (Dean *et al* 1979; Secondary Heads Association 1979b).

A second issue concerns the place of parental choice, and the extent to which it is consistent with an orderly response to falling rolls. In areas subject to substantial migration, the decline in numbers will be much sharper than in the country generally. For example, it is estimated that in the Inner London Education Authority secondary enrolments will fall from a total of 180,300 in 1976 to no more than 106,056 in 1990, a decline of some 40 per cent. How will the inevitable closures that follow from such a fall in numbers be managed? There are those who contend that parental choice and the market should exercise the predominant influence. To do otherwise, on this view, is to incur unsupportable political costs. Unfortunately, free parental choice makes local authority planning very difficult. Without the right under existing legislation to declare a school 'full', and thus to bring about a planned reduction in numbers leading to phasing out and the eventual orderly transfer of remaining pupils to a viable and suitably located school elsewhere, authorities are hamstrung (Newsam 1978). Yet in other systems it has been found that properly resourced forward planning is essential if closures and mergers are to be brought about with minimum disruption to the education of the pupils concerned.*

Such planning, however, is likely to conflict with the principle of maximising parental choice of school. Fiske has documented the effects that unrestricted parental choice will have on the intakes to individual schools. In Manchester, there is one school with 25 per cent of its pupils having non-verbal quotients of 115 plus and only 8.1 per cent below 85, and another school with 31.3 per cent below 85 and none at all above 115. Fiske (1977) argues that the time has come to think and talk more about the needs of children rather than the rights of their parents, and that a child's needs for secondary education can be said to include some certainty of a place in a known secondary school; the opportunities to transfer with established friends; reasonable continuity of teaching and curriculum on transfer from the primary to the secondary stage; admission to a comprehensive secondary school with as balanced an intake as possible, and a system in which there is high morale among all the teachers. Although a system of unrestricted parental choice can produce impressive overall figures in terms of the number of first and second choices that are capable of being met, it does not satisfy many of the criteria that Fiske suggests as important.

The Secondary Heads Association argue that to maximise parental

* 'The National School Boards Association suggest that long range plans look five to ten years into the future, and suggest the Highline (Washington) school districts approach as a model. Suburban Highline which peaked at 31,000 students in 1967, is now down to 18,000 and will lose 3,000 more by 1982. It has closed eleven schools, with eight more – including a High School – to be phased out in the next four years . . . Highline's massive retrenchment has gone smoothly, at least in part, because of the carefully articulated plan divided into "phases" each with its own timetable, purpose, method and special concerns' (Divorky 1979).

choice, whilst recognising the concern which parents have about the quality and the character of their children's education, 'would be relatively expensive and socially divisive. It would cause "sink" schools to develop, often for reasons quite unrelated to the quality of education being offered by the school, and in these schools the problems of redundancy and redeployment of staff would be acutely concentrated' (Secondary Heads Association 1979a). The Association admits it is equally untenable to maintain the opposite policy of arguing that every secondary school must continue in existence and that catchment areas should be systematically redrawn to enable a viable distribution of numbers.

Briault (Briault and Smith 1980) argues for the retention of large schools by a policy of planned amalgamation, recommending Authorities 'to provide by 1991 the smallest reasonable number of secondary schools and the largest sizes of schools, having in mind the distance between schools . . .' (p. 245). Critics of the traditional sixth form and of large schools have taken issue with this prescription, suggesting that it is based on outmoded notions of 'subjects' as distinct from curriculum 'areas' and that the 'logic of whole curriculum planning is a common 11 to 16 curriculum in single institutions of modest size, followed if necessary by 16 to 19 education ideally in a tertiary college' (Holt 1980).

The eighties are likely to see a series of compromises, both of principle at national level and in the practice of authorities, involving complex processes of collecting and analysing the relevant facts, consulting parents, communities and teachers, reconciling political and professional preferences and reaching judgments, rather than adherence to predetermined formulae.

Contraction and the curriculum

Some indications of the implications of falling rolls for the curricula of primary and secondary schools have been given in the preceding section. Fortunately, we now have much more information than a few years ago about how schools organise their curriculum, and on the deployment of the teaching staff. Surveys by the Burnham Committee and by the Inspectorate, together with the reviews of local authority arrangements initiated by the Department of Education and Science, have all produced large quantities of useful facts and figures. The specific effects of falling rolls have been documented in detail in a sample of schools by a research team at Sussex University led by Professor Eric Briault (Briault and Smith 1980). This research indicates that in some cases schools have been hard hit by declining numbers, with the sciences no longer taught as separate subjects, only one foreign language offered and the disappearance from the curriculum altogether of subjects such as music which are vulnerable to the departure and the non-replacement of specialist teachers. These problems are not restricted to secondary schools. Farmer (1978) points out that in junior and middle schools, music, French, craft and home economics are seen by many as 'peripheral in terms of both their content and the skills which can be developed through them'. He suggests that the shortage of specialist teachers in these subjects, and the fact that the 'heavy and light crafts' and home economics require split classes mean that, especially in small schools, it will be impossible to deploy staff in such a way as to maintain a suitable range of offerings.

The effects of the random loss of specialist teachers can to a certain extent be offset by careful planning, in-service training for 'second subject' specialists, spreading staff reductions over several years, permitting otherwise unjustifiable pupil-teacher ratios in circumstances where these are necessary to protect aspects of the curriculum, and consciously embracing interdisciplinary subjects (such as Integrated Science) where resources are no longer available to permit greater specialisation.

The problem of deploying staff efficiently among individual schools will probably lead to some slowing down in the trend towards decentralisation of timetabling and curricula decision-making. Just as in some authorities, the right of secondary school heads to appoint their own staff on the basis of public advertisement has been withdrawn in the face of threat of redundancy and the need to manage staff redeployment over the system as a whole, so in individual schools it will be necessary for the central administration to control the use of time.

There will be less incentive for 'block' timetabling that has given subject Faculties opportunity to use time allocated to them more flexibly for e.g. a mixture of team teaching, class teaching, year lectures and audio-visual presentations, small group work and individual tuition. In this sense, falling rolls are likely to compound the effects of the back-to-basics movement, and to encourage a focus upon certain key areas of the curriculum, such as those identified by the Inspectorate in recent surveys.

One factor that may have positive effects upon teaching and learning in schools of diminished size is the greater availability of space. The built environment of most institutional forms is a powerful constraint upon change. As many teachers have discovered, it is not easy to introduce team-taught, mixed ability, individualised instruction into buildings designed in a climate of educational ideas that stressed homogeneous ability groups, single teacher classrooms and classes of uniform size.

What Victorian three-deckers, between wars brick piles and generous post-war designs had in common was a certain amount of 'wasted' space. Such space was extremely useful when a teacher wished to divide students into smaller groups, develop a resource collection, and to find somewhere for individual work. Since the early fifties, however, every penny spent on buildings has been counted. Most modern buildings have little by way of surplus square meterage. With falling rolls in the eighties, space may once again become available for purposes other than housing classes of 30 from nine to four. The eighties may see a relaxation of the space restrictions to which many teachers have been subject for the past quarter century, with significant effects on curriculum and pedagogy.

Falling rolls will be one of many factors that will influence curriculum change in the period up to 1990. Concern for all those activities that can be loosely grouped under the heading of 'curriculum development' is unlikely to abate, but it may take a somewhat different direction from much of the work of the sixties and seventies. Both central and local government have begun to take greater interest in curriculum. As Lawton indicates in his chapter in this volume, motives for such interest are mixed. There is an element of disillusionment with the performance of schools; a wish on the Right to contain the spread of what are seen as 'subversive' ideas in schools (the incidence of which is much exaggerated) and, on the Left, not to seem complacent and soft in the face of such concern; a recognition of the widening gap between the best and the worst that our schools can offer; a wish to see some benefit from the relatively large sums spent on curriculum development projects and activities; a feeling that many teachers, recruited on a largely unselective basis during periods of chronic shortage, without adequate grounding in scholarship or in technique, and subject to the multiple pressures of a society that inevitably expects too much from its schools, have in many cases been unable to cope; irritation on the part of politicians and administrators with the apparent insensitivity of the teachers' organisations to criticism; and the impact of what can be labelled 'Benthamite-technological' thinking upon school organisation (in the shape of accountability) and on curriculum (in the form of objectives and competency based instruction). All these have played their part in forming the climate in which discussion and action about curriculum will develop during the eighties. Falling rolls create conditions that will facilitate some developments and inhibit others. The direct effects are likely to be felt via resources, staffing levels, and the viability of teaching groups. The indirect effects will derive from broader social and economic changes referred to in an earlier section of the chapter. They may be no less significant for the values and content of what is taught and learned.

Contraction and careers in education
Contraction has important consequences for the structure of teaching

as a career. Every decision to close a school or college or department means one less headship. To combine smaller schools into larger units and tertiary colleges into polytechnics reduces the number of top jobs available.

As far as promotion is concerned, age structure and rate of recruitment are critical factors. In the universities, the rapid expansion of the late sixties and early seventies has produced a distribution skewed towards the younger end of the age range. In the mid-seventies, well over a third of university staff with ten years service or more were still in lecturer grades. For those with more service, there were substantial differences between subject groups. For example, 18 per cent of applied science staff with twenty years of service or more had not yet achieved senior lecturer or above, but for social scientists the proportion was only 6.7 per cent, for science 11.9 per cent, and for arts 12.8 per cent.

At about the same time, nearly half the teachers in maintained primary and secondary schools were below the age of 34. Only just over one fifth were over 50. In other words, two and a half times as many were in the first third of their careers as in the last third (DES 1979b). Age profiles like these mean that promotion prospects will in future be less good than in the recent past.

In schools, as elsewhere, the most serious effects are likely to be felt by those individuals who have already achieved their 'career grade'. In the words of a DES report on teachers' promotion prospects (Quoted Secondary Heads Association 1979a):

> . . . to a large degree, future occupiers of these posts are already there, and having reached their present level of seniority, in many cases very quickly, they must expect to wait a long time – perhaps 15 years on average – for further advancement.

Expectations tend to be based upon past experience. It is the relationship of expectations to opportunities, rather than any absolute number of promotion posts, that is most likely to affect morale and attitudes. Spooner (1979) has argued that morale may not be much affected by general promotion prospects:

> I do not believe that teacher moralè was low before the war, when there was virtually no promotion ladder but a sudden jump to Deputy or Head. Usually, low morale results from working for an institution that is thought to be in decline.

One short-term consequence of reduced promotion prospects is to bring into sharper focus the career and promotion structures charac-teristic of particular schools, colleges, or universities. Any regulation or requirement which limits the number and proportion of promotion posts comes under scrutiny. In the universities, the application of the 40–60 ratio, which decrees that only 40 per cent of staff may occupy posts of senior lecturer or above, the remaining 60 per cent of appointments requiring to be in lecturer or lecturer-related grades, has attracted particular criticism. In schools and public sector colleges, the Burnham points scheme prescribes the number of senior posts that may be held in institutions of particular size and with certain levels of work, and teachers' organisations have argued the need for the basis of points allocation to be reviewed in the light of falling rolls.

The effect of contraction is not simply to reduce promotion prospects within institutions, but also to limit the number of administrative, advisory and support posts. Between 1974 and 1978 the decline in the number of advisers per head of population was 30 per cent in large authorities, 5 per cent in small, 10 per cent overall. Despite these reductions, nearly all local authorities maintained adviserships in such subjects as physical education, music and art and craft, but only just over half had subject advisers in religious education, the one compulsory subject in the post-1944 school curriculum (Doe 1978). During the sixties, colleges of education recruited heavily from among successful and experienced teachers, to whom, generally speaking, they offered improved conditions of service and higher salaries. Cut-backs in teacher training have largely removed the possibility of moving to such work.

A number of suggestions have been made about ways in which the effects of contraction on career prospects might be counteracted. Whitehorne (1977) has argued that in universities a lectureship should be the career grade, all promotions being on a temporary scale, with the holder, if his or her position is not renewed, reverting to that point on the lecturer scale that would have been reached had he or she not originally been promoted. Those lucky enough to obtain a second or third 'term' might then achieve permanent promoted status. In an unpublished paper, Bragg has suggested a system of flat-rate payments for academic staff, retaining existing grades, but with compensation for the higher ranks in the form of time off rather than enhanced salary. Thus a senior professor would draw a flat-rate salary for only, say, one and a half days work per week in the university, the rest of his time being free for research, scholarship or other employment.

Fewer opportunities for advancement leading to reduced turnover, and smaller intakes resulting in a higher average age need not all be disadvantageous. During the sixties young teachers poured out into the schools, keen enough for the most part, but without opportunities for a proper induction into life in classrooms, and sometimes without sufficient appreciation of the problems they would have to face. What mattered was to get someone in front of the class at the beginning of each year, each term, even each week. Many heads had the experience of starting the school year with a staff half of whom were absolute beginners. In the cities children were taught by a succession of temporaries, many of them short-term residents from overseas.

Contraction has changed all this. On the whole, experienced teachers are better at the job than beginners. They have learned how to handle the variety of children and groups they meet in the course of a day, a week or a year. They are better able to cope with mixed ability classes, to help individuals with their learning difficulties, to recognise lack of understanding or failure to keep up and to know what to do about it. Being more mature they are less liable to be thrown out of step by the personal and domestic problems they encounter, more likely to offer the right kind of guidance and help.

With smaller annual turnovers, heads can get to know and to balance the strengths and weaknesses of their colleagues. Longer serving staff build up loyalties to the school, form more cohesive working groups and provide each other with more effective mutual support. Ideas and techniques learned through attendance at courses and conferences have a better chance to be assimilated into daily practice. Some in-service training can be based on individual schools, with heads and teachers sitting down together to identify and work on their problems with the aid of consultants from the local authority and the universities. There will be enough experienced teachers to ensure that the much reduced number of newcomers get the help they need to make a success of their first year. As far as children are concerned, there will be more continuity of teaching – the question, 'Are you going to be with us next week, Miss?' will be asked less often.

All these are gains. Experience, maturity and continuity are all needed. Nonetheless, there is no denying the costs involved in an aging profession.

Less wastage, lower rates of turnover and smaller numbers of mature entrants to teaching mean a diminishing proportion of staff with experience of the world beyond the classroom. There is evidence that older teachers are more conservative, less innovative, likely to stick with old and tried methods even when these have been shown to be ineffective. There is less new blood coursing through the professional veins. Older teachers are less flexible, less likely to be sympathetic to teenage tastes and values.

The adventurous and the entrepreneurial will have fewer outlets for their talents. Unless the economy picks up there will be little encouragement for those who find teaching uncongenial to move to other employment. The successful teacher who does receive an attractive offer from elsewhere may hesitate to make a move if he/she is unsure of being able eventually to return to the classroom, especially if a possible loss of seniority is involved. Teaching is tiring work. Older

35

people tire more easily, and show the effects more quickly. Large-scale early retirement, which might help to unblock promotion and create new opportunities for younger men and women, may prove too expensive for many systems to afford. As a result, there may be many teachers in mid-career who have lost interest in their own prospects and have an unhappy feeling that they are blocking those of their younger colleagues.

Yet not all the problems of an aging profession arise from structural and biological causes. The residue of a cultural history which placed emphasis upon speed and strength, and a more recent period of rapid technological change in which recency of training counted for more than experience and accumulated wisdom, have combined to over-stress the importance of youth and to diminish the contribution of older members of the work-force. In these respects, we are to some extent victims of the biological metaphors we employ to conceptualise our experience. We have become accustomed to regarding institutions and societies, like individuals, as being characterised by processes of conception, birth, dependent nurture, youth, maturity and age. Each generates sets of socially patterned behaviour expectations, some kind of 'fit' with which is required if a sense of order and rhythm in life styles is to be achieved.

Deeply rooted although such expectations may be, there are signs of change. Women are tending to have their children later, after several years of outside employment, and are making more use of crèches and baby-minders in order to remain employed. Universities make financial and other provision for a proportion of mature students. Middle-aged faces can be seen in many undergraduate classes. Industry, commerce and the armed services are willing to a greater extent than heretofore to release senior staff for research or advanced study. Retirement after 20 years from military service, from the police and overseas appointments makes it possible for some men and women to undertake in their forties the systematic full-time training they missed at 18.

The solution to the problems posed by contraction is not to be found merely in advising alternative structures that protect the possibilities of career advancement and promotion, or waiting for expectations to adjust themselves to the realities of a smaller system, but through adapting attitudes towards the pattern and sequence of career development, enhancing the possibility of changing tracks in mid-career, maintaining possibilities for intellectual excitement and pro-fessional renewal up to and beyond the point of retirement from full-time employment. Our present notions of what constitutes for people of a given age an appropriate life-style and career point are an amalgam of the values and expectations of an agricultural, pre-industrial society and the imperatives of industrialisation in its early and middle period.

Such values may have made sense when hard physical labour took its toll at an early age, when manipulative skills were at a premium, when rapid economic growth stressed the innovativeness of youth rather than the trained judgment of the middle years. They are decreasingly appropriate to a world in which a majority of individuals are employed in service occupations, the micro-processor and robotisation are in process of altering the nature of skills, and minimum wage legislation no longer confers such a substantial economic advantage upon the beginner.

Conclusion

The response that a society makes to the problem of falling rolls in its schools is not just a matter of how much money is available to cushion the effects of closures and declining employment opportunities, or the skill with which planning can avoid distortion in curriculum and diminished educational opportunities. It is also affected by the extent to which economic and social momentum can be maintained in other sectors, by attitudes to education, by the speed with which engrained conceptions of age-appropriate behaviour can be modified. When growth is the highest value, when positive affect is directed principally towards youth, there are inevitable costs to pay in unfulfilled expectations and in the identification of non-growth, non-youth states in almost wholly negative terms. There are too many important and worthwhile educational tasks to be undertaken in the eighties to permit a surrender to the values and attitudes of run-down and decline. Some of the alternatives to such a surrender are suggested in the chapters that follow.

2
Work, Leisure and Life Styles

Harold Entwistle

At the beginning of the nineteen sixties, projections for the future of work and leisure covering the following two decades were essentially optimistic. The prevailing political myth was that advanced industrial societies had 'never had it so good'. Predictions were of exponential growth in human knowledge and, especially, in scientific and technological innovation, which seemed to augur a proportionate improvement in the standard of life. Educationally, the correlate of these trends seemed to be one of indefinite expansion of educational provision, especially in the fields of higher and further education. The only problem seemed to be that of 'future shock'; a question of whether or how human beings might learn to live with change of such magnitude and pace. Thus, it was reasonable to expect that on the threshold of the eighties we should be celebrating man's technological achievements, his improved standard of living and the possibility of improving the quality of schooling at all levels within the educational system: that is, projections for the next two decades might reasonably have anticipated further confident strides into an increasingly affluent future.

In reality, however, the mood on the threshold of the eighties is sombre, more often evoking the economic history of half a century ago, than optimistically assessing the creative possibilities inherent in technological innovation for bringing the good life within reach of increasing numbers of our fellow men. Evidently, any review of the educational implications of future trends in patterns of work and leisure has to confront the facts of economic and political constraint as represented by crises in the supply of energy, industrial recession, and the swing towards governments committed to 'monetarism' and retrenchment of the social services. In particular, current economic realities seem to threaten those educational aspirations which once seemed within reach of realisation, consequent upon those technological changes which reduce the demand for labour. For example, recurrent education has been proposed as the only 'constructive alternative for societies which can produce goods without a need for a vast labour force' (Houghton 1974 p. 8). But proposals to meet the declining demand for places in higher education resulting from demographic trends by transferring redundant resources to adult education seem likely to be an early casualty of retrenchment of educational expenditure. However, even without direct government action upon educational expenditures, the ideal of lifelong education that people should have the freedom 'to drop out of school and into work, and out of work into school' (O'Toole 1975 p. 15) is threatened by economic recession. Dropping out of work into school looks less attractive when mounting unemployment makes it much less likely that one can readily drop back into work at will.

In face of the dilemma of whether to engage with the realities of the short term or with expansionist expectations of the longer term, this chapter will discuss some implications for work, leisure and education of optimistic expectations that technology can transform the quality of life, whilst also, where appropriate, noting the implications of the current recession, including the possibility that this must also colour our expectations for the more distant future. For, given certain assumptions about what constitutes the good life, our current predicaments are a blessing, not a curse.

Mechanisation, automation and work

In the literature of post-industrial society,[1] the assumption has been that the secular trend is towards an 'age of automation'. This conception epitomises a shift away from the economic and technical organisation characteristic of the first industrial revolution based upon the mechanisation of industry, with a semi or unskilled work force operating as machine minders. This intensive mechanisation of industrial production involved the minute division of labour. Production, divided into the simplest of processes, involved the worker in only one, or some few, simple operations repeated incessantly throughout the working day. The human implications of this kind of industrial organisation were effectively satirised in Chaplin's *Modern Times*. Under intensive industrial mechanisation tied to the conveyor belt, workers are employed directly in production, but in subservient roles, as slaves to the machine. From the point of view of education it is evident that even the most rudimentary of skills learned in school (even minimal literacy and numeracy, as well as craft skills) make far greater intellectual demands of the pupil than those he is likely to be called upon to meet in industry for the remainder of his working life. Even the backward in our schools achieved levels of literacy and numeracy far beyond the demands which working life makes on them. Indeed, much industrial activity is counter-educational, the graveyard of literacy and manual skill. If schooling has any vocational relevance at all (and this essay is written from the assumption that it ought to have), it is not surprising that a child, perceiving himself to be destined for a life in the mechanised factory, should often be so little motivated towards learning in school.

By contrast with mechanisation, automation seems to have different implications for the deployment and development of knowledge and skill in work. Essentially, automation removes workers from direct participation in the production process. Whilst mechanisation created an army of unskilled machine minders and operatives, automation makes these redundant. Machines can now mind themselves. Through computer and electronic feed-back techniques and the use of mechanical transfer, it is possible to have conveyor-belt production serviced largely by machines; it becomes possible to produce quite complex articles untouched by hand.[2]

In attempting to project the educational implications of this 'post-industrial' trend from mechanisation to automation, the effects of the latter have to be assessed both qualitatively and quantitatively. Will automation increase or decrease opportunities for finding work; and what will be its effect upon the quality of the working life in terms of the demands it makes upon intelligence and skill, upon knowledge and upon the aesthetic and moral sensibilities of workers? Answers to these questions will also have implications for the availability and quality of leisure.

With reference to the quantity of available work consequent upon automation, the fear is that this trend will drastically reduce the opportunities for employment. For massive unemployment does appear to be the likeliest consequence of technological innovation which hands over machine minding to machines themselves. But this pessimistic conclusion is often challenged by two optimistic assumptions; first, that the automation of industry will inevitably increase opportunities for leisure, an assumption which will be examined later. Second, that technological innovation increases rather than decreases employment opportunities. It is true that, in the past, revolutionary technological innovation has not diminished opportunities for employment, partly because of the expansion of industrial output which technological advance makes possible, but also because the new technologies themselves generate compensatory employment in ancillary industries and in research, planning and design. The modern aircraft industry, in which gestation periods of up to ten years are required before the first prototype takes the air, provides an example of how prolific novel technology can be in its consumption of pre-production labour.[3] Technological innovation which reduces the numbers of workers required in one role tends to have compensatory effects in increasing the demand for different kinds of workers. With automation it is the incidence of human labour within the productive process which has shifted. However, although we have experience that unemployment is not the inevitable outcome of the development of labour-saving technological innovation, dramatic new departures in this direction revive fears that modern technological change is unfriendly to human employment. For example, The Council for Educational Technology has attempted to estimate employment prospects consequent upon the development of micro-electronic technology. It concludes that 'the rate of contraction of demand for labour as a result of new technology is likely to be substantially greater than any rate of economic growth that can be achieved, so that in the transitional period there will be a sharp reduction in the demand for labour, whether or not this is a long term feature' (Council for Educational Technology 1978 p. 4).

However, past experience has also given cause for belief that technological innovation which has made possible significant improvements in the material standard of life on the basis of a contracting industrial labour force, also makes possible a considerable expansion of that tertiary sector of the economy which is concerned with the provision of services, especially in education, health and welfare, recreation and the arts. From a quantitative point of view, it seems a reasonable expectation that so long as there is disease or ignorance, malnutrition or inadequate housing, personal misfortune, public squalor or misery of any kind (especially with reference to the Third World), there should be work to do for everyone who wants a job.[4] We have unemployment, not because all human needs and wants are satisfied, but because we lack either the will or the skill to organise the economic system differently. In fact, the question of whether technological innovation increases or reduces opportunities for employment is not primarily itself a technological problem: it is a question to do with economic and political institutions and with the moral choices we make as individuals and communities. This is especially true of the demand for public sector service occupations within the economy. Although an expanding public service sector is, in part, a spin-off from technological labour-saving innovation, it is, no less, a function of the demands which citizens make upon the public services and, often a contradictory influence, their willingness to pay for such services through taxation. With respect to the latter, the factors determining the level of employment opportunities are political and economic. Of relevance here is the debate engendered by some Social Democrats (e.g. Roy Jenkins and the late Anthony Crosland) about the optimum combination in a mixed economy of public and private investment. From an economic point of view, at the time of writing and on both sides of the Atlantic, the preferred monetarist solutions to problems of inflation and recession involve considerable retrenchment of expenditure on the public services and a consequent reduction of opportunities for employment in the public sector of the economy. And, evidently, this retrenchment has little to do with the question of the kind and scope of public services which people really need. In a number of contexts we shall return to this point that questions about the future of work and leisure are as much political and economic as they are technological and, so far as this raises educational issues, these are as much concerned with political and moral education as they are with vocational (including professional) education or education for leisure.

Future prospects for the quality of life at work in an automated society have been assumed to be positive: that is, in the direction of making work more congenial, intellectually demanding, autonomous and creative for an increasing number of workers. In the traditional factory, work was too often mechanical, mindless, soul destroying, even brutalising. Increasingly, it is assumed, new work roles will demand greater knowledge and intellectual skill. The shift we have noted from unskilled manual work ancillary to the machine towards management, planning, research, supervisory and maintenance functions within industry, and towards professional and para-professional occupations in the public and tertiary sectors of the economy, is assumed to involve an upgrading of work. This shift is usually epitomised as one from blue collar to white collar occupations. And, traditionally, the latter are assumed to be more dignifying, more demanding of knowledge and intelligence, giving the worker greater autonomy on the job and greater security of employment. The educational correlate of this ought to be the need for better general education and the expansion and improvement of technical and professional training in further and higher education. And, indeed, educational innovations of the past two decades have been a response to these expectations. The reorganisation of secondary education was intended to raise the general educational standards of adolescents, partly in preparation for further vocational education beyond the school. The need for an expansion of further and higher education has been advocated as investment in technical and cognitive skills required for economic growth. Again, it is the assumption of this essay that vocational imperatives of this kind are necessary and legitimate demands upon educational institutions, especially as an integral part of claims that education should minister to the growth of students as persons.

However, the notion that automation and the shift to white collar work axiomatically makes for a qualitative improvement in working life is subject to increasing scrutiny and criticism. No doubt there is a growth in professional and para-professional occupations in both the public and the private sectors of the economy, but there are those who argue that many of these newer professionals have little of the status and autonomy traditionally associated with the learned professions (see Rinehart 1975). With reference to the lower levels of the white collar work force, doubt is also thrown on the assumption that, especially with increasing automation, office work is now more demanding than blue collar work, even assuming that it ever was. It is odd that this myth of the superiority of white collar work should have gained currency even in traditional industrial societies. It is not clear how, or why, the work of a typist or book-keeper should be deemed to require greater skill, intelligence or knowledge than that of a carpenter, a plumber, a farm worker or of the many skilled manual jobs in the engineering industry. The 'superiority' of many routine white collar jobs only ever derived from the social context of the job (being staff, being in contact with management and sharing some of its privileges, etc.) rather than from the technical, intellectual or aesthetic demands of the job itself. And with reference to the assumed post-industrial mushrooming of white collar occupations, it is argued that many of these threaten to be as routine, soul-destroying and non-creative as unskilled and semi-skilled blue collar work has been in the past. Many office jobs, it seems, appear like nothing so much as a reversion to the conveyor belt, requiring less training and fewer opportunities for flexibility and autonomy at work than even traditional routine office work like typing or book-keeping. Formerly, an efficient shorthand typist or general clerk required a high degree of literacy and knowledge which resulted from a good general education. But, it is argued, the most recent intrusion of technology into the office – word processing – seems effectively to diminish the demands made by work on this group of white collar workers.[5]

A realistic conclusion about the quality of work likely to be available in a post-industrial society would be that there is undoubtedly an expansion of professional and quasi-professional work opportunities which require post-secondary schooling, and which offer greater opportunity for the deployment of knowledge, intellectual skill and creativity at work as well as giving the worker greater autonomy and flexibility. Whatever the magnitude of the shift from unskilled and semi-skilled manual work towards professional or quasi-professional white collar occupations, one educational correlate of this ought to be that more children will require the kind of literate and cognitively oriented secondary schooling which has traditionally constituted the liberal education of the professional middle class. It also seems evident that any expansion of professional and para-professional employment opportunities in modern economies would require an expansion of facilities for professional and technical training within Further and Higher Education. At the same time, routine, undemanding work on a large scale will probably not disappear with a shift from blue to white collar. Instead, the trend towards unionisation of white collar workers suggests that these increasingly suffer occupational discontents of the kind which have prompted blue collar unionisation over the past two centuries. Some of this discontent may arise from the fact that educational standards have risen at a pace which far outstrips the capacities of modern economies to provide upgraded work opportunities commensurate with this broadening of educational opportunity. In the United States it has been estimated that 'the expansion of professional, technical and clerical jobs absorb only 15 per cent of the new educated workers; 85 per cent accept jobs previously performed by individuals with fewer credentials' (O'Toole 1975 p. 15).

Here we confront one of the contradictions of capitalism in that its educational ideology commits us to the complete and harmonious development of every individual's human potential, whilst its economic arrangements are incapable of generating work opportunities for the majority which even begin to honour this educational axiom. The conventional liberal educational wisdom attempts to pick us off the horns of this dilemma through the pretence that education should have nothing to do with the work people are destined to do – 'education is for living, not earning a living'. But on the assumption (to be argued below) that 'living' and 'earning' cannot be dichotomised in this way, the alternatives facing us if we are to avoid the problem of 'over education' are either regressive or radical. One implication of the persistence of undemanding occupations is that it would be a mistake to improve the quality of schooling for those destined to continue to suffer alienation at work: indeed, raising their educational standards would probably only deepen their alienation and perhaps we ought to put the clock back to something like the days when most future workers only had elementary education. Alternatively, acceptance of the conclusion that there should be some kind of fit between achievement in school and performance at work would be viewed as posing a radical challenge to our civilisation: the imperative to create alternative economic, cultural and social institutions which more fully enlist human potential to address human needs and bring the good life within reach of increasing numbers of our fellow men.

However, the conclusion that with different economic and social arrangements, work might be upgraded to fit improved educational achievements falls foul of another item in the received view of education. This is the belief that educational standards have not risen in the recent past: on the contrary, they have declined. On this view, it is questionable whether sufficient new entrants to the labour force can be trained to fill future upgraded work roles efficiently, given the conventional wisdom about the distribution of intelligence and, hence, the capacity for post-secondary education within the population. It is often assumed that even the expansion of white collar occupations which has taken place since World War II has been possible only by recruiting personnel who would have been considered unsuitable for white collar work half a century ago. This is the conclusion that 'more means worse', and the enlarged student body in higher and further education is frequently dismissed as only semi-literate. The assumption is that there appears to be insufficient latent ability within the population to upgrade industrial and professional skill on the scale required by an automated economy: although we need 'silk purses' it seems that the only human raw material we have consists of 'sow's ears'. Twenty years ago, however, the Newsom Commissioners addressed this problem with greater optimism. Recalling Macaulay's belief that the supply of genius is subject to the same laws of supply and demand as any other commodity, they concluded, with him, that the supply of ability and talent available to a community may be 'diminished by restrictions or multiplied by bounties' (Newsom Report 1963 p. 6). If this is the case, children's own perceptions of the possibility of a more challenging vocational future might well call forth motivation towards greater academic achievement. But similar perceptions from their teachers are also required. Too often, their point of reference in terms of their expectations of children is their own blinkered perception of the dynamics of technological change. Even educational conservatives who oppose educational equality are apt to recognise that many of those who perform society's chores are capable of better: 'The canvass of equality cannot be pressed too vigorously in case the result turns out to be some sort of Dodo race in which everybody wins and vital services are left to be done by those *too overeducated* to undertake them' (Wilson 1975 pp. 20–24; emphasis added). With reference to school leavers, there seems hope that an industrial economy demanding more of intelligence, knowledge and skill from new entrants to the work force need not be disappointed in its expectations.

This discussion of the future of work in both quantitative and qualitative terms has concentrated upon changes likely to be related to an intensification of automation. But although there are increasing numbers of workers in automated work roles (in manufacturing industry, commercial and business enterprises and in space engineering, for example) traditional work patterns persist. Alongside computerised industrial production, there still exist traditional handicrafts as well as heavy manual industrial processes which expose the worker to dirt, disease and danger. In spite of the spread of domestic refrigeration, men still deliver milk on to doorsteps daily in all kinds of weather. Refuse is still disposed of unhygienically in dustbins emptied manually and men still shovel snow and sweep streets and the Underground. Moreover, this persistence of traditional work roles is also reflected in daily life experiences where the traditional and the modern co-mingle. Via space technology, television brings the entire world nightly into our living rooms but, in personal experience, most of our lives are circumscribed by the limits of the immediate locality. A recent Gallup Survey showed that even in the most advanced industrial society, fewer than half the teenagers in America (and fewer still in some regions) have flown on a commercial airline. This probably reflects the limited extent to which the 'jet age' affects personal travel experiences. Even in affluent industrial societies, it is probably true that a majority of people have never even experienced what it means to fly. Paralleling the occupational mix of traditional and post-industrial technologies is a similar mixture of daily life styles which is significant for any consideration of leisure.

A second relevant phenomenon is the revival of artisanship, as represented by those, mainly young, who set up stalls in public places, university precincts and shopping malls to merchant their own products – works of art, pottery, jewellery, paintings, candles, hand made clothing and furniture, etc. Department stores are also apt to offer for sale 'unique' artefacts manufactured by established artists and artisans. What this phenomenon represents as a proportion of the working population or how enduring a trend it will continue to be is uncertain. Much of this artisanship is concerned with production of non-essential or 'luxury' goods (however modestly priced) which could be a casualty of economic recession. But, in part, the phenomenon is also related to the revival of aspirations and values which are significant for any discussion of the quality of life, especially the quality of work. On the other hand, one suspects that many of these young artisans do not, and do not expect to, eke out a comfortable living from these kinds of work which, for economic reasons, can be no more than part-time occupations possibly combined with traditional forms of regular work. This is a reminder of the existence of 'moonlighting' and 'black economies', phenomena which inevitably fudge any statistics relevant to a consideration of the trend of work opportunities and assessments of the kind of satisfactions people derive from their work.

The phenomenon of revived artisanship, even if manifest mainly in part-time occupations, is an affirmation of traditional values and aspirations which has to be taken into account in discussion of the quality of life and, especially, of work. Some discussions of the effects of technological change seem predicated on the assumption that this has its own logic and imperatives for the future of work and leisure. There are futurists who assume that if a particular technological innovation is possible it ought, axiomatically, to be engineered. Connected with this is the tacit assumption that technological change cannot but be in the best interests of people, and that a kind of 'false consciousness' or 'bad faith' is at work when they resist change. But it is not obvious, for example, that because travel in space is possible, people ought to want to go to the moon. Conservatism with reference to some experiences may represent not ignorance or fear or a 'nostalgification of reality' but a rational, educated response to the implications of change.

Leisure and employment

As with the future of work, the future of leisure can also be discussed from both a quantitative and a qualitative point of view. One assumption which has grown out of acceptance of post-industrial technological innovation is that it will greatly expand the spare time available to most workers. Indeed, it is often assumed that the shift towards automated, labour saving technologies has put us on the threshold of a Golden Age of Leisure. If diminishing opportunities for employment seem to be a consequence of the kind of technological innovation characteristic of the post-industrial society, it seems only rational to assume that work could be spread more thinly amongst those in the labour market, making for a radical reduction in the working day or the working week; or, perhaps, there is the possibility of longer vacations, even 'sabbatical' leaves for industrial workers.

However, it is only by thinking about work and leisure in an economic and political vacuum that it is possible to conclude that opportunities for leisure will increase dramatically as a consequence of automation. Without considering political and economic constraints it does appear axiomatic that if the application of new industrial technologies should spell redundancy for large numbers of workers, this ought also to lead to reorganisation of the work force so that everyone benefits from the dramatically increased productivity which is implicit in the new industrial techniques. Unfortunately for this analysis, 'Western' societies are rooted in free enterprise, capitalist economies in which (as a matter of fact – this point is not made polemically) production is for the sake of profit and not for the satisfaction of human needs. No doubt, satisfying human needs and wants is often also profitable (in making a profit the baker, the shoe and clothing manufacturer, the builder, the show business entrepreneur are all meeting human needs and aspirations), but if satisfying a particular need is not profitable, it remains unfulfilled in a free enterprise capitalist society. People are in business to make profits; they are not, on the whole, philanthropists. This is, essentially, why we develop mixed economies: the rationale for developing the public sector is that there are human needs (in the areas of education, health, etc.) which would not be addressed in any economy which is primarily fuelled by the profit motive. Indeed, a major justification of socialism hinges on the notion that the quality of life depends upon the public provision of goods and services, the universal provision of which private industry would not find profitable. Gorz has concluded that even scientific research is decreasingly devoted to projects concerned with the elimination of poverty and disease or raising the standard of life: 'the main purpose of research and innovation is to counteract the tendency of the rate of profit to fall and to create new opportunities for profitable investment' (Gorz 1978 p. 164).

The point of this insistence that in capitalist economies the profit motive ultimately overrides human need, is that the worker's need for more spare time (or, when threatened with redundancy, his need for a job) is not a 'service' which industry can provide consistently with the pursuit of profit. The fundamental weakness of the view that with the intensification of automation, vastly increased 'leisure' is an imminent probability, is that it can bear little relationship to the facts of life in capitalist economies. Under capitalism, labour-saving innovations are made to reduce costs and increase profitability, not benevolently to create leisure for workers. As the managing director of Standard Motors once put it: 'We are not installing £4 millions worth of equipment in order to employ the same number of men. We can't carry people for fun' (Quoted by Lilley 1957 p. 129). Given this kind of economic imperative, technologically induced 'leisure' becomes merely a euphemism for unemployment. For however productive an economy may be, potentially, from a technological point of view, so far as technological innovation requires a significant reduction in the work force it operates to reduce effective demand for goods and services. Unless compensating opportunities for work are created in other private or public enterprises, the only way we have of financing mass 'leisure' is through the dole, welfare benefits or pensions. Technologically induced redundancy is not an invitation to leisure so much as an imperative towards finding another job elsewhere in industry or in the public sector of the economy. Hence (this constitutes a further reason for assessing the work–leisure relationship in terms of particular economic and political systems) structural redundancy in a capitalist society also creates the problem of maintaining a satisfactory level of economic activity through its effect on demand for goods and services. In a market economy, people have to be in receipt of an income in order to keep industry in business. Yet the rhetoric of futurism often seems predicated upon the assumption that an increased capacity to supply goods and services automatically generates its own effective demand. In fact, as we have already observed, the maintenance of effective demand for labour is partly a function of political and economic decisions affecting the level of public expenditure. And if such decisions are to be properly democratic this, in turn, depends upon the quality of political education which is available to the community.[6]

In qualitative terms, the future of leisure is also inseparable from the quality of work. One common assumption about the relationship between work and leisure, is that leisure can compensate for alienation at work. Education for leisure is apt to be proposed on behalf of those whose work appears to be routine and mindless. To the extent that such people might experience a reduction of the time spent at work, it is thought desirable to ensure that their spare time is filled profitably and creatively. The assumption is that the average man lacks the personal cultural resources towards that end. Advocacy of education for leisure tends to focus upon the need for initiation into a variety of pursuits, usually of a 'play' or 'recreational' nature. No doubt there is often a genuine concern that the quality of a person's life should be enriched in this way. But one critic of what have been called 'professional leisurists' sees the emphasis upon developing 'leisure industries' and 'leisure training' as a modern version of the nineteenth century's concern for 'gentling the masses': leisure is to be the new opium of the people. As Parkin puts it, in a modern society subtle ways are found of 'ensuring social discipline and conformity by entrusting this task to the welfare professions in their capacity of moral entrepreneurs' (Parkin 1979 p. 18). One apologist for 'professional leisurists' has argued: 'Since the average citizen is unable to invent new uses for his leisure, a professional élite shares a heavy responsibility for discovering criteria for ways of employing leisure and creating enthusiasm for common ends within the moral ends of the community' (Quoted by Parker 1971 pp. 128–129). As Parker observes, this point of view is not only élitist: the notion of 'moral ends of the community' also implies 'that only certain kinds of leisure are to be promoted and that they are intended as a means of social control' (Parker, *loc. cit.*). There is also an implication of change for the sake of change in the criticism that the average man is incapable of inventing '*new* uses for his leisure'. This presumes, without explanation, that *old* uses for leisure are somehow inadequate.

It may be, of course, that the way in which many people in our society occupy their spare time leaves much to be desired from the perspective of what constitutes an educated life. A conclusion of this kind necessarily involves value judgements about the kinds of activities which are considered worthwhile components of the good life. And although these judgements which are made about other people's lives are apt to be dismissed as élitist or paternalistic, they are inescapable for social reformers and, especially, for educationists. In one form or another, the judgement that most people make less than the best use of their spare time is commonplace amongst scholars and intellectuals. Sociologists and historians from Engels down to the present day (often actively involved in the working class movement) have pointed to the deleterious effect of industrialism upon popular culture, and to the tendency of the working class to search for irrational, escapist solutions to the problems of life. However, in correlating the prevalence of mechanical, escapist, soul destroying spare time preoccupations with the existence of a particular kind of industrial and economic organisation, these sympathetic critics of the quality of much activity spent outside the workplace are also pointing to the unreality of the compensatory conception of education for leisure; the assumption that you can redeem people from the de-humanising effects of their work by teaching them how to make constructive and profitable use of their spare time. For there is an air of unreality about a notion of education for leisure which assumes that you can educate a man whose work is trivial and repetitive away from the pursuit of trivial, mechanical, spare time activities and towards those which are intellectually and aesthetically demanding. A number of modern industrial sociologists have concluded that the relationship between work and leisure has to be one of correspondence. As W.E. Moore has put it: 'leisure is a problem where work is a problem and probably proportionately. The "constructive" use of leisure is likely to depend in considerable measure on the constructive definition of jobs'. Life-styles, that is, are a package of essentially sympathetic activities, at work, at play, domestically, politically and culturally.

This conclusion opens the way towards a conception of leisure richer than one which conceives it merely as a vacuum which remains to be filled when the economic imperative to earn a living has been accommodated, and which poses the problem of education for leisure as one of helping people 'to fill their leisure hours' consequent upon a reduction of working hours or even 'the enforced leisure of unemploy-ment'. It is more fruitful to conceive of leisure as itself a way of life, a manner of conducting all life's various activities. It is mistaken to conceive of work, play and recreation, home life, political activity and social service as discontinuous. Work, especially, cannot be circum-scribed from the rest of life. Whether or not work provides intrinsic satisfactions it tends to determine one's style of living. Work frequently determines the character of our personal relationships, our friendships and, hence, the quality and pattern of recreational activity. It may be the mainspring of our activity as citizens, determining whether and how we perform social service, as well as our political allegiances. To change one's work is often also to alter one's entire pattern of life.

This conclusion that work is integral to life and, especially, to leisure is shared by diverse intellectual, religious, political and popular traditions within Western civilisation. Variously, work is regarded as an opportunity for worship and for sharing with God the Worker the task of creating and renewing the universe; as the essentially human activity which distinguishes him from the beasts; as the *raison d'être* of social organisation; as the mainspring of human culture, especially of the arts (Entwistle 1970, Ch. 2). The educational implications of this assumption that work is the central life activity, since a civilisation is the creation of human work, are most rigorously pursued in the principle of polytechnical education, the theory and practice of education in Marxist states. Dewey's educational theory and the Project method which he inspired are also rooted in the assumption he shared with Marx that what brings people together in a community is the organisation of different economic tasks to minister to human welfare. This celebration of work by different cultural traditions is paralleled by the common and widespread fear of unemployment. This is not simply a fear of economic deprivation which could be overcome by generous welfare handouts. As Lord Beveridge put it in his classic report, *Full Employment in a Free Society*: 'idleness is not the same as want, but a separate evil, which men do not escape by having an income. They must also have the chance of rendering useful service and feeling that they are doing so'. Nor is it only a matter of enabling a person to contribute towards the common good. Especially in the kind of society where a good deal of political power is exercised through the major economic institutions both capital and labour, those cut off from these institutions are also politically impotent. Pundits heralding the eighties have concluded that people will have to accept the fact of unemployment and there is even talk in 'official' circles of education for unemployment. One is at a loss to understand what this last could possibly mean, but it is inconceivable that educationists should even contemplate this notion. What the bland insistence that people can be persuaded to accept unemployment as inevitable leaves out of account is its political implications. According to what principles do we select those who are to be denied employment, not only as a source of political power, but also as the only means to an economic existence beyond mere levels of subsistence? The prevailing political and moral climate remains one where social insurance payments have to be kept at a level which is not a disincentive to work. Those fortunate enough to remain in employment will need considerable persuasion to agree to the diversion of revenues from taxation towards welfare benefits capable of sustaining even a moderately affluent standard of living for the unemployed.

The conclusion that leisure is linked closely to work and, indeed, that leisure is most profitably conceived as a way of life compounded of a variety of sympathetic life activities is underlined by the notion of a leisured class. Historically, the leisured class was not a social group without the obligation to work, dedicated to idleness and the mere pursuit of pleasure. The leisured class pursued 'honourable employments', as landowners managing their own estates, for example, thus providing employment for others, as well as government and the administration of justice at various levels in the State (Entwistle 1978, Ch. 6). The leisured class was also the ruling class. Its work was in government and the management of a rural economy, functions having economic significance. But although in one sense leisured class employments were obligatory (its continued privileges depending on the provision of good government and work for others), the essence of its leisure consisted in the freedom with which it could pursue its distinctive work. Freedom or flexibility about how and when work can be done is the essence of leisure.

In this connection, freedom was for Marx a necessary condition of the worker's delivery from alienation and it is interesting that his brief description of the ideal working life in a Communist society should evoke the lifestyle of the leisured class:

> In Communist society, where nobody has one exclusive sphere of activity but each can become accomplished in any branch he wishes, production as a whole is regulated by society, thus making it possible for me to do one thing today and another tomorrow, to hunt in the morning, fish in the afternoon, rear cattle in the evening, criticise after dinner, in accordance with my inclination, without ever becoming hunter, fisherman, shepherd or critic.

Idyllic and redolent of upper class life as this is, it has been taken as a point of departure for modern reflection upon the ways and means of improving the quality of working life and, hence, of the quality of leisure. Dahrendorf has asked, why not 'collect people's taxes in the morning and repair their cars in the afternoon, assemble television sets in the morning and go to polytechnic in the afternoon?' (Dahrendorf 1975 p. 76). This notion of redeeming workers from the alienating effects of industrial specialisation by sharing society's work so that everyone enjoys creative tasks and suffers the unpleasant chores is central to neo-Marxist prescriptions for the future of work. Evidently, this would require an entirely novel mode of economic and industrial organisation and, so far as this kind of flexibility could be a possible outcome of technological innovation, it posits a need for political education as a necessary component of vocational education.

This is to say that vocational education must be conceived more widely than in its pejorative identification with technical training for manual occupations. Even in that context, as in historical examples of apprenticeship, there was a moral dimension to the training of craftsmen. As well as the 'mystery' of his craft, the apprentice was expected to acquire a cultural orientation in which acceptance of moral and social responsibility towards the client, the community and the fraternity of one's craft was of major importance. Also, to the craftsman the notion of 'a job well done' had aesthetic overtones: especially, the aesthetic dimension was implicit in the creation of art forms associated with these economic communities, particularly drama and music. And prior to the imposition of industrial discipline which accompanied collecting craftsmen into factories, the work patterns of industrial artisans shared some of those characteristics of 'leisure in work' (especially in relation to timing) that we have suggested are the prerogatives of a leisured class.

Thus, to have a vocation in its traditional sense is to do a job in a cultural context requiring an appreciation of the close connection between technical skill, personal taste, citizenship, morality and, perhaps, religion. In this sense, vocational education requires technical and professional training, but also political, aesthetic and moral education. It is this necessary reference to other cultural dimensions, as well as to the individual's capacity for acquiring 'technical' skills, which can ensure that vocational education becomes a liberating experience. A liberal education is one which frees the learner from whatever constraints might hinder his development as a person. And if our repeated conclusion throughout this essay that future problems of work and leisure are likely to be as much a matter of political organisation and of the choices we make about what constitutes 'the good life' (including the obligation to make that available to as many as possible of our fellow men) as they are of the commercial and industrial management of technological innovation, then political and moral education are inescapable components of vocational education and education for leisure.

No doubt all this points, conservatively, to something like the traditional, humanistic, liberal curriculum, suitably modernised to encompass new forms of knowledge and properly concretised to speak to a variety of student interests, talents, aspirations and needs. But as is often the case in periods of normative confusion, a return to educational first principles may be the most appropriate way of finding our way out of current social dilemmas and of establishing signposts towards ways of harnessing technological innovation for the humanisation of work and leisure.

Notes

1   The use of this term has been criticised, especially for implying technological homogeneity in modern societies where the most advanced production processes co-exist with other industrial processes, including traditional crafts. However, the term is a useful shorthand for characterising an economy in which modernisation increasingly employs cybernetics, computers and micro-electronic technology.

2   This distinction between mechanisation and automation is elaborated in Entwistle, 1970. Other issues dealt with only summarily in this essay are also examined there in detail. See also Entwistle, 1978, Chapter 6.

3   For statistics illustrating the scale of the shift to work roles preparatory to production with reference to the Ford Motor Company, see Galbraith, 1972.

4   Demographic trends in relation to education are the subject of another paper in this book. However, what has been called 'the greying of the future' (the calculation that fifty years hence the number of pensioners to be supported by every active worker will be doubled) has obvious implications for any discussion of available employ-

ment in the future. Apart from the fact that the contraction of the demand for labour will be matched by a diminishing supply of workers, it is also a fact that the retired population will make increased demands upon public services concerned especially with health and welfare.

5   See Rinehart, 1975; the historical trend to diminish the status and remuneration of clerical workers to a point close to the bottom of the occupational ladder is outlined by Braverman, 1974, Chapter 15.

6   This argument that technological innovation does not automatically make increased 'leisure' available to workers does not preclude the possibility that associations of workers may bargain for a reduction in working hours as a part of the continuing struggle of labour with capital for a larger share of industrial revenues. But any shortening of the time at work has to be seen in the context of that struggle, and not as the inevitable outcome of technological change. Moreover, although industrialists sometimes willingly reduce working hours in response to Hawthorn-type research, this is done in expectation of higher productivity and profits, not in terms of the employee's intrinsic need for more 'leisure'.

3
Educational Policies for a Multi-racial Britain

Alan Little

Immigration control and anti-discrimination legislation have been the twin political responses to a multi-racial Britain; the inconsistency between the two pieces of policy – immigration control motivated by colour consciousness and anti-discrimination legislation that seeks to eliminate discrimination by colour – has not escaped critical attention. Nevertheless, in the political arena (and also in the public mind) the policies are seen to be inter-related. A Labour Home Secretary summarised his Government's policy as 'an absolutely firm and determined front . . . against any form of discrimination within our society, accompanied by the recognition that there is a clear limit to the amount of immigration this country can absorb. That being so, the maintenance of a strict control is very much in the interests not only of the majority but the minorities' (House of Commons Debates 912 col. 112). To which his Conservative shadow agreed that 'closely linked problems of immigration from the New Commonwealth and race relations' (House of Commons Debates 912 col. 86) were disturbing to the community at large and should be seen as the two sides of race relations. Control of immigration and anti-discrimination legislation have been imposed with the support in principle and usually in practice of all three major parties.

What is lacking in current race relations policy is the establishment of a set of social policies responsive to the needs of a multi-racial society and designed to achieve equality of conditions and opportunity between different racial and ethnic groups. The need for such policies was recognised in the 1975 White Paper on Racial Discrimination: 'What is here proposed for a further attack on discrimination (i.e. the 1976 Race Relations Act) will need to be supplemented by a more comprehensive structure for dealing with the related and at least equally important problem of disadvantage' (Home Office 1975 para. 26) – a point the Home Secretary was careful to emphasise on the Second Reading of the Race Relations Bill in March 1976: 'a wide range of administrative and voluntary measures is needed in order to give practical effect to the objectives of the law. These measures are needed not only to combat discrimination and encourage equal opportunity but also to tackle what has become known as racial disadvantage' (House of Commons Debates 906 col. 1548).

Education's contribution: 'develop potentialities and understanding'

The area of social policy of particular importance for achieving a racially just and harmonious society is education. This point is recognised by government. For example, in its response to the Select Committee on Race Relations and Immigration, while admitting that 'it would be wrong to suppose that education alone could achieve all the objectives on which society may set its sights, or that it could function unaffected by conditions in society at large', government policy was 'that the education service has important contributions to make both to the well-being of immigrant communities in this country and to the promotion of harmony between the different ethnic groups of which our society is now composed. This is because first the education service is made responsible to assist citizens of all ages to develop their opportunities to the full and within that responsibility has a special obligation to children who for one reason or another are most at risk of not achieving their true potential, and second education would be a potent instrument for increasing understanding and well being between races' (Home Office 1974 para. 1). These point to the potential twin contributions of education, identifying and meeting the special needs of black pupils and communities, and preparing all pupils for life in a multi-racial society.

What factors should educational policies for achieving relative justice between racial groups take into account? In my view, amongst the wealth of fact and opinion about the educational situation of black children, eight points stand out in determining their educational needs:

1 CONCENTRATION

Ethnic minority communities make up a relatively small proportion of the total population (around 5 per cent) and a slightly larger proportion of the child population (around 7 per cent of births are to women who were born in the New Commonwealth). The concentration of black people in relatively few areas means that proportions in particular schools and local authorities are much higher. Several years ago, when the DES was counting the numbers of immigrant children in schools (immigrant children were defined as children born outside the UK, or born to parents who had been in this country for less than ten years), two local authorities had more than 25 per cent of their pupils defined as immigrant, five between 20 per cent and 25 per cent, and a further six between 15 per cent and 20 per cent. In addition, some authorities with few children of immigrant origins overall had certain schools with large percentages; for example, nearly one school in 33 in 1972 had more than a quarter of its pupils of immigrant origin (Little 1975).

Current population figures take this point further (Office of Population Census and Surveys 1977 Table 4). Places like Bradford, Birmingham, Leicester, Wolverhampton and the entire GLC area currently have a fifth or more of their school entrants born to women from the New Commonwealth and Pakistan. In areas like these the black child is not a small proportion of the school population but a sizeable element and the issue of their progress in school is a major one facing the school and the Local Authority. The practical policy consequence of uneven distribution of multi-ethnic communities is that the issues and problems of special need are unevenly shared and therefore certain authorities require support from outside.

2   NEWNESS
Insofar as some of these children's difficulties stem from newness to this country, and the fact of cultural and language difficulties, one should not be just looking at the coloured community but at all immigrant groups. For example, in the ILEA recently, 7 per cent of all live births were to women from Ireland, 23 per cent to women from the New Commonwealth and Pakistan, and 12 per cent to women from other countries. Four out of ten (41 per cent) of all births were to immigrants. In the borough of Brent the total in 1975 was 64 per cent (18 per cent, 38 per cent and 8 per cent). Kensington and Chelsea had 50 per cent and four other London boroughs had a figure of a half or more (Office of Population Census and Surveys 1977 Table 4). In areas like these, immigrant groups generally and the coloured groups in particular make up a large element of the child and family populations. They are a significant part of the client group for pre-school and school services; newness, language, cultural and religious differences make up the new social situation that public services must respond to.

3   VARIED NEEDS
Different areas (and, in particular, different schools) will have different sorts of educational needs as a consequence of the presence of children of different migrant groups, and therefore the nature of the response of the educational system may well have to differ. Reviewing ILEA's experience, its leader, Sir Ashley Bramall, said: 'Inner London has 25 per cent of the West Indian population of the whole country: in Spitalfields 40 per cent of the population is Bengali and of 28 children taken into one primary school in the area this September, 23 knew no English at all; in one Church of England school in Soho, 50 per cent of

the children are Chinese; in North Kensington and Paddington hotel owners are recruiting ever-increasing numbers of rural Moroccans whose children arrive in schools without even the most rudimentary knowledge of urban life' (*Education* 3 December 1976). Different groups with differing needs and requiring varied educational responses. A second but related point is that most of these schools are racially mixed and have pupils from the indigenous population as well as children of migrants. Five years ago in the ILEA (one of the areas of highest concentration of migrants and especially coloured migrants) eight out of ten black children were in schools in which the black pupils made up less than one fifth of the children of the school. Without doubt schools exist which are largely Chinese, Asian or West Indian, but these are rare. What does exist is a large number of schools with an ethnically mixed pupil body, and educational policies must reflect this: multi-racial education must enable black and white pupils to have equality of educational opportunity in an atmosphere of mutual tolerance.

4   SOCIAL DISADVANTAGE

The areas with concentrations of black people tend to be areas of urban decay and social disadvantage. Black people have not created the problems of the inner cities but for a variety of reasons (not least racial discrimination) they have been forced to live in them. The Department of the Environment's analysis of the 1971 census was that 70 per cent of the black community are concentrated in 10 per cent of enumeration districts in which they constituted roughly a fifth of the total population. When these 10 per cent of enumeration districts are compared with others on measures of housing deprivation, the Department found that they contain nearly three times the proportion of households which share or lack hot water, twice as many sharing or lacking a bath, nearly three times as many households living at a density above the statutory over-crowding level, and twice as many without exclusive use of basic amenities (Department of the Environment, unpublished research; see also Holtermann 1975). Of the top 12 urban areas with the greatest incidence of urban blight, nine were amongst the areas with the highest proportion of immigrants. These are the multi-racial inner-city areas of urban decline, and the educational consequences of this are profound. Professionals in these areas have had to respond to the long-established problems of social disadvantage and to this has been added the issue of race relations. They have responded with only limited aid from Local Authorities, training institutions and central government.

5   THE BACKLASH

The school problems are a combination of social and racial disadvantage. Policies must recognise this. The important question is why they have failed to do so. In a review of policies for dealing with racial inequality in housing a CRC study concluded that there were 'two major restraints on policy . . . central government restrictions and the need to take into account the reactions of the majority population' (Community Relations Commission 1976a p. 40). The majority attitudes, according to the report, 'did not always act as a restraint on policy, but it was certainly part of the context in which policy was formed'. The term used in the US for this is 'fear of the white backlash' (see Glazer 1975, Ch. 5).

Recently the House of Commons debated a proposal for creating a special fund to assist Local Authorities meet the need of ethnic groups and create conditions for equal and harmonious race relations. Although the majority of speakers were in favour of the Bill, opponents kept coming back to the issue of the backlash. One speaker warned that: 'It is no good thinking that ordinary, white, working-class people who exist in all the inner cities and who feel they are deprived, are not keenly aware that there is a form of discrimination that is likely to be codified . . . the broad mass of white people in inner cities stand on one side and there are enclaves of coloured people to whom preferential allocation of funds will be made . . .' Another member drew attention to the danger of 'appearing to discriminate in favour of certain groups . . . it offends the majority of the population and thereby sours rather than helps race relations' (House of Commons Debates 964 cols. 101, 134).

Noting this resentment is not new: a Circular from the DES to Local Education Authorities in 1965 put this sentence in italics: 'It would be helpful if the parents of non-immigrant children can see that practical measures have been taken to deal with the problems in the schools, and that the progress of their own children is not being restricted by the undue preoccupation of the teaching staff with the linguistic and other difficulties of migrant children' (DES Circular 7/65). Behind the official words the meaning is clear: political and administrative anxieties about the reactions of the indigenous population in multi-racial areas both to the presence of coloured pupils and policies to help them. Policies in the area of race relations must take note of these reactions – that is the message that politicians and administrators have received – and it is reasonable that they should respond to people's fears and anxieties. However, not every response need be to reinforce or follow them. Politicians have a responsibility to lead and inform public opinion, not merely to follow or fuel it.

6 MINORITY DEMANDS

The white backlash is not the only reaction that has to be taken into account. Increasingly the reactions of minority communities themselves must be noted in policy development. A significant pointer in that direction is the Community Relations Commission study of the 1974 general election, indicating the potential and actual political influence of the minority vote (Community Relations Commission 1975). This study concluded that without the support of ethnic minorities, Labour would not have won an overall majority in the October 1974 election. Despite this, when questioned on how Asians might vote in an election, the then Prime Minister, James Callaghan, is quoted as saying, 'It is not a matter which I wish to discuss. I do not think we should discuss these issues on a question of race at all' (*The Times*, 3 January 1978). But insofar as certain issues are directed at racially distinct sections of the community, and insofar as the perceived anxiety amongst the majority population inhibited professional, administrative and political action on race relations matters, no one should be surprised (or dismayed) when minority communities themselves react in a vocal and organised manner on issues that affect them as ethnic minority groups.

7 UNDERFUNCTIONING

There is no comprehensive information about the performance of children in schools, and therefore the data on the comparative performance of white and black children come from a limited number of studies. The best known of these have been undertaken by the Inner London Education Authority (Little 1975). Several findings are of profound significance for developing an education policy for multi-racial areas. (a) There is a wide gap in performance between the children of minority backgrounds and the indigenous population. At the end of primary schooling, the children of New Commonwealth migrants in the ILEA had a reading age of approximately one year below the national norms for their age groups. (b) The most important factor in determining educational functioning appears to be length of education in the UK, but even pupils fully educated in the UK are not functioning at the same level as the indigenous population. At transfer to secondary school, the ILEA bands pupils into three broad groups (top 25 per cent, middle 50 per cent and bottom 25 per cent) on verbal reasoning, English and mathematics. The percentage of immigrant children fully educated in the UK in the top 25 per cent are given in Table 1 for the three years 1966, 1968 and 1971:

TABLE I

	Verbal Reasoning	English	Mathematics
1966	12	13	14
1968	10	12	12
1971	13	12	12

Educational policies for a multi-racial Britain

In all three years the percentage of immigrant children in the top 25 per cent is roughly half what should be expected, and half what the indigenous achieve. Further, there was little change over the five year period under review (1966–1971). Admittedly, in one sense this is a relatively short time period to expect change, but in educational terms it is a long period, insofar as it is nearly the length of a child's primary schooling. (c) Children from different ethnic backgrounds who are fully educated in this country appear to be functioning at different levels. Of the two main immigrant groups in the ILEA (West Indian and Asian), Asians who have completed all their primary education in this country appear to be doing as well as the indigenous population.

TABLE 2

Percentage of pupils fully educated placed in the upper quartile on transfer to secondary school, 1968

	English	Mathematics	Verbal Reasoning
West Indian origin	9.2	7.4	7.2
Asian origin	19.3	20.2	21.1
Indigenous	25.0	22.9	19.8

Studies on smaller samples of secondary schools reinforce this conclusion. Comparing boys from South Asia with indigenous whites at the end of secondary schooling in Newcastle, Taylor confidently states: 'Asians do better' (J.H. Taylor 1976). As one committee notes, 'Taylor shows that both educational achievement and commitment to educational success was a great deal higher amongst the South Asian respondents than it was amongst a matched sample of English boys' (Driver and Ballard 1979). In a study of a 16 plus cohort in Leicester, Singh found that the achievement of Asian pupils in 16 plus examinations was 'no worse than their white peers', despite the fact that 42 per cent had not received their primary schooling in Britain. Further, a very much higher proportion of Asians than whites transferred to grammar school to take sixth form courses, and over half of those who left school enrolled at a college of further education (Brooks and Singh 1978). Brooks studied Asian school leavers in Walsall and concluded: 'It is the similarities between white and Asian educational performance which is impressive, rather than any difference' (Brooks and Singh 1978). In a study of three schools with large numbers of Asian pupils, Driver and Ballard report that, with the exception of English language, the South Asian pupils consistently out-performed their English classmates. For example, in maths 'their superiority could hardly have been more marked'. They also found in one school that 'while at 13 plus the South Asian children came a full

61

year behind the English children in mean reading age . . . by 16 plus the situation had changed completely' (Driver and Ballard 1979).

There are two reasons for the better performance of Asians than pupils of West Indian origin, one of which is speculative, and one of which can be documented. The speculative one is what children bring to school, the empirical one what they receive there. Asian children come from stable cultural backgrounds with their own languages, religions, cultures and values which include prizing learning for its own sake and encouraging striving for self-improvement. This gives the child a clear sense of its own ethnic identity and personal worth quite independent of the dominant culture's reaction to it. This is not true of West Indians, whose cultural background is essentially a variant of the dominant culture, which to no small extent disparages, and even rejects, their colour. Asian pupils bring to school a positive sense of their own worth. (How long that will be preserved if the system fails to support its survival is another question.) In a different way, Driver and Ballard make a similar point: they contend that South Asian pupils have been much less 'socialised to failure' than their white classmates, and ethnic affiliation, far from being a handicap or disadvantage 'must surely be regarded as a positive resource' (Driver and Ballard 1979).

Further, it is not difficult for the educational system to identify and respond to the more obvious needs of Asian pupils. It is easy to see that non-English speakers require additional help with the English language, and it is relatively simple to create the political climate within which this can be achieved. The same cannot be said for the needs of West Indians, which are much more difficult to identify, subtle in nature, and possibly more threatening to the white culture. Local authorities have made considerable strides to meet Asian needs, but not those of West Indians, and this is one of the major conclusions of Townsend and Brittain's study of school responses to the presence of black and brown children (Townsend and Brittain 1972 p. 135).

It is apparent that the teaching of English to non-English-speaking pupils is seen by multi-racial schools as their major task. Schools deal with this task in many different ways according to their own philosophy and to the resources available by local education authorities. What is not so clear is the level of proficiency in English at which schools decide that no further special arrangements are necessary. The question of 'second stage' English, following the initial achievement of literacy, appears as yet to be imperfectly understood in either the need or the approach. Equally misunderstood perhaps are the need for, and approach to, teaching pupils of West Indian origin to use the English idiom, pronunciation and intonation.

(d) There is no evidence to suggest that the situation of West Indians is improving with the children's progress through school: the ILEA Literacy Survey tested the same children aged 8 plus, 10 plus and 15 plus between 1968 and 1975. At age 8, the gap in the mean reading score between West Indians and indigenous was 10.5 standard points, at the end of primary school it was 11.2 and at 15 plus 12.3 points. If reading standards are an adequate indication of intellectual development (and there is considerable evidence to suggest that they are), one must conclude that the gap in performance is widening with school career. Certainly there is no evidence of these pupils catching up, or narrowing the gap. (e) West Indian children are functioning at a level not only below indigenous population, but also below socially disadvantaged sections of it. To take one example, a comparison on a standard reading test between West Indians fully educated in the UK tested at 8, 10 and 15 and children from unskilled working class backgrounds, on mean scores:

TABLE 3

	West Indian fully educated	Children of un-skilled background	Difference
8 +	89.9	93.7	4.2
10 +	88.7	93.5	4.8
15 +	87.1	92.1	5.0

At each age, the unskilled working-class child is on average reading at a significantly higher level than a child of West Indian origin. Given the wealth of evidence in the literature on the under-performance of white working-class children, this is a disturbing finding. This (and other points made earlier) has been confirmed by a study of 11 plus year olds in eight multi-racial schools in one Outer London borough. The report notes that these schools are mainly situated in the poorer parts of the borough, and so, 'the indigenous pupils as a group scored below the national average. The Asian pupils as a group scored significantly below the whites, and the West Indians scored significantly below the Asians. Bearing in mind the fact that the Asian group would include some very poor English speakers, the score of the West Indian pupils gives real cause of concern' (Redbridge, CRC 1978). This point was reinforced by an example of one secondary school in the borough: of first year pupils, over one quarter (27 per cent) received remedial help. Of children of West Indian origin, this figure was nearly half (46 per cent). By the time of 'O' level/CSE the average number of passes for all grades was 4.2 for white pupils, and 1.0 for students of West Indian origin. (f) The gap in performance between black pupils and socially-disadvantaged whites can be demonstrated early in the pupil's school career. Stages I and II of the English Picture Vocabulary Test (i.e. the infant school and junior school stages) were used in the ILEA Educational Priority Study (Barnes 1975a) and the results are given in Table 4

TABLE 4

| | Level 1 | | Level 2 | |
	N	Mean	N	Mean
All pupils	1341	94.5	1551	90.9
Non-immigrant	957	97.9	1162	92.9
West Indian	298	86.9	250	85.5

Several interesting points emerge from this analysis: pupils in schools defined as EPA score over five points below the national norm on Level 1, and nine points below on Level 2. West Indians in infant schools (and therefore pupils who are likely to have a full United Kingdom education in the future) score 13 points below their national age peers, and 11 points below their indigenous classmates. In junior schools, the gap between them and their national age peers is nearly 15 points, and with class peers, over seven points. What stands out is that even at a very young age (i.e. in infant schools), the indigenous white pupil in the EPA school is performing at a significantly higher level than his black classmate but at a significantly lower level than his national age peer. It is worth noting that this finding is confirmed by a study completed in another EPA area using the pre-school version of the English Picture Vocabulary Test: 63 non-immigrants in the area (mean age of 4 years 7 months) had a standardised score of 84.1 (Barnes 1975a). This indicates that the gap in passive vocabulary pre-dates school entry. A similar point has been carefully documented by Pollack; in her Brixton survey she found that children of West Indian parentage were found to be developmentally disadvantaged at three years old, compared to indigenous children living in the same inner-city working-class neighbourhood; on tests of adaptive behaviour, language and personal/social development given to three year olds in Brixton, West Indian children scored lower than other children (Pollak 1972).

(g) The teaching profession is concerned not only with the educational performance of children of West Indian origin, but also with their behaviour in school. Research by Rutter and colleagues shows that teachers report a higher incidence of maladjusted behaviour in school (Rutter *et al* 1974 pp. 241–262, 1975 pp. 105–124). In a study in South London, they found that: 'West Indian children showed rather more behavioural difficulties at school, but they did not differ from other children in terms of disorder at home. Nor did they differ from other children in terms of emotional disturbance in any setting'. A clue to the link between school performance and behaviour is given by a study by Varlaam, which examined the relationship between reading standards and maladjusted behaviour: the conclusion was that 'when the two conditions (reading retardation and behaviour disorders) are found together, there is a better chance that reading retardation preceded behaviour difficulties than the other way round, and second, that such a chance is particularly strong when the children involved come from large families or have a West Indian background' (Varlaam 1974). Educational failure may create the maladjusted behaviour schools report.

8   DISCRIMINATION

A final point to be taken into account is the fact of racial hostility and discrimination. This affects children at school in various ways: initially they experience the consequence of discrimination on their parents (who have had limited job opportunities, poor housing, etc.). As a result, their own upbringing is less favourable than it might have been. We know, for example, that the incidence of multiple disadvantage is three times as high in the West Indian community as in the general population (Community Relations Commission 1976a p. 15). Later, young people leaving school face discrimination in the labour market; the Office of Population and Census Survey is following up matched pairs of black and white school leavers, and it has shown that it takes four times as many interviews in careers offices to place a West Indian school leaver as his white counterpart, despite similar qualifications and education experience (Select Committee on Race Relations and Immigration 1976). Schools contain pupils of all ethnic groups, who have grown up in a prejudiced world, and are therefore prejudiced themselves: the development of racial prejudices and stereotypes, even in young children, has been extensively documented, and David Milner has shown how feelings of rejection threaten the identity of coloured children, and generate learning problems for them (Milner 1975).

Finally, aspects of the school experience (the curriculum, teaching methods, etc.) may unintentionally intimidate many coloured pupils. While, for example, the content of history or geography courses may be offensive, because of cultural biases, probably the most important influence is the attitude of the teacher: Elaine Brittain argues from her research that 'the needs of multi-racial schools were not being fully understood and recognised by the teachers' and, more disturbing, she found amongst teachers interviewed, evidence of 'large scale stereotypes of West Indian pupils'. It is clear (she argues) that teachers perceive West Indian pupils as 'of low ability and creating disciplinary problems' (Brittain 1976). Therefore, in addition to anything else, educational policy must respond to the fact of racial discrimination and negative stereotypes, some of which is contained in the schools.

The official responses: 'Trying to avoid tension and hatred?'

I THE GOVERNMENT

What has been the 'official' educational response to the policy needs of multi-racial areas? The first indication of Government interest in what was happening in schools in multi-racial areas came as a result of an angry meeting in Southall in 1963 when the then Minister of Education, Sir Edward (now Lord) Boyle faced a large group of English parents who protested vehemently at the number of immigrant children in two particular primary schools. In what appears to have been a panic measure taken to defuse the situation, the Minister recommended in Parliament that no school should contain more than about 30 per cent immigrants, and promised his support for any Authority which tried to spread its immigrant pupils throughout its schools.

Shortly after Boyle had announced Government policy, and as a result of the Inspectorate's necessary involvement in advising LEAs on the educational needs of immigrants, the Ministry issued its pamphlet No. 43 *English for Immigrants*. This recommended the use of specifically-trained teachers of English as a second language, and gave general suggestions of educational arrangements for immigrants. In Circular 1/65 it invited Local Authorities to put in requests for permission to employ above quota 'staff in multi-racial schools', although no additional financial assistance was made available.

The next Government statement on the education of immigrants and the last for six years, was Circular 7/65, issued in June 1965. The main recommendation of this circular was that the number of immigrants in any one school should be kept to a maximum of one-third. The recommendation was based on the premise that 'As the proportion of immigrant children in a school or class increases, the problem will become more difficult to solve, and the chances of assimilation more remote . . . Up to a fifth of immigrant children in any one group fit in with reasonable ease, but if the proportion goes over about one-third, either in the school as a whole or in any one class, serious strains arise.'

Two points are interesting about this: first, of the handful of LEAs who implemented a policy of 'dispersal', in one of these the Race Relations Board subsequently (1975) formed the opinion that they were acting in breach of the Race Relations Act, and at least two others were investigated by the Race Relations Board. Secondly, it is ironic that detailed research in the ILEA of the performance of black and white children aged 8 and 11 concluded that 'there was no evidence to justify – on the grounds of academic attainment – the limiting of immigrant intake into a school, either by housing or controlled entry, or of attempting some kind of social engineering' (Mabey 1974).

The 1965 Circular further emphasised the importance of English language teaching, and the need for follow-up or 'second stage' help, for children who had received basic tuition in English. It also hinted at the needs of dialect speakers, without actually mentioning West Indians. Much emphasis was put on 'Commonwealth teaching' and 'Education for International Understanding' – more an optional extra to the curriculum than a reorientation. Classes for adult immigrants were also recommended, and local authorities were offered some elementary advice on how to publicise such courses.

The first Government intervention to bring assistance to multi-racial areas was through the Local Government Act, 1966. Section 11 of this Act enables central Government to pay to local authorities making 'special provision in the exercise of any of their functions in consequence of the presence within their areas of substantial numbers of immigrants from the Commonwealth whose language or customs differ from those of the community' grants for expenditure in respect of the employment of staff. Originally such a grant was at the rate of 50 per cent of expenditure, but this was later increased to 75 per cent. In applying this Section, the Home Office required local authorities to provide evidence of the number of immigrants in their area, and the Department of Education and Science statistics were used as a measurement. In fact, the education service has been the major user of Section 11 funds.

The Association of Metropolitan Authorities, while welcoming Section 11, in evidence to the Home Office, thought it suffered from a number of disadvantages. First, payment is always after the event (and so there is no immediate source of finance to meet unforeseen difficulties). Its limitation to cover only staff makes it too restrictive, and a limited definition of 'immigrant' further curtails its use. As a result, 'authorities are in certain respects inadequately reimbursed'. Hardly, in their view, an adequate policy, and to these disadvantages a working party of the Chief Education Officers, convened by the Community Relations Commission, added two further points:

(a) Uneven take-up. Some LEAs take considerable advantage of the Section 11 fund, whilst others, with similar proportions of ethnic minority children, take very much less.

(b) Lack of strategy. No requirement is placed on local authorities to ensure that Section 11 appointments concerned with needs of minority groups are related to any general appraisal of the need in their area for special provision or any strategy to meet this need.

Because of this, the working party concluded: 'As far as education services are concerned, *the DES as the central department concerned has not been directly associated with the LEAs to the extent necessary to achieve the identification of needs, desirable levels of provision and objectives. Perhaps for this reason no national policy on ethnic minority education has emerged during the period of nearly ten years in which the Section 11 fund has been administered.*' (Community Relations Commission 1976b, pp. 4, 6).

Without having a funding or educational policy on multi-racial education, the DES continued to produce statements on the education of immigrants, in *Potential and Progress in a Second Culture* (Education Survey 10, 1971), *The Education of Immigrants* (Education Survey 13, 1971) and *The Continuing Needs of Immigrants* (Education Survey 14, 1972). These dealt respectively with assessment of attainment and intelligence of immigrant pupils, general policies and practices in the education of immigrants, and the need to continue special help for immigrant pupils after the initial stage of English teaching. In Education Survey 13, the Department considerably modified its views on dispersal, while leaving it to local education authorities to decide which policy was the most suitable for their situation. It stressed that no policy affecting groups of children should be allowed to take precedence over the reasonable wishes of individual parents in the matter of choice of school. A quotation from the Chief Education Officers' report for the CRC summarises their view of the DES's position: 'Little attempt appears to have been made either to formulate a national policy other than in the most general terms, or to estimate the cost of an adequate ethnic minority education programme'. Many of these points were accepted by the recent Labour Government (and also by the Conservative Party in opposition). In March 1979 the Government presented to the House of Commons a bill designed to replace Section 11 and, as its spokesman said, to meet its commitment to support 'a comprehensive attack upon racial disadvantage' (House of Commons Debates 964 col. 55). The Minister's speech also saw the need for a comprehensive strategy; he said that the Bill outlined the strategy for allocating resources to combat racial disadvantage and 'therefore repairs two deficiencies of the 1966 Act. It provides for three grounds upon which the local authorities must incur expenditure in furtherance of their function. The first is in the removal of disadvantage from which an ethnic group suffers. The second is in securing that a local authority's services are as effective in relation to ethnic groups as they are to the rest of the community. The third and final ground is the promotion of good relations between ethnic groups, and between those groups and the rest of the community.' The Opposition front bench spokesman, while recognising 'the limitations of Section 11, which the Minister fairly outlined' and re-emphasising the party's 'strongly held view that measures to remove disadvantage and deprivation suffered uniquely by ethnic groups can and should be supported' argued that they had 'two major fears about the Bill, which the Minister's speech did not dispel. First, there is scope for positive discrimination towards any group, and that discrimination could be on a large scale. Secondly, the Bill perpetuates, and encourages the perpetuation of, the separateness of the immigrant and the ethnic minority community.' As a consequence it would be 'bitterly resented by many people. It would be regarded as offensively patronising by many members of the ethnic minority groups themselves.'

2 LOCAL AUTHORITIES

Turning now to local education authorities, Townsend's 'Immigrant Pupils in England – the LEA response' shows the range of provision made by 71 authorities (Townsend 1971). All of them made arrangements for the teaching of English as a second language at secondary stage, all but four at junior stage, and all but twelve at infant stage. The arrangements ranged from the provision of an extra peripatetic teacher spending a few lessons a week with withdrawal groups, through full-time language classes within schools, to part-time and full-time language centres. One authority had a highly-organised peripatetic service of nearly 100 teachers. Oddly, the scale of the special arrangements did not always bear a relation to the size of the ethnic minority population in schools, and neighbouring authorities catered for similar situations in widely differing ways. For example, no other authority with a large Asian population provides language teaching to infants on the same scale as Bradford, and the West Indian Supplementary Service in Waltham Forest has no parallel among other authorities with sizeable West Indian populations. Similar diversity is seen in the distribution of immigrant children in ESN schools. Some London authorities have high disproportions of West Indian children in such schools, while other authorities, mainly outside London, do not.

A further example of the varied response of local authorities can be seen in the take-up of Section 11 grants: neighbouring authorities with similar racial compositions make very different claims, Ealing, for example, claiming twice as much per immigrant as Brent, Coventry only a third of Nottingham (Community Relations Commission 1976b p. 11). A simple explanation of the disparity is that those authorities with a higher expenditure per head of immigrant population are also those which have developed more intensive programmes for the education of minorities. There is no evidence that this is so, and difference may well reflect a greater awareness on the part of some authorities of the possibilities of Section 11, and political and professional willingness to use it. But the Department has not seen fit publicly to pressure authorities actively to use Section 11.

LEA response has therefore been patchy and (with the exception of initial language training) limited: a conclusion the CRC came to when it followed up the main recommendations of an early Select Committee report. The Select Committee recommended more in-service training in race relations and the teaching of immigrants, the appointment of special immigrant education advisers and educational social workers to encourage home-school links, and more teachers from minority ethnic groups. Out of 49 LEAs with more than 2 per cent immigrant pupils, only a fifth were frequently providing the in-service training recommended. Less than one-third had an adviser on immigrant education, a half left home visiting to the education welfare officers. Two out of three saw no special reason to employ teachers from minority ethnic groups (Community Relations Commission 1974).

3   TEACHER TRAINING
Teacher training institutions were slow to respond to the training implications of multi-racial education systems: it was only in the second half of the 1960s that colleges of education began to pay some attention to the needs of immigrant pupils. When the Robbins Committee reported in 1963 they declared one of the aims of higher education was 'the transmission of a common culture and common standards of citizenship', but it seemed clear that they had only the indigenous culture and its standards in mind, and saw no need at that time to relate to a multi-cultural society. The James Committee, in 1971, concluded that 'an understanding of the multi-cultural nature of society should feature in any general education'. Some ten years after the Robbins Report, the Select Committee on Race Relations and Immigration, reporting on education, held the view that 'all students on initial and postgraduate courses can and should be made aware that, wherever they teach, they will be doing so in a multi-cultural society.'
In 1970, the Community Relations Commission published an analysis of the influence of the multi-racial nature of many of Britain's schools on the syllabuses of colleges of education. The findings were that, by 1968, 'a significant number of colleges were paying systematic attention in their courses to the problems of immigrants', and that this was being done through two major areas of study – the education of children from immigrant communities, and the teaching of all children, in a multi-cultural society. However, experience shows that only a very small number of students emerge from college having been given any assistance in understanding the demands that will be made upon them when they teach in multi-racial urban areas. In 1974, a Joint Working Party of the CRC and the Association of Teachers in Colleges and Departments of Education produced a report *Teacher Education for a Multi-Cultural Society*, which looked at provision for all students, specialist options in initial training, postgraduate courses and in-service training and gave some detailed examples of courses

actually being offered in certain colleges. It recommended that all students should be given an awareness of the educational implications of a multi-cultural society; that this awareness should also be incorporated in courses for other categories of students studying in reorganised institutions of higher education; that specialist options should be provided in initial training for students who plan to teach in multi-racial areas, that colleges should use their expertise and resources to provide a variety of in-service courses, in co-operation with the local education authorities. There is still little evidence that training institutions are approaching the education of minority groups in more than a haphazard way. While there are some notable examples of colleges where this issue is given serious attention, they are in a very small minority.

The Select Committee's National Programme: 'Grasping the scale of what we have taken on'

Earlier the judgment of a Chief Education Officers' Working Party that 'little attempt appears to have been made to formulate a national policy . . . or to establish the cost of an adequate ethnic minority education programme' was quoted, and it is a conclusion that is equally pertinent for many local authorities and training institutions. Three limitations of existing policies stand out: lack of systematic educational strategy to tackle the problem on a local level, insufficient advice and support from central government to LEAs and from local education authorities to schools and inadequate financial aid to authorities and schools under stress. The Select Committee put its finger on all three in 1973 when it recommended: 'First, that consideration be given to the establishment of a central fund to which local education authorities could apply for resources to meet the special educational needs of immigrant children and adults; second, that local education authorities should be required, as a condition of using the Department's resources and services, to report regularly and fully on the situation in their area and what they are doing about it; third, that an immigrant education advisory unit should be set up in the Department of Education and Science' (Select Committee on Race Relations and Immigration, Education, 1973, Report p. 226). These are the pre-conditions for effective local authority and school action but these were turned down by the Department of Education and Science for reasons given in the Government's reply to the Select Committee (Home Office 1974 paras. 2, 3). On the development of a special advisory unit the Government accepted 'the fact of immigration and its continuing consequences'. However, the fall in immigration will mean 'an ever-increasing proportion of the children of immigrant descent entering the schools will have been born in this country, many of them to parents settled here for many years or indeed themselves born here. It is true that some of these children may have been reared in the language and customs of the country of origin and may need the same sort of help as a newly arrived immigrant child. *But, where immigrants and their descendants live in the older urban and industrial areas, the majority of their children are likely to share with the indigenous children of those areas the educational disadvantages associated with an impoverished environment. The Government believes that immigrant pupils will accordingly benefit increasingly from special help given to all those suffering from educational disadvantage.'*

The main argument is that the needs of minorities (with the exceptions of the problems of newness, language and culture differences) can best be met by general policies for the disadvantaged. There is a great deal in this argument: black communities share with a large section of the white population the problems of persistent and chronic inequalities, and so their situation would be considerably improved by general and radical social improvements. Policy makers are also faced by the problems of being seen to favour minority communities and ignoring the needs of the numerically larger host community. Therefore general programmes for social equality would be desirable politically. But would they meet all the needs of the black communities? First, it must be noted that the exceptions (newness, language and culture) would still justify a serious advisory and support effort if needs are to be met effectively. Secondly, the argument underestimates the extent to which the history of racial discrimination creates problems that schools must respond to and the difficulty of creating the political climate for generating that response. Many of the difficulties facing black children are the result of long histories of colonial exploitation and the existence of colour prejudice and discrimination in contemporary Britain. Schools cannot change these things: but the educational system can try to help black pupils develop as black people in a largely white society with a sense of their own personal worth and identity. It can create additional resources and reallocate existing resources to support positive developments that will encourage the development of an educational atmosphere for both black and white pupils of mutual understanding and tolerance. These are some of the special dimensions of racial disadvantage. Schools and authorities need support and encouragement to develop and implement special programmes for dealing with it, not least because of the uneven distribution of black pupils.

All these issues are well documented in David Milner's *Education and Race* (1975). But the implications of an ethnically mixed child population affect the whole school and all the children and staff in it and call for attention to be given to the teaching methods, materials, curriculum, staffing, relations with the community and in-service staff training. The working party of Chief Education Officers concluded,

'*Being responsible for multi-racial schools means making political, administrative and educational decisions about inter-group relations, allocation of resources, the possibility of positive discrimination and involvement with agencies outside the school.*' (Community Relations Commission 1976b p. 3). It is for these reasons this working party endorsed the Select Committee's recommendations on a special fund and an advisory unit.

The government response to the suggestion of a special fund was:

The Government have given consideration to the case for a central fund for the education of immigrants. The case for a central fund seems to rest on two arguments. The first is that the presence of large immigrant populations places a burden on local authority services (among them, education) which falls more heavily on some local authorities than others because of the uneven pattern of immigrant settlement.

The second is that local education authorities will not take initiatives to improve the education of immigrants unless there is an earmarked Department of Education and Science fund on which they can draw to meet the cost. The first of these arguments has been accepted by successive Governments. It is for this reason that they have maintained the provisions of Section 11 of the Local Government Act 1966. The Government do not believe that the second argument is borne out by experience. *The public provision of education is, for the most part, the responsibility of the local education authorities.* It is financed like any other local authority service largely through the rates and Rate Support Grant. *It is the job of the local authority to decide how best to use its resources of staff and money to meet the needs of its area.* If specific grants for particular aspects of education in which the local authorities have previously enjoyed discretion were to be introduced, the effect might be to reduce the scope of local responsibility. Since the Government believes that such responsibility is essential to the vigour of local government, they would be reluctant to do this, and their policy is to channel special assistance through Section 11 and the Urban Programme (use of the latter is not confined to immigrants) which apply to a wide range of local services, thus giving the authorities the opportunity to set their own priorities (Home Office 1974).

What this response underestimates is the extent to which local authorities have not met or cannot meet their special responsibilities created by the presence of black people on a scale commensurate with need, in part because of the limitations of Section 11 discussed earlier. The Select Committee justified its recommendations on the grounds of 'regional variation, flexibility, equity, credibility' and these points still stand. The concentration of minority communities in local authorities least able to afford additional expenditure creates the need. The evidence of school and job performance of youngsters of West Indian origin illustrates this problem (in February 1977 the all party Select Committee, after lengthy meetings with black and white groups, and local authorities, concluded 'young blacks present a critical challenge to all those working for the improvement of race relations. The alienation of some of the young blacks cannot be ignored and action must be taken before relations deteriorate further and create irreconcilable division' (Select Committee on Race Relations and Immigration, 1976, para. 154). The patchy and limited provision of educational services relevant to a multi-racial community has been documented by the Select Committee, the Community Relations Committee and the National Foundation for Educational Research, and indicates ways in which the response has been inadequate. To say that local responsibility would be reduced by a special fund is to repeat conventional administrative wisdom: the reality is that local needs are not being met and will not without effective external support (both financial and advisory). Clearly there is weight in the argument about 'local responsibility'; it is the particular circumstances of multi-racial areas that make it unconvincing. The uneven distribution of black communities, concentrated in socially disadvantaged areas, and the existence of racial hostility means that many areas have neither the resources nor the political will to take the necessary action to achieve general educational objectives like equality of opportunity.

In special circumstances surely the main local responsibility is to ensure that needs are being effectively met and not to generate the resources to do so. Generating resources to meet needs that are unevenly distributed is the responsibility of the central agency (they even have a word for it in the rate support grant, 'equalization'), and the strict limitations and lack of overall strategy of Section 11 mean that as it stands it does not serve the purpose. In other contexts special centrally financed educational programmes have been introduced (e.g. the Adult Literacy Resource Agency) with considerable effect without destroying local responsibility.

Towards an effective policy at the local level: 'a national approach that will avoid racialism, distortion, hatred'

The starting point for an effective educational policy in multi-racial areas must be improved by support and advice from central government and adequate funding for the special dimension of racial disadvantage: these would seem a framework that would encourage local authorities to develop comprehensive and coordinated strategies for these areas and in turn schools could begin responding most effectively to changing needs. What should be the substance of such local strategies? Clearly, it must respond to the salient facts which are:

1 The fact of under-performance of children of West Indian origin and of special educational needs (language, culture) of children and adults from all minority backgrounds, i.e. the need for special educational programmes.

2 The fact of racial prejudice, hostility and discrimination within the majority population both child and adult, i.e. the need for teaching programmes on race issues for all sections of the school population.

3 The fact of early detection both of under-functioning amongst minorities and the emergence of racial stereotypes amongst majorities, i.e. the need for early intervention.

4 The fact of variation of need within and between different local authority areas, i.e. the need for local diagnosis and programmes.

5 The fact that we are ignorant about the scale of needs and more important ways in which they can be met, i.e. the need to improve our knowledge base for action.

6 The fact that given the nature of race relations, special provision cannot be imposed upon communities (either majority or minority) but must carry the communities with it, i.e. the need to involve communities in the diagnosis of need and provision of services.

7 The fact that racial disadvantage co-exists with general social disadvantage, i.e. the need for a coordinated and comprehensive approach to community development.

Perhaps the most significant fact is the uneven distribution of recent settlers in the system, and as a result efforts cannot be left to the initiative or resources of individual schools or local authorities but should be part of a national programme. This is why the government should reconsider its relationship with local authorities which have relatively heavy concentrations of peoples from minority backgrounds. To no small extent the initiative for action lies with it (as do the necessary resources) and it has the responsibility to ensure that action is both taken and systematically evaluated. Further, any programme should combine development and research with action; we are ignorant not only about the nature of the disadvantages of the black population (i.e. these needs cannot adequately be diagnosed) but about effective ways of improving our present efforts. Equally we are ignorant about the social and psychological origins of prejudice and how it can be best combatted in schools: therefore action and development must go in parallel.

The last government acknowledged that it was its responsibility to take action to achieve racial equality: in its 1975 White Paper on racial discrimination it said: 'It is the government's duty to prevent these morally unacceptable and socially divisive inequalities from hardening into entrenched patterns. It is inconceivable that Britain in the last quarter of the twentieth century should confess herself unable to secure for a small minority of around one and a half million coloured citizens their full and equal rights as individual men and women' (Home Office 1975 para. 12).

My point is that this will not be solved by words alone, only by positive policies, and these require commitment and resources. An educational programme for multi-racial education is vital if racial equality and harmony are to be achieved: the words of the present Chairman of the Commission on Racial Equality (while still an MP) sound a warning: while welcoming the government's new law to eradicate racial discrimination he said: 'Economic and social disadvantage is an even greater problem than racial discrimination' (House of Commons Debates 1027 col. 1613).

If the educational system does not respond effectively to this challenge it will reinforce these economic and social disadvantages. For the system to respond requires the government to have an educational policy for multi-racial areas that is not just part of a general programme for the educationally disadvantaged. Without special programmes, educational policy will be responsible for creating a further twist in the cycle of racial disadvantage, with serious damage to race relations. The White Paper on Racial Discrimination recognises this: 'The possibility has to be faced that there is at work in this country, as elsewhere in the world, the familiar cycle of cumulative disadvantage by which relatively low-paid or low-status jobs for the first generation of immigrants go hand in hand with poor and crowded living conditions and a depressed environment. *If, for example, job opportunities, educational facilities, housing and environmental conditions are all poor, the next generation will grow up less well-equipped to deal with the difficulties facing them. The wheel then comes a full circle, as the second generation finds themselves trapped in poor jobs and poor housing.* If at each stage of this process, an element of racial discrimination enters in, then an entire group of people are launched on a vicious downward spiral of deprivation' (Home Office 1975 para. 11).

What is lacking are policy initiatives from government to prevent this downward spiral. Without such initiatives the warnings of a *Times* leader (1 February 1978) that 'if we cannot give a fair place in our society to the generations of immigrant descent born in Britain, then Mr Powell's dark forebodings may indeed be fulfilled' may prove true.

4
From Policy to Practice — Some Problems and Paradoxes of Egalitarian Reform

John Gray

> The essential fact of twentieth century educational history is that egalitarian policies have failed
>
> (Halsey 1972 p. 6)

There has always been something peculiarly attractive about the idea of equalising opportunities through education. Like economic growth it offers a way of redistributing society's resources relatively painlessly. Unlike many other reforms, investment in children's futures promises a measure of social change at comparatively little cost to the present generation. It is not difficult to see how the idea of social change through education has maintained a measure of political consensus for much of the twentieth century.

In the last two decades, there have been signs of that consensus breaking down. Waning enthusiasm for the belief that educational reforms would lead to more equal educational opportunities was already apparent during the late fifties. The late sixties saw the beginnings of scepticism about what education alone could achieve. By the mid-seventies the view that egalitarian policies had 'failed' had become part of the conventional wisdom of educational policy-making. To raise the issue as central to educational policy for the next decade, therefore, runs the risk of seeming either quaint or utopian. Yet it is hard to see how such discussion can ignore what has been termed 'the most prolonged issue of twentieth century educational history' (Silver 1973 p. xi).

To understand the basis of the charge that egalitarian policies have 'failed' one must know something of the history of educational expansion over the period, of the educational reforms that have been launched in the name of equalising opportunities and of the influence of social class upon educational opportunity at every level of the educational system. I shall be outlining some of these factors in the course of this chapter. But I shall also argue that it is difficult to convince oneself that many of the reforms that have been launched were predominantly *egalitarian* in character. They may have adopted the rhetoric of equality but they have often lacked the substance. I shall conclude that if egalitarian policies have hardly been tried, they can scarcely be said to have failed.

Expansion or equality?

Probably the single most important feature of twentieth-century education is that it has expanded – there is more of it, at every level. Two underlying expansionary trends may be identified. First, at least in the period since World War II, there have been more children in every cohort and still more predicted. Indeed, it was only in the mid-seventies that government began to take seriously the fact that the birth-rate had been dropping steadily since 1964. For most of this time demographic statisticians had been predicting that an upturn in the birth-rate was imminent, with the implication that resources would continue to be under pressure. Second, parents have demanded or been supplied with more education for their children. The school-leaving age was raised to 15 in 1947, with the result that successive generations have undergone longer periods of compulsory education. More children have stayed on voluntarily beyond the minimum age; more have obtained more qualifications; more have gone on into some form of tertiary education and, at the apex of the educational system, more have entered university. In each succeeding generation, the greater proportion of children have received a lengthier education than their parents. It is difficult to resist the conclusion that educational opportunities have improved – for everyone.

Yet, at the same time, educational policies and budgets that have been largely committed to planning and increasing the stock of buildings, teachers and places have had little slack available for the pursuit of policies related to the equalisation of educational opportunities. A succession of government reports in the fifties and sixties including Crowther (1959), Newsom (1963), Robbins (1963) and Plowden (1967) have embraced the rhetoric of opening up greater opportunities for working class children. There has been no corresponding attempt, however, to give substance to these calls by monitoring the outcomes of government policies systematically. Government statistics on education tell a story of growth but a story of improvement in class-chances in education is conspicuous by its absence from them. This absence of an official record must make one wonder whether equalising educational opportunities has been a focus of government policy after all? Returning to government statements on the subject one discovers that frequently the sharp edge of 'social class' is missing. Concern has been expressed that the country was wasting its talents and that the pool of able children was larger than had previously been realised (Crowther, Newsom and Robbins).

There has been a strong inference that social class factors in the form of support offered by the home were responsible (especially in Plowden). But, at the end of the day, policies have tended to be formulated in terms which embraced social class at best indirectly; opportunities were extended to all who were able to benefit from them, regardless of class.

In short, if one focuses on the context of educational policy-making, and in particular its expression through government-sponsored reports, it has often appeared laudably egalitarian in intent. If, on the other hand, one examines the expression of those same sentiments in terms of the actual development and implementation of educational policies, one discovers that there is nothing necessarily egalitarian about expanding the number of opportunities at the top unless, at the same time, one operates on the criteria by which places are allocated. Indeed, it was not until the late seventies that a government policy document began to embrace this problem directly pointing out, as one of five policy options for responding to declining enrolments in higher education, that the opportunities for mature and working class students *might* be increased (DES 1978). In absolute terms there are, indeed, more working class children in the advanced stages of education than ever before but are there relatively more? Has expanding opportunities meant equalising them?

Class chances in education

The tradition of 'political arithmetic' has tried to document the nature and extent of changes in the chances of children from different social class backgrounds reaching particular stages of the educational hierarchy. A pioneering piece of research in this tradition was conducted by Gray and Moshinsky (1938). They examined the unequal distribution of children from different social classes in different types of secondary school, pointing out that large numbers of able children from working class backgrounds were being denied access to the type of secondary schooling for which they were eminently qualified. Bringing together data from a variety of published sources, Little and Westergaard (1964 pp. 301, 315, 321) were also concerned to provide a picture of the 'operation of social selection in education, from school to university' and to establish whether there had been changes between the pre- and post-war periods. They concluded that there had been only small reductions in 'social inequalities in access to secondary education'.

One of the frustrations of research on class-chances (and, indeed, of much research on the effects of educational policies in general) is that it is rarely up-to-date. One is often obliged to extrapolate data collected a number of years previously to provide present-day trends. The most recent and possibly the most ambitious attempt to document changes in class-chances in education was launched in 1972 by a team of researchers at Oxford, as part of a study of social mobility under the direction of Halsey and Goldthorpe. They based their research on a very large sample of males and from the information provided we can examine the period of educational history from the early thirties to the late sixties in some detail. Regrettably, studies of social mobility have been steadfastly tied to documenting the careers of males, so no correspondingly detailed information is available on females. I shall attempt to make some limited inferences about the position of women at the end of this section.

Table 1 spans the period from the early thirties to the late sixties. It is based on data drawn from the Oxford study and provides the percentages of boys from different home backgrounds who reached particular stages of education (Halsey, Heath and Ridge 1980). For their analyses Halsey *et al* defined *three* social classes (in contrast to the middle/working class, non-manual/manual dichotomies that are typically adopted). These were as follows: a 'service' class composed of those whose fathers were in professional, managerial or supervisory jobs, making up just over one-in-ten of the population; an 'intermediate' class (fuller details of which are contained in the footnotes to Table 1), making up just over three-out-of-ten; and a 'working' class,

TABLE 1: *Trends in class-chances in education among males*

Staying on till 16 or later	Percentage of the social class staying on till this stage of education during the:			
	thirties	forties	fifties	sixties
Service class	52	61	77	79
Working class	9	10	20	32
Ratio of class chances	5.7	6.1	3.9	2.5
Staying on till 18 or later				
Service class	16	20	32	38
Working class	3	2	4	6
Ratio of class chances	5.1	8.7	8.5	6.0
Attending university				
Service class	7	16	24	26
Working class	1	1	2	3
Ratio of class chances	8.0	13.3	10.3	8.5

Notes
Adapted from Halsey, Heath and Ridge (1980), Tables 8.10, 8.11 and 10.8. The figures for the intermediate class have been omitted. Missing information means that each of the tables is based on differing numbers but all are based on approx. 8,000 cases. All percentages in the table have been rounded but the ratios have been calculated on the basis of the unrounded percentages. For greater detail the reader is advised to return to the source.

including skilled, semi-skilled and unskilled workers, making up the remainder (just over half). In the interests of brevity and clarity, however, I have confined the following discussion to the service and working class categories only.

Definition of social class
Service class: Higher grade professionals, administrators, managers and proprietors; lower grade professionals, administrators and managers, supervisors and higher grade technicians.

Intermediate class: Clerical, sales and rank-and-file service workers; small proprietors and self-employed artisans (the 'petty bourgeoisie'); lower grade technicians and foremen (the 'aristocracy of labour').

Working class: Skilled manual workers in industry; semi-skilled and unskilled manual workers in industry; agricultural workers and small-holders.

During the thirties, some 52 per cent of boys from service class background stayed on at school until they were 16 or older; only 9 per cent of those from working class backgrounds did so. By the sixties, these figures had risen to 79 per cent and 32 per cent respectively. In other words, whereas almost six (5.7) service class boys stayed on in the thirties for every working class boy, by the sixties the disparity had been more than halved (2.5:1). In short, at this stage of education, there would appear to have been considerable moves towards equalising class chances. Of course, by 1974 with successive legislative efforts to raise the minimum leaving age the disparity evaporated. Service and working class boys had an equal chance of staying on till 16 by legislative fiat. This observation prompts the question whether there was any particular significance in the later decades in staying on till 16? It may well be that what was more important was staying on beyond the statutory age and that whereas 16 served as a benchmark during the thirties, by the sixties this had shifted to 18.

Examining the figures for those staying on at school till 18-plus a different picture of class-chances emerges. Again there is an increase in the percentages staying on but there is no corresponding pattern of class chances being equalised to match that at 16. Indeed, in the thirties the ratio was 5:1 and in the sixties 6:1. At university level, a thirties/sixties comparison also suggests little change but this particular comparison masks the fact that for a while working class chances actually declined; the improvements only look important if one examines the differential impact of the war years on

81

the two classes. By the late sixties, despite the fact there had been a fourfold increase in the proportion going to university, the working class were still sending a percentage of their children that was only half that the service class had been sending during the thirties.

This picture is the simplest and in some ways the most optimistic that can be painted. It is also among the more favourable to the case that opportunities have become more equal. If, in contrast, we look at the absolute gains for each class rather than the relative ones, then the service class has made greater progress than the working class at all three levels, including staying on at 16. There are also additional complications that can be taken into account, such as the fact that the size of the service class has almost doubled during the course of the century. But, whatever adjustments we attempt to make to the figures, the overall picture looks pretty similar. Where progress towards equalising educational opportunities has been made at the lower levels, this has not been matched by parallel improvements at the higher levels. The universities, in particular, have remained comparatively inaccessible to the working class. By the end of the sixties, 26 per cent of service class boys were attending them compared with only 3 per cent of the working class.

As far as one can tell from the limited data available, the story for girls parallels that for boys. Girls have benefited in much the same way as boys from the general expansion of educational facilities, except in one major respect. Whilst they have had much the same chances as boys of entering selective schools they have had much smaller chances of entering university (Little and Westergaard 1964 pp. 301–315, Tuck 1974 pp. 141–50).

Shifting definitions and changes of emphasis

So have we moved closer to equality of educational opportunity? This depends, in part, upon how the concept is defined and how rigorously that definition is applied to practice. Coleman *et al* (1966), offers five definitions and Bowman (1975 pp. 73–89) seven, albeit somewhat fancifully with respect to two of them. The existence of such competing definitions should alert us to the need to be explicit about which we are employing when we discuss the impact of educational policy. Two have, however, dominated public discussion in recent years and it is these I shall consider in greater detail.

The evidence on class-chances indicated that there was still a considerable measure of inequality between the service and working classes. It also told us that at the lowest level (staying on until 16 or later) there had been some progress. This emphasis on the *results* or *outcomes* of education has dominated much academic and policy-related discussion throughout the seventies. In terms of this radical definition, a society may be said to have equality of educational opportunity when the average member of any social class has the same chance of reaching a particular stage of education as the average member of any other social class. On this definition we should have to conclude, bearing in mind the evidence in Table 1, that there had been little progress towards equalising opportunities.

The liberal definition posits that equality of educational opportunity exists when children of equal *merit* have equal *access* to the various stages of secondary and tertiary education. Much, of course, hangs on the crucial question of what is meant by 'merit'. Where earlier studies treated the concept as largely unproblematic, later ones have suggested that there are problems in reaching acceptable definitions. Nevertheless, without some such definitions one cannot make much sense of either pre- or post-war 'egalitarian' policies. An egalitarian concern, for example, played a part in the decisions to abolish fees for grammar schooling, introduce comprehensive schooling and expand higher education. But such reforms have had a wider appeal as well since they could also be seen as fostering 'talent' and removing barriers to 'unfair' educational competition. In consequence, liberal definitions of equality of educational opportunity have been able to command a measure of political consensus which more radical definitions could not.

Given this consensus, it is perhaps surprising that it has been the radical definition that has somehow slipped into the popular wisdom about educational policy-making during the seventies. The Coleman Report on *Equality of Educational Opportunity* in the United States made the important observation that 'schools bring little influence to bear on a child's achievement that is independent of his background and general social context' (Coleman *et al* 1966 p. 325). Similar conclusions could be drawn from British analyses of data collected around the same time for the Plowden Report (Peaker 1967, 1971; Acland 1973). A few years later, however, this finding had hardened into the conclusion popularly associated with Jencks's study *Inequality* (1973) that 'schools don't make a difference'. At precisely the time when the political climate was perhaps most favourable to some initiative the terms of the debate changed. The research evidence itself had scarcely altered, but the values of interpretations that were brought to it had.

This is not to deny that Jencks's message was an important one for some of those involved in developing policies for the American 'War on Poverty' and its more modest British equivalents. It disabused them of the idea that educational reforms alone could abolish poverty and lead to social change. The gains from attending the 'best' schools as opposed to the 'worst', assuming they could be translated into educational strategies, would lead to at best minor reductions in inequalities in educational performance; and, anyway, educational performance was not as strongly linked to subsequent life-chances (defined in terms of occupational status and income) as the popular wisdom about a 'tightening bond' might have led one to suppose. Cast against this social background, the differences between schools did, indeed, seem very modest. But whilst Jencks's arguments were powerfully marshalled, one is left with the suspicion that it was a 'straw man' he had demolished.

A working class 'handicap'?

Do working class children have to run just that little bit harder to reach the same destination as their more privileged counterparts? The idea that they might be 'handicapped' in the educational competition has been the focus of considerable sociological investigation, although the reasons why they might be handicapped have been surrounded in controversy. Explanations have been based on the different types of support (both material and motivational) available to children from their homes; on the differing ways in which they have been treated by their schools; and on whether the way 'merit' has been defined was appropriate.

Boudon (1974) has demonstrated that even relatively small differences in the propensity of different social classes to stay on within the educational system may lead to quite marked differences in the representation of different social groups in the selective stages of education. His model is based on theoretical assumptions about how the system operates but it seems to fit the British case. Until the seventies, one of the crucial hurdles was at 11-plus and selection for grammar school; more recently, with the deferment of selection till 16-plus, it has shifted to the point of entry to the academic sixth form. Just staying on in the system seems to be particularly important for subsequent entry into high-status occupations. Bowles and Gintis (1976) show that one of the most important predictors of occupational status has been the sheer length of schooling (measured in years) completed rather than one's 'intelligence' or 'ability', although obviously one must have a modicum of these. Similar conclusions may be drawn from a study based on British data (Psacharopoulos 1977). Staying on also brings its own more short-term rewards. More was spent on pupils at grammar schools than secondary moderns; more is spent on sixth-formers than fifth-formers; and in higher education the disparities become still more marked. It costs about ten times as much to educate a university student as a primary school child. In short, given the structure of post-compulsory education and the opportunities associated with it, there are both short- and long-term benefits associated with staying within the system.

Assuming some sort of handicap is operating, for whatever reasons, establishing its size is more problematic. If one looks back to the fifties and sixties, however, the criteria along which selection for secondary education was conducted were more explicitly delineated. Tests of so-called 'intelligence' featured prominently in the procedures. By comparing the way one might have expected the allocation of places in selective institutions to operate, if purely 'meritocratic' criteria were dictating outcomes, with the way it actually did, one can obtain some rough estimates of the size of the working class handicap. There are some problems with such an approach. Are we, for example, to judge the extent of 'bias' in the system by employing criteria of so-called intelligence and aptitude which have themselves been highly criticised? In doing so we should be aware of the limitations of evaluating the educational system in terms of its own (unstated) criteria. The exercise is, nevertheless, instructive and Halsey *et al* (1980) provide some estimates which will serve our purpose. Confining discussion to a comparison of service and working class boys, they suggest that the working class handicap in competing for places in grammar or technical schools was about seven IQ points; assuming boys survived beyond this stage, it was about ten points at 16; about ten points at 17; about eight points at 18; and about seven points at entry to university. Depending on the assumptions one makes the figures could be a little larger or a little smaller.

Two misconceptions of what I am arguing will spring to mind. First, I am not suggesting that the educational system *deliberately* discriminated against working class pupils. On the contrary, I would assume that, other things being equal, selectors at the various stages of the system scrupulously selected those who were best qualified in terms of the established criteria, regardless of background. And second, I am not suggesting that working class pupils were in any sense 'deficient' in terms of their cultural background. There are a variety of competing explanations all of which might contain more than a grain of truth. What these estimates do indicate, however, is that to square the expected and observed take-up of places in selective secondary schools and post-compulsory education, one must postulate the existence of some sort of handicap of the order of five to ten points. In other words, there is a gap to be made up which could serve as a focus for policy.

The effects of schools
Schools differ in their effectiveness. It is a matter of debate by how much because it is not just enough to focus on the outcomes of schooling, such as examination results or standardised test scores. As Coleman (1975) has suggested, 'it is the *increment* in achievement which the school provides which should be the measure of the school's quality'. Public discussion, in contrast, frequently falls into the trap of comparing schools with very different intakes as if they were the same;

even when some allowance is made for differences in intakes and social context, it is rarely enough.

Jencks (1973) estimated that the most effective fifth of American elementary (i.e. primary) schools boosted children's performance by between five and ten points on standardised tests when compared with the least effective fifth of schools. Similar estimates can also be obtained from British studies (Acland 1973, Barnes and Lucas 1975). Studies of secondary schools, both in America (Jencks 1973) and Britain (Ainsworth and Batten 1974, Rutter *et al* 1979), suggest figures of a somewhat smaller order. Gains of this size are also, on Halsey's estimates, to be obtained from sending one's son to a minor independent school (always assuming one can afford it) rather than the local secondary modern. If we think in terms of examination results, public discussion talks in terms of schools which 'produce' pupils with one or two 'A' levels apiece as opposed to others which average only one or two 'O' levels/CSE grade Is. In fact, if we take into account the extent to which intakes to different schools differ and make allowance for this in considering their examination results, a very different picture emerges. Schools still differ in their effectiveness but the range is by no means as dramatic as public discussion would suggest. Pupils in the most effective school obtain just over three examination passes more than pupils in the least effective school. Such differences are by no means negligible but they represent the extremes. Over two-thirds of schools 'produce' pretty much what one would have expected from knowledge of their intakes, give or take an 'O' level pass (Gray 1979a). The search for more effective schools must therefore concentrate on relatively subtle approaches if the effects of schools are to be better understood.

In brief, if we judge these estimates of the effects of schools against the radical definition of equality of educational opportunity, it becomes clear that schools 'don't make much difference'. If, however, we employ the liberal definition we could argue that they 'make all the difference', since the estimates of the working class handicap on the one hand and the effects of more as opposed to less effective schools on the other seem fairly similar. Indeed, it is worth noting in passing that parents who can afford to buy educational opportunities for their children by entering the private market seem to be gaining an average advantage of this sort. To sustain this assumption, however, we must also be prepared to argue that, on average, working class children attend less effective schools. This is a more difficult assumption for which to produce evidence, given the very limited number of studies available, but one which the Plowden Committee (1967), for example, seemed to embrace. In putting forward proposals for 'positive discrimination' in favour of the educationally disadvantaged they declared that the 'first step must be to raise the schools with low standards to the national average. The second, quite deliberately to make them better'. There is one major flaw in this set of assumptions, as far as developing educational policy is concerned. One must assume that educational practitioners know how to identify effective practice and how to implement it in other settings. Jencks (1973) was sceptical about their skills in this respect. He wrote: 'We can see no evidence . . . that they know how to boost test scores (i.e. educational perform-ance)'. Some British work tentatively confirms this impression (Crocker 1974, Barnes 1975b, Gray 1979b). In short, there is evidence that schools vary in their effectiveness but also that our understanding of how and why they vary is limited. It should come as little surprise, therefore, to discover that many of the egalitarian reforms that were implemented during the sixties and seventies had unintended con-sequences for educational opportunities because the knowledge-base upon which they were implemented was less secure than was originally realised.

Some paradoxes of reform

Pre-schooling has been one of the politically most popular forms of intervention. It was backed, for example, by the Educational Priority Area action-research teams who had been funded as part of the Plowden initiatives. They described it as 'the outstandingly economical and effective device in the general approach to raising standards in EPAs' (Halsey 1972 p. 180). Certainly the evidence they assembled suggests that something useful could be done at this stage (Halsey 1972, Smith and James 1975). Unfortunately, the initiatives that were being canvassed in the name of *pre*-schooling did not match the prevailing traditions of *nursery* schooling. Initially at least, nursery school teachers often resisted the very parts of the pre-school programmes that were most likely to have some impact (Halsey 1972, Barnes 1975b) and government commitment was at best lukewarm. Left to their own devices, local education authorities often im-plemented piecemeal policies in disadvantaged areas. The nursery school programmes they backed seem to have been notable chiefly for their lack of specific effects, either good or bad, in comparison with other approaches (Tizard 1974). Most importantly, perhaps, a pre-school programme has yet to be discovered which benefits working class children more than those from other backgrounds. Since children from all backgrounds have been increasingly exposed to pre-school experiences, little overall change has occurred.

For a while, some local authorities (notably the Inner London Education Authority) channelled extra resources to primary schools servicing educational or social priority areas. It was assumed, naturally enough, that head teachers and their staff were the persons most competent to decide how such extra resources should be spent. The

EPA research teams monitored some of the outcomes. They discovered that in the Dundee area the teachers resented the fact that their schools had been designated as being in need of extra help (Town 1974). Disadvantage might well exist, but not in their schools. In Inner London, the heads mostly felt that everything possible was already being done (Barnes 1975a). It may have been that these were merely realistic comments on the relatively marginal resources being offered but it is obvious that, in certain cases, teachers' attitudes and willingness to examine their own practices represented something of a stumbling block to further progress.

At the same time, several major weaknesses in the overall strategy for positive discrimination were identified (Barnes and Lucas 1975). First, it had been assumed that the majority of children in need of extra help were to be located in a relatively small number of 'disadvantaged' schools. This was an administratively convenient assumption but it turned out to be falsely based. Only two out of every five target children were found to be in EPA-designated schools. Second, assuming the extra resources were having some impact (an assumption about which there were some genuine doubts) it turned out it was most probably 'disadvantaged' *middle* class children who were likely to benefit relative to their middle class peers rather than disadvantaged working class children relative to theirs. And third, there was no straightforward relationship between teachers' enthusiasm for particular innovations and their measured impact on the children's progress. In short, there is good reason to suppose that 'positive discrimination' in favour of disadvantaged children had, at best, limited effects on equalising opportunities, even when some political commitment and resources were available.

Further examples of the unintended consequence of reforms that were partly justified on the grounds of equalising educational opportunities may be drawn from the secondary sector. Much discussion has focused on the point of transition from primary to secondary school and the mechanisms of selection. To date, however, we lack good research on the overall effects of the introduction of comprehensive schooling, in part at least because this has been a politically explosive area where good research designs have been hampered by political intervention (Ross *et al* 1972 p. 159, Wright 1977 p. 88). Such actions may, in turn, have been based on a belief that the comprehensive movement was too young and vulnerable for anything definitive to be produced. But they were also, doubtless, based on the fact that large parts of the educational system continued to be 'creamed' well into the seventies and that many schools were 'comprehensive' in name only. Meanwhile, a number of studies have reminded supporters of comprehensives that dismantling the old tri-partite system represents only the first of a number of stages. Streaming, it is feared, may have delayed but not negated the effects of selection (Ford 1969); 'hidden' curricula and teachers' categorisations of pupils may need to be tackled (Keddie 1971, Woods 1979); whilst there are even those who would argue that in the attempt to remove class barriers 'the effects of those (same) barriers have become obscured from view' (Westergaard and Resler 1975).

Two recent research studies on the effects of comprehensive reorganisation (which at the time of writing were both awaiting publication) suggest that the effects of comprehensive schools on pupil performance to date have been comparatively modest.

A study by the National Children's Bureau, based on a large national sample of pupils followed up on a longitudinal basis, indicates that the most able 20 per cent of pupils (defined in terms of performance on an intelligence test taken at 11) did equally well on tests of reading and maths at 16, regardless of whether they went to comprehensive or grammar schools; those who just missed selection for grammar schools apparently did less well in comprehensives than their seemingly similar counterparts in grammar schools; whilst for the less able, comprehensives seem to have provided a better alternative than secondary moderns (Steedman 1980).

A second study (with which the present author has been associated) by the Centre for Educational Sociology at Edinburgh University supports the view that comprehensive reforms may provide some modest benefits for less able pupils. For a number of reasons comprehensive schools have been established for a longer period of time in certain parts of Scotland. This study was based on a very large cross-sectional sample of Scottish school-leavers. It suggests that pupils in the comprehensive sector did slightly better in terms of average examination passes than pupils in the unrecognised selection sector. But the average also masks the way in which these overall attainment levels were obtained. In the comprehensive sector fewer pupils left with no public examination passes; in the selective sector slightly more left with the Scottish equivalent of 'A' levels.

Neither study can be regarded as definitive, although from the point of view of the present discussion there are two reasons why they are instructive. First they allay fears that comprehensive reforms imply some lowering of standards. This is an important criticism to counter. Second they underline the limitations of school reforms as an instrument for egalitarian reform. It is unlikely that such reforms will bring about any sudden transformation of education and opportunities.

In the short term, however, the effects of reorganisation or equalising educational opportunities remain unclear. Virtually all former secondary modern schools have become comprehensives but by no means all grammar schools. Since the working class were already handicapped in the competition for grammar school places and since comprehensive schools have, in many cases, quite properly decided to provide opportunities for many more of their children rather than 'sponsoring' their most able, the 'handicap' suffered by able working class children may well have increased. At the same time, while direct grant schools have now been phased out, there has been some growth in the independent sector. If, for whatever reasons, independent schools have been more successful in boosting the chances of their pupils at the borderlines for selection to higher education or employment, then the abolition of the direct grant and grammar schools (which deliberately undertook the same kind of activity within the state system and thus provided some effective competition) may also have reduced the chances for such working class children as would formerly have gained access to them. In brief, it is difficult to convince oneself that half-finished schemes for reorganising secondary schooling have the same effects on educational opportunities as planned or completed ones.

The expansion of higher education during the sixties and seventies confirms the impression that egalitarian reforms have rarely been straightforward in their consequences. In 1963 the Robbins Committee recommended that 'courses of higher education should be available for all those who (were) qualified by ability and attainment to pursue them and who wish(ed) to do so' (Robbins 1963 p. 1). Again, there were hopes that educational opportunities for the working class would be expanded as universities doubled their numbers of students. This did, indeed, happen; more working class pupils went to university. But a study by Hutchinson and McPherson (1976) shows that in Scotland at least, where there was already a slightly higher proportion of university entrants than in England, it was the middle class who benefited most. In particular, better qualified middle class women took up a larger proportion of the expanding places than working class men, since they were stronger competitors for places in the arts and social sciences, which had traditionally been entry points for working class males. There seems to have been a similar trend in England (Open University 1977). There was no overt discrimination here – it was just that no-one had instructed the universities to alter, in the course of raising their numbers, the application and admission procedures they had been employing. One type of inequality, therefore, competed with another.

Conclusion
The weight of this evidence would appear to support the case that egalitarian reforms have failed. But such a view is premised on the assumption that egalitarian concerns have, in fact, been consistently pursued by post-war governments. This seems more doubtful.

Before we can realistically assess the fate of any egalitarian policy, we must ask the question what shape it would have to take in order to have even limited chances of success. First, it would need to be based on an adequate theory of how inequalities were generated in the educational system. Second, it would require a set of policies to be developed that flowed directly from the theory. Third, those charged with implementing the policies would require the power, resources and commitment to undertake them. And fourth, there would need to be some attempt to monitor those same experiences in order to establish a still firmer basis for action.

If we employ this model to evaluate the logic and record of 'egalitarian' policies it rapidly becomes obvious that few, if any, have begun to meet these criteria. The theories that have been adopted have usually been incomplete; they are, perhaps, better described as plausible bases for action. The policies that have been based upon them have frequently been only loosely linked to the ideas from which they have claimed parentage. Poorly-conceived policies have, in turn, often failed to secure the resources necessary for their implementation; many of those which have been funded have been counteracted by initiatives (both public and private) at other levels of the educational system. And finally, there has been little evidence of systematic attempts to evaluate policies and learn from them. In other words, what little has been known about the effects of schools has not been turned into a set of coherent policies and practices.

Are these criteria too stringent when applied to the development of educational policies? I would maintain not, since their application to policies aimed at expanding opportunities within the system suggests that such policies have, indeed, been successful in achieving their objectives. What they highlight is the rather woolly-minded way in which it has been assumed that potentially egalitarian reforms can be piggy-backed upon expansionary ones. In the process, a number of pertinent questions are raised. Have successive governments embraced egalitarian objectives for education or have they, in fact, been unable or reluctant to pursue them? Has there been a massive investment of resources in policies with predominantly egalitarian (as opposed to other) objectives or has the entire annual commitment amounted to less than the cost of running a small university? If the latter, it is less surprising that one encounters difficulties in detecting results. In sum, if so-called egalitarian policies have failed to have any egalitarian consequences, it seems reasonable to ask in what sense they were egalitarian?

5
European Unity and National Systems

Nigel Grant

We are all assumed to be in favour of unity, just as we are all supposed to be against sin; but in either case there is a difficulty of definition as well as performance. Not all, perhaps: the idea of unity as the gradual relinquishing of national peculiarities is usually shared by opponents of EEC membership, who resist assimilation in the name of national sovereignty. The intention of this chapter is to argue that this model (and its rejection) is far too simple.

As far as it can be identified, the conventional wisdom of the European Community appears to favour a common European educational system, eventually. Degrees of enthusiasm vary (the idea is put forward with notably less vigour than a few years ago), as do attitudes towards method (Halls 1974 pp. 211–220, Fragniere 1979 p. 311). Though some would prefer to press on with regulation, others rely on the indirect mechanisms that seem likely to make for homogeneity. Thus, though the Treaty of Rome does not pronounce directly on education, two of its provisions are potentially important. The more obvious concerns the 'harmonisation' of professional qualifications (EEC 1957a). Though the numbers involved are a small minority, the structure of their courses is particularly influential because of the well-known 'filtration of influence'. Faculties of law, medicine and (on the Continent at least) engineering have a prominent position in most universities; these in turn are widely imitated by other higher institutions; entry to higher education influences what the secondary schools do, and not only in the courses taken by those likely to go further; and so on through the whole system. Higher professional qualifications are thus a particularly sensitive part of any system.

The second is the provision of free movement of labour within the community (EEC 1957b). Mobility, or even the prospect of it, has long been a strong force for assimilation. The likelihood of having to seek educational or professional advancement elsewhere puts a premium on skills and qualifications marketable outside the system – hence the devaluation of (say) Irish or Breton in favour of metropolitan

92

tongues, or the adoption of English curricular patterns in Northern Irish or even Manx schools. Inward mobility can have a similar effect if the incomers are sufficiently numerous or influential. Examples of this include the dilution of Basque by the influx of workers from other parts of Spain, or the influence of English and US academics on Scottish and Canadian universities (and therefore on the educational systems themselves, Bell and Grant 1977). Such influences, helped on by vaguely ecumenical European sentiments, would seem to favour the eventual creation of a common system, an optimal blend of those of the United Kingdom, France, Belgium, the Netherlands, Luxembourg, the Federal Republic of Germany, Denmark, Italy, the Republic of Ireland – and, in time, Spain, Portugal and Greece.

It is worth spelling out the actual and potential member states at this stage, to emphasise how enormous – and, at the same time, how limited in conception – such a task would be. What about the rest of Europe? Austria and Switzerland have common languages and close cultural links with their neighbours. As for Eastern Europe, connections fluctuate according to the international temperature, but can they be discounted altogether? Their systems are becoming rather more diverse, and although the Soviet model is still dominant, educational planners are also looking at western developments (Anweiler 1969, Grant 1969, Mitter 1979). Norway, Sweden and Finland have closer links and more affinities with Denmark than do most EEC countries, and the Nordic Council also has provision for educational harmonisation. In education, as in other things, the arrogation of European identity to the Common Market alone raises problems that go beyond organisation; the closer the unity within this *part* of Europe, the less chance there is of broader unity in the future.

But even if this is left aside for the moment (which is rather hard on the Danes, who belong to *two* supranational groupings with pretensions to 'harmonisation'), further difficulties arise even within the limited compass of the EEC. Accepting that educational practices, especially in methods and curriculum, can and do cross frontiers with greater ease, can we still contemplate total *unification*? Perhaps it is just possible. France and England might come to agree about centralisation, curricular uniformity and prescription from above. Denmark and West Germany might, somehow, agree about comprehensive schooling or the role of central regulation. It might be possible to harmonise policy about the independent sector in England (where it has long provided an élite and is now to be strengthened in this 'creaming off' role by an injection of public funds), West Germany (where it is peripheral and experimental), France (where it is church-linked and not highly regarded) and Denmark (where it enjoys generous state support and is extremely varied socially, pedagogically and ideologically). Most systems have taken a century or two to come to some arrangement about Church schools, all different; possibly the next stage could be the creation of a common policy, but the obstacles would be immense. There has been a general trend to some kind of secondary comprehensive reorganisation in the post-war decades, but this has been very uneven; compare Denmark's all-through *folkeskole* up to the age 16 with the retention of selection at ten in most West German *Länder*, where comprehensive schools are few and ideologically suspect. The manner of change has varied too; the systems of the British Isles have kept the primary-secondary division at 11 or 12 and combined the secondary schools, but Spain (like Denmark) has developed a common school up to mid-adolescence and kept differentiation thereafter, a model common in Scandinavia and Eastern Europe, while France and Italy have developed a comprehensive middle stage. The pace of change differs also: even with the same government, Scotland and Wales went comprehensive much more quickly than England, and more completely too – the coexistence in the same area of comprehensive and selective schools is a largely English phenomenon. As for higher education, there is more common ground here, functionally at least, though here again the French *grandes écoles* might be difficult to relate to institutions elsewhere, while the UK structure would be difficult for continental systems to assimilate or even understand; it is little enough understood even within the United Kingdom.

One could go on, but it would seem that unification is a long way off. Even if agreement could be reached in such questions of structure, content and control (to say nothing of philosophy), it has to be asked how such a unified system could be administered. National systems have very different approaches to administrative theory and practice. Either these would need to be homogenised, with bureaucratic complexities that can be imagined all too well, or the member states would be allowed to continue in their own ways, in which case we would have a set of co-ordinated systems, not a unified structure – and without that, uniformity of content and method could not be guaranteed either.

But it also has to be asked whether this would be desirable in any case. If education has to respond to social need, and do so more readily as the pace of technological and social change quickens, it is hard to see how a uniform system could do this. The problems of the Ruhr and the Midlands are not those of Western Ireland or the Italian Mezzogiorno. Given the tendency of the metropolitan centres within nation states to dominate, misunderstand or simply ignore the peripheral areas, the dangers of exacerbating this in a unified system must be obvious enough.

As for the indirect influences and interactions between systems – mobility, communications, cultural factors of all sorts – these operate beyond the Community or even Europe; the influence of North America is particularly obvious. Further, outside influence acts on different European countries to different extents and in different ways, and many of them operate independently of policy or power. The chances of retaining uniformity, even if the legal basis exists, are therefore limited.

But there is a further and possibly fundamental obstacle: few of the countries are themselves culturally homogeneous. Even though some try to ignore this at present, it is likely that further integration into a supranational structure will throw the issue into sharper focus.

Outside Western Europe, multi-cultural societies are commonplace; they are the norm, not the exception. The extent to which this is allowed for in the organisation of education, however, varies a good deal. In the United States, the structure of the system – state sovereignty, strong local participation and control – has little to do with multi-culturalism, but is rather the product of ideology and geography at a formative period, and had little difficulty in coexisting with a remarkable degree of homogeneity into which immigrants from the Old World were blended. The rejection of the 'melting-pot' approach is recent; the provision for mother-tongue instruction in Spanish or Amerindian languages, the reassertion of identity among the descendants of immigrants, the quest by many blacks for such an identity – these are not the outcome of the loose federal structure or the growth of education at the 'grass roots'. Canada, too, is federal, but here the situation is different. At federal level, the country is officially multi-cultural, but education is a matter for each province, only one of which is bilingual (New Brunswick). Quebec and Ontario, though they do have substantial minorities of English and French speakers respectively, and do provide schooling in the minority language, do so within an officially unilingual structure (Ray 1978 pp. 19–32, Harley 1978).

In the USSR and Eastern Europe, the official policy is one of multi-lingual education, but with more limitations on other aspects of the cultures. In the Soviet Union, for instance, where Russians are now less than half the total population, the major nationalities at least can be taught in their own languages: and though this may extend to artistic modes, it does not to social and philosophical, nor to customs, and emphatically not to political content. Federal the system may be, but power remains at the centre. It is much the same in the other East European countries; cultural variation is allowed, even fostered, as long as it is not thought to imperil the social system or the integrity of the state, dangers that many of them seem quick to find. Thus, East Germany encourages the tiny Serb minority, educationally and culturally, but Romania is much more wary of the large and once dominant Hungarian population in Transylvania (Grant 1969, 1979).

Yugoslavia is an extreme case, consisting essentially of minorities; the Serbs are the biggest single group, but are outnumbered by the others put together. Nor does the complexity stop with the various South Slav people – the Croats, Slovenes, Bosnians, Montenegrins and Macedonians; there are many non-Slav nationalities as well, of whom the Albanians, Hungarians, Turks, Romanians and Italians are the most numerous. Pluralism in this case has strong political arguments behind it, as attempts before the war to impose a unitary Serbian state proved disastrous. Accordingly, each nationality is entitled to education in its own tongue: and the commitment to decentralisation (under the name of 'socialist self management') places education in the hands of the six republics (within broad federal guidelines), all of which devolve considerable responsibility further down the line. There is nothing quite like this in any other East European country. There is nothing quite like it in the West either, though Switzerland comes close in the correspondence between cultural group and unit of control. There *is* a clear majority here – German-speakers make up over 70 per cent – but the other languages, French, Italian and Romansch, have equal status, are used in the schools, and are not the subject of tension largely because so much power rests at local level anyway. Belgium and Luxembourg are both bilingual, but in the case of Belgium the tensions between French and Dutch *have* given rise to considerable problems, and have been dealt with by an uneasy truce; the Walloon and Flemish areas use their own languages in the schools, and Brussels is in the officially bilingual area.

The other members of the Community, actual and potential, present a more uniform appearance at first glance, but a closer look shows a more complex picture in most of them. Cultural identity, however, is easier to assert than to define. It can rest on various criteria, of which one or two may stand out. The most obvious are language and religion, as these are usually conspicuous and emotionally charged. But these may represent a more complex cluster of criteria, or they may not feature at all – Europe has many groups not much different from their neighbours in speech or faith, but which nevertheless insist on their distinctiveness. It may be useful, therefore, to look at some of the major cultural variants as they affect identity and education within the larger community.

Language is the most conspicuous for several reasons; apart from emotional considerations, and its role in communication and teaching, it affects the speaker's very perception of reality (Stephens 1979, International Review of Education 1978, Ray and Lamontagne 1977, *Compare* 1978). Virtually every member state, present and future, has some degree of internal linguistic variation, though some try to ignore or suppress it. West Germany and the Netherlands are probably the least affected (though there are dialectical differences), but they do have substantial numbers of *gastarbeiter* or immigrant workers from Turkey, Yugoslavia, Spain, Greece, Italy and elsewhere, while the Netherlands have an Indonesian minority as legacy of a colonial past. Italy has a small German-speaking population in the Alto Adige (South Tyrol), and of course some of the Italian variants, notably Sicilian, Neapolitan and Sardinian, are distinct from the Romanised Tuscan that has become standard Italian, and have vernacular literatures of their own. Of the future entrants, Portugal is relatively homogeneous. Greece still has Turkish, Slav and Albanian minorities left over from more than a century of border-change and warfare, and has only recently sorted out the wide discrepancy between the official purist form (*katharevoussa*) and the kind people actually speak (*demotiki*). As for Spain, it has emerged from the imposed uniformity of Franco's rule with a variety that calls to mind the old term of 'The Spains' from the days of the *Reconquista*. Catalan, as close to French as to Spanish, is spoken by some six million people, and has a literary heritage dating from the Middle Ages. Andalusian, originally a form of Castilian, has developed an identity of its own, and the Galician of the north-east is akin to Portuguese. Basque, quite unrelated to any Indo-European language, survives in the Atlantic provinces, and seems to be enjoying a revival too (Diez *et al* 1977). The expansion of the Common Market will bring in not only three new member states, but many other groups conscious of their own identity.

In two cases, indeed, they are in the Community already, for there have been Basques and Catalans in both France and Spain since before either modern state took shape. France (ironically, the most unitary state in the EEC) has the largest number of minorities (Sérant 1965, Bec 1963, Villemarqué 1977). Apart from the Basques and Catalans, there are the 'overspills' from other states in Europe – the Dutch speakers of Westhoek (Artois), the German speakers of Alsace-Lorraine, the Corsicans (who speak a variety of Italian): and the Bretons, over a million of them, speak a Celtic tongue, probably brought over by British refugees from the Saxon invasions. Then there is the group of Latin languages – Provençal Gascon and others – usually grouped as Occitan, with strong Catalan and Italian affinities and, again, a literature of considerable antiquity. Additionally, France now has a sizeable Arabic-speaking population, mostly from Algeria and Morocco.

Even Denmark, having accorded home rule to the Faeroes and Greenland, still has Germans in south Jutland, a large number of immigrants, and wide differences between Jutlandic (*Jysk*) and the official Danish of Zeeland. Luxembourg is officially bilingual in French and German, but also has its own spoken Luxembourgeois, though the schools take little account of it. Ireland recognises both Irish and English; the former enjoys official sponsorship and is fostered in the schools, but is the mother tongue of only a small minority in the *Gaeltachta* of the West. Elsewhere, perhaps 20 per cent have a reasonable competence in it.

In the United Kingdom, the position is more complex (Bell and Grant 1977). It is a union of three countries and one province, but in no case is the population distinct by reason of language: as the great majority are monoglot in English, the roots of identity will have to be sought elsewhere. But there is a linguistic element. It is most prominent in Wales, where about 20 per cent speak Welsh, and even among those who do not there is some sense of connection between language and nationality. This is much less so in Scotland, which has been a multi-cultural nation since the early Middle Ages. Gaelic is still spoken by perhaps 100,000, mostly concentrated in the Western Isles and West Highlands where they form a majority (though there are some in the Lowlands too). Lowland Scots is still used, but has broken into a series of regional dialects since its decline as a court and literary tongue (though there have been revivals in its literary use). Most, however, use English with distinctive pronunciation and some specific vocabulary.

Ironically, the language difference, technically at least, should be the easiest variant to cope with in the educational system. True, it often becomes the symbol for a range of other characteristics, but of itself it need not affect content or structure. As we have seen, the USSR manages to provide a substantially uniform curriculum through different vernaculars, but there are examples nearer home. Scottish education differs from English in organisation, content and to some extent in philosophy, but not essentially in language; but the Welsh system, administered as part of the English until the 1960s, is practically identical in curricular structure and in organisation, language being the main difference. Language, therefore, does not *necessarily* imply other variables.

Religion can also serve as a badge of identity, but does not commonly assume this role within the Community. There are Catholic and Protestant divisions within Germany and the Netherlands, coinciding to some extent with regions, and strong enough to justify the Dutch tripartite system of Catholic, Protestant and secular schools. There are church schools in France, and the differences between the English and Scottish churches once loomed large in the school systems of both countries; but are now not the main issue – Scottish–English contemporary differences have little to do with theology. Likewise, being Catholic is not the main thing that distinguishes a Breton or Bavarian. The chief exception is Northern Ireland, where religion has become the symbol of the two embattled communities, but even here it has at least as much to do with their historical antecedents and contemporary allegiances as with their beliefs; no one seems to be trying to *convert* anyone. Whatever its strength elsewhere, then, religion seems to have lost much of its force as the *primary* feature of identity in Western Europe.

Since the obvious criteria do not always apply, then, others must be at work. What is it nowadays that makes Austrians not Germans, Montenegrins not Serbs, Scots and Welsh and Irish not English? The feeling of distinct identity is there, whether reflected in separate institutions or not. Montenegrins have their own republic within the Yugoslav Federation, and the Irish in the Republic have statehood, but elsewhere the position is more complex. At present, none of the countries comprising the United Kingdom has its own legislature; the Westminster Parliament ceased to be the English Parliament in 1707, a fact of which many of its members seem unaware. But all have some other institutions of their own. Scotland and England have their own national churches and legal codes, while Wales does not, a reflection of the ways in which Union came about – Wales was conquered and incorporated, Scotland was not. There is also some *administrative* devolution (including education) through multi-purpose Scottish, Welsh and Northern Ireland offices, though not in England: departments there are either all UK in their remit, or specifically English only when the functions of the smaller countries have been devolved (a matter of some confusion, as witness the ambiguous role of the DES).

But it would be rash to claim that having their own institutions is what *makes* these countries distinctive: on the contrary, they would seem to have acquired their institutions *because* they were distinctive: and Europe is studded with minorities which have been denied even the semblance of their own institutions for centuries, but which still feel they exist. At the risk of a cliché, we may have to fall back on some concept like 'historical awareness', an identity based on common experience that does not depend on any of the clearer cut criteria (though it may include them). Within England, for instance, the North–South divide leaves the Northumbrians with, in some respects, more in common with the Scots than with the Home Counties; but history has created a sense of being English that overrides all local identities, with the possible exception of the Cornish, who are historically not English at all.* In Scotland, there are a number of clear distinctions between Highlands and Lowlands, Gael and Gall, East and West, Protestant (of various kinds) and Catholic, and there are other distinctive regional identities less well known – Fife, the Borders, the North East, Orkney and Shetland; yet all of these groups

---

* Cornwall retained its Celtic language until the eighteenth century: it has been revived (on a small scale) in the twentieth. Anglophone Cornish people, however, are usually reluctant to accept the designation 'English', *legally* correct though it may be.

(with the probable exception of the last two*) consider themselves as primarily Scots. Some general concept of identity is needed to explain this, vague though it is. It can also explain why other divisions (like Highland and Lowland) were more important in the past, and why the Northern Isles still jib at being called Scots at all.

Faced with internal diversity, states have adopted different stances, ranging from outright repression through neglect to tolerance or even encouragement. Of these, repression has been by far the most common up to recent times. At present, France is the clearest example of the imposition of the metropolitan language and culture, making no allowance for diversity within the school system. True, children are no longer flogged for speaking Basque or Breton, but they are stigmatised; it is now possible to take these languages (and Catalan, Corsican, Occitan) as *subjects* in the *baccalauréat*, but nowhere can they be used as the teaching medium. This policy can be traced to the Revolution, when local particularism was seen as a threat to the new régime, of whatever political complexion, ever since. Until recently, France was by no means alone in this. Until Franco's death, Spain also denied recognition, in education or anything else, to the Basque, Catalan or Galician cultures, and noticed their existence only to seek to extirpate them – not, as it turned out, very effectively (Marks 1976 pp. 199–218).

But this has been the story in the British Isles as well through most of their history. The attempts to suppress Irish from Plantagenet times onwards are tolerably well known; less familiar, perhaps, are the attempts to teach out (or even beat out) Gaelic, Welsh and Lowland Scots during the nineteenth century and well into the present one. Nor can this be laid (entirely) at the door of English cultural imperialism. The earliest attempts to root out Gaelic were made by the government of an independent Scotland (Bell and Grant 1977, McKinnon 1974, 1977, Thomson 1978, McClure *et al* 1980, Jones 1966, Dodgson *et al* 1968, Cuív 1969, Corkery 1968). It took pressure on *their* identity, from England, to lead the Lowland Scots to make any kind of common cause with their Celtic compatriots. It should be noted, too, that many parents in Brittany, Occitanie, Ireland, Wales, the Gàidhealtachd, etc., acquiesced in the process, on the assumption that knowing their own language would interfere with their children's mastery of English or French (or whatever) and thus hold them back – particularly as the minority areas have often been both peripheral and impoverished, and 'success' has been equated with escape. This process was also helped on by the assumption, virtually unchallenged until relatively recently, that 'progress' was an indivisible package deal, and that the customs of

†Orkney and Shetland were transferred to Scotland by Norway in the sixteenth century in payment of a bad debt; the Norse language of these islands (Norn) died out in the nineteenth century, but the islanders still insist on Norse rather than Scots identity (see Linklater 1971).

the metropolitan cultures, from language and dress to cuisine and curriculum, were valid for the entire human race – an assumption which many among the minorities themselves came to share.

But in most cases this stance has been at least modified, partly under political pressure, partly because some of the metropolitan cultures are not quite as confident as they were, and partly because of the growing body of evidence that multi-lingualism may actually be an educational asset. The centralist, unitary model has therefore been abandoned by many countries in favour of a more pluralistic one. In Spain, for example, Catalunya and Euzkadi (Catalonia and the Basque country) now exercise control over political as well as cultural and educational matters within the Spanish state. In Belgium, communal tension has made the dual French and Dutch school system one of the means of political survival; Italy has devolved much power to the historical regions, and West Germany has since its foundation left a wide range of matters, including education, to the constituent Länder.

Some states actually encourage minorities. The record of the UK has been mixed on this. Nowadays, on the whole, detailed policy is left to the local authorities. Policy regarding Gaelic and Welsh is left to the Scottish and Welsh Offices, whose stance might be called hesitantly supportive (a contrast to former open hostility). In Wales, this varies from assiduous fostering to ill-concealed hostility, and in Scotland the regions vary similarly. Comhairle nan Eilean (the Western Isles Council) has adopted a policy of complete bilingualism: Strathclyde (which has some Highland areas) is supportive also, while Highland Region is suspected of 'benign neglect'. (Almost nothing, however, has been done anywhere about Lowland Scots.) The Irish Republic has strenuously promoted the Irish language since independence. Strictly speaking, this is not seen as encouraging a minority, as the aim is to restore it as the *national* language; but since the preservation of the Gaeltacht (the native-speaking area) is central to government policy, it could be seen in that light.

This case, indeed, illustrates the limitations of policy: just as Franco failed to stamp out Catalan, the Irish Republic has failed to restore Irish, for other factors are at work. Irish was certainly suppressed in the past, particularly by the Tudors, but mobility proved more effective, notably the Plantation of Ulster with English-speaking colonists by James VI and I and the Great Hunger of the nineteenth century, which half emptied the country, especially in the Irish-speaking West, and began the Irish diaspora which has continued to the present. Irish education (puerile self-laudatory 'Irish jokes' notwithstanding) has for over a century been unusually effective for a relatively poor country, but essentially an education for emigration, with the resultant stress on skills usable abroad. Much the same has happened in Scotland (internally and externally), Wales, Brittany,

Corsica, the Mezzogiorno and so forth. Areas thus affected need not be depressed: the Isle of Man, net importer of population though it is, lacks any higher education, and thus has to prepare students to seek this elsewhere (usually England) and also draws its teachers from outside. The independent Manx system, therefore, is much more like the English than the non-independent Scottish system. (This is true of the Channel Isles also, see Pickering 1973.)

Cultural domination, in the broadest sense, is no respecter of frontiers. Dublin can receive BBC and Ulster TV just as easily as Radio Telefis Eirean (RTE), the Irish Television Service, and of course programmes shown in Scotland and Wales are from the UK network, a potent force for 'normalisation' despite the specifically Scottish and Welsh material. (There is now a move to phase out Scottish schools broadcasting and use only centrally produced material.) Much the same happens in publishing, since authors are interested in maximising their readership: the process that led Hume (who spoke Scots) to write in English has also made terms like 'O-level' and 'Public School' (in the sense of a private one) widely current in Scotland, inappropriate though they are. When the textbook industry is taken into account, it is small wonder that the very content of teaching in Scotland, Ireland and Wales has undergone some Anglicisation.

A variant of this process is the use of models in educational innovation, since total originality is extremely rare. German and French models spread almost everywhere in nineteenth-century Europe, as American models have been widely used in Asia (and parts of Europe) in the twentieth. Likewise, élite schools in Scotland and Ireland owed much to their English prototypes, and the same frequently happened in higher education. The minority system does not always copy the majority, if the majority lacks a model of its own for some innovation; thus, the nineteenth century English civic universities looked to the Scottish, and more recently such innovations as the Keele Foundation Year or the Open University credit system drew on and adapted Scottish as well as North American experience, since there was little precedent in the English system. More commonly, though, the greater tends to influence the lesser. Mobility, wealth, size, economic and cultural hegemony – all of these, quite apart from political control, seem to favour increasing homogenisation. This assumption is certainly widely held, even by many among the minorities. Internally, at least, natural forces would seem to favour unity of the incorporating kind.

But other factors are present also. The reassertion of identity, by minorities in Europe and North America, has been a widespread phenomenon in recent years. It may take a political form (moderate or radical) or may concentrate on cultural or linguistic revival, or any combination of these. Contrary to the conventional dismissals of such developments as 'provincial', out of keeping with an age of greater internationalisation, it can be argued that this assertion of identity is a logical concomitant of the growth of supranational complexes like the EEC and the Nordic Council.

Culturally as well as politically and economically, the nation state is not the self-contained entity that it once seemed, and therefore less convincing *internally* as a homogeneous unit. Now, if total *international* assimilation is not possible or even desirable – and we have already looked at some of the obstacles – then some other kind of international co-operation has to be developed. (One might add that the EEC, let alone Europe, is rather large an entity to identify with completely.) But if pluralism is acceptable within an international co-operative framework, then it can work *within* nation-status too. From this point of view, variety (linguistic, cultural, structural, curricular, etc.) is not only compatible with European unity, but is an essential aspect of it.

To construct such a model will be a difficult task, conceptually as well as practically. Ironically, the United Kingdom could have some contribution to make from its own experience, but has consistently mishandled the issue of pluralism, largely because influential sections of opinion (perhaps a majority) in England have never grasped the difference between union and incorporation. (A host of examples could be offered, but one will serve, namely the frequency with which 'England', 'Britain' and 'the UK' are used as if they were synonymous, and the puzzled surprise when Scots, Welsh and Northern Irish refuse to be described as English.) Space does not permit anything like a full account here of the latest attempt to sort this out, culminating in the 1979 Referendum; but just in case the impression has been given that the Scots and Welsh rejected home rule or even their own identities, some points need to be made. The specific Acts were full of confusion and hamstrung by limitations. The Scottish Assembly, for example, was to have control over the educational system, but not the universities; these, influential as they are, were to remain in the province of the DES, that is, in effect, of the English Ministry of Education (Grant and Main 1976). The Welsh Assembly was to have no legislative powers at all. There was a great deal of this, which limited enthusiasm even among supporters. Unlike the 1975 Referendum on EEC membership, this was conducted in the absence of any clear factual information from the Government, leaving the way clear for the wildest allegations (such as border controls, which of course were never contemplated). In spite of all this, a majority of voters in Scotland approved the Act. Parliament had, however (again, unlike the EEC referendum), invented a special rule whereby 40 per cent of those on the register (including the abstainers, the indifferent, the double entries, the removed and the dead) had to vote Yes. The Government fell in the row that followed, and its successor (which had been trounced at the polls in Scotland) repealed the Act. The '40 per cent rule' was, of course, unique. If it had been applied in the 1975 referendum, the UK would not now be in the EEC; and if it had applied in general elections the present Government, like most of its predecessors, could claim no mandate. The whole affair produced a good deal of bitterness and cynicism in Scotland, and demonstrated that the UK stands closer to France than any other member of the Community in insisting on the maintenance of a unitary state.

But the issues will not go away. The UK minority systems continue to have their own structures and problems and are still run by their own bureaucracies (responsible to Westminster). It must be said that there is little evidence of governmental sensitivity to those problems: indeed, the practice of legislating for education for the whole UK simultaneously, with Scottish provisions added as an afterthought, seems to be catching on. Central policies are being pushed harder than they were, with some odd consequences. To cite but two examples: the 'Assisted Places Scheme' (whatever may be thought of it in England) is quite at variance with the Scottish tradition and system, as the private sector is much weaker in most of the country; and decisions taken on university finance seem to have taken little account of the different course-structure in Scotland. It is also proving more difficult to establish international links (most of these go through the DES), which is hardly healthy if the system is to develop in its own way in the larger community.

The continued reluctance of the UK and France to recognise adequately their internal variations does not augur well for their acceptance of diversity at the international level; and indeed there is little evidence of serious moves towards harmonisation either. While this lasts, the European educational systems are liable to be left to the blind forces of interaction, with the occasional act of 'normalisation' on specific points, without thinking through their implications for education as a whole. Unity, in any meaningful sense, cannot be achieved in this way.

What is needed is the recognition that we are all minorities now; someone else's identity need not be a threat to one's own. The logical outcome of this is to create effective autonomy for all internal minorities to develop their educational systems in their own ways and make them responsive to their own particular needs. Within the UK, this means that mere *administrative* devolution of education is not enough; without political organs, civil service departments are in danger of being mere instruments of remote control.

Nor will it be enough to revive the 1979 Acts; they left the Scottish universities under DES control (thus hobbling the Assembly's capacity for overall policy-making in education), and offered the Welsh little more than the shadow of control of anything. Next time, the political structures will have to be less pusillanimous about letting the Scots and Welsh develop their own systems (which includes financial powers). There is also a case for English devolution, of course, if only to clarify the present confusion between all UK and specifically English functions (as with the DES). The form, of course – unitary or regional – is for the English to decide.

At the same time, it has to be recognised that no educational system exists in a vacuum. Teachers and students do move about, raising the need for some machinery of coordination, if only to ensure recognition of qualifications on the one hand and reasonable chances of higher education entry on the other – both matters which the UK has still not managed to sort out even internally. Externally, exchange of students and teachers is still limited, but could grow in the future and should be prepared for. As for joint research, and pooling of expertise and resources in teaching, this too could (and should) be an area of growth. It will therefore be desirable to work out equivalences at critical points of the schooling process – the end of compulsory schooling and entry to employment, the end of upper secondary school and entry to higher education (a model such as the International Baccalaureate could be useful here (Peterson 1977 pp. 77–81)) and first degree level. This is a logical extension of the harmonisation of professional qualifications, and would still allow individual systems to develop in their own idiom within this framework, if flexibly enough conceived.

But this could not be left to agreement between the member states. Some of the minority systems are already structurally different from majority ones, and would need direct representation. Further, such systems have a particular need for international contact to avoid becoming too inward-looking; for their own health, it is important that the systems of Scotland and Wales and Brittany and Catalonia cross-fertilise directly, and not have to communicate through London or Paris or Madrid: they have stood in the shadow of one neighbour for too long already.

Looking further ahead, there would need to be some coordination of social policies in education. This could not be pushed too far; it would not be realistic or reasonable to forbid Scotland or Denmark to pursue egalitarian policies or England or France selective ones. (This is near enough what happens in the UK, which is bad enough; extending it internationally implies a degree of overall control that no state would lightly accept.) But it should be possible to find *some* common principles within a pluralist framework. The rights of minorities is one possibility, and has to some extent been acted upon already. (The provision of mother-tongue instruction was designed to meet the needs of citizens of the Community living outside their own countries, but has implications for indigenous minorities which have yet to be fully explored (Steedman 1979 pp. 259–268). Parental rights is another area (Beattie 1978 pp. 41–48); continuing education could be yet another. Some degree of sovereignty might be lost, but membership of the Community already involves that. The important thing would be to achieve a balance between effective ground-rules and essential autonomy all round.

These are structural questions, hideously difficult but not insoluble, given the will. But content will have to be considered too, and here again we run into difficulties. Some systems, like the French, accept prescription from the centre, whereas others, like the English, suspect even the idea of a core curriculum. But this cannot be avoided indefinitely; it would therefore make sense to agree on a common core, delimit its boundaries, and clarify the principles underlying it. There is no point in expecting agreement, for example, on the place of religion, but it should be possible to agree that education should enable people to function as members of the Community; and this would mean (if the arguments adduced already have any force) the acceptance of multiple identity (Grant 1977 pp. 139–150).

This was a familiar enough conception in the Middle Ages, obscured by the dominance of the nation state in the last couple of centuries. But it is still there, and fits the idea of an international community where people still belong to nations. It is perfectly possible to be (say) human, 'western' European, British, Scots and Highland simultaneously and to endow these roles with meanings that reinforce rather than contradict each other. Education, then, has to begin at least to provide the capacity to fill these roles. This requires the cultural and linguistic knowledge and skills to understand the immediate environment, the wider national heritage, and the foundation of contact with and understanding of the international community. (The natural environment and the international language of science have a place too, of course.)

Naturally, there are limits to what the school can do; a sound basis in the student's own culture does seem feasible, however, as do firm points of contact with the national and international mainstream culture, using one's own as the foundation. But not everything can be attempted. Continuing education, then, will have a major part to play, not only on the vocational grounds often urged, but to develop the interconnected identities of the child, the young person and the adult.

Admittedly, the task is as difficult and complex in concept as in realisation, but there is no real alternative. Uniformity is not feasible nor can cultural autonomy offer retreat from a complex wider world, and an education limited to either perspective will not meet the needs of the member of the rich and varied mosaic of European cultures. The opportunities for innovation, participation and development are great, and with intelligent planning there is no reason why this should be incompatible with the maintenance of standards or the other instrumental tasks that education is called on to fulfil. It has no hope of success if learning is seen as a once-off process – but that will not, in any case, be an adequate model for the education of the future European, or of anyone else.

PART TWO

6
The Curriculum and Curriculum Change

Denis Lawton

Maurice Kogan, in 1978, wrote about the end of consensus in education in the mid-1960s and the development of conflict in the 1970s. One of the best examples of the move from consensus to controversy was the school curriculum and especially changes in the curriculum. Throughout the 1940s and 1950s it could comfortably be assumed that not only was education 'a good thing', but that it was in safe hands. The curriculum was little discussed, being considered uncontroversial to the point of dullness, and it was generally taken for granted that the curriculum should remain the responsibility of individual schools and teachers. Other contributors to this volume touch upon some of the specific events behind the 'loss of faith' in education – such as the William Tyndale dispute, and the growth of the accountability movement. Many of these events are directly connected with curricular issues. Two general issues emerged during the seventies which will certainly continue into discussions about the curriculum in the eighties: the content of the curriculum, and its control. Underlying both these issues are two very different approaches to the curriculum, which may be referred to as the behavioural objectives and the cultural analysis models. The former focuses on 'efficiency', the latter on justification.

The behavioural objectives model tends to take the existing curriculum pattern more or less for granted, but aims to improve it by clarifying objectives, relating these to specific changes in pupils' behaviour, and to evaluation. In that sense (and some others) it is a conservative model, likely to appeal to those worried about standards, measurement and minimal competency.

At the other extreme, the cultural analysis model is concerned with radical, fundamental questions such as 'what are schools for?', 'what is knowledge?', 'what knowledge and what kinds of experience are most worthwhile?', 'what do pupils need in order to be able to participate in our society now and in the future?'. A preference for one model rather than the other may depend on deep-rooted values, priorities and prejudices, but each has certain strengths and weaknesses which should be carefully noted.

The behavioural objectives model

The objectives model has a long history in the USA and has something in common with the 'payment by results' approach adopted after 1862 in England. From the first decade of the twentieth century, American educationists such as Bobbitt, attempted to apply to school systems the industrial techniques of F.W. Taylor. This involved listing specific objectives and costing teaching processes. The results achieved by pupils were the only acceptable criteria of success. This view of curriculum planning was given a new lease of life in the late 1940s by the theoretical work of Ralph Tyler. His *Basic Principles of Curriculum and Instruction* (1949) was extremely influential in curriculum theory. Tyler identified four fundamental questions which must be answered in connection with any teaching programme:

1   What educational purposes should the school seek to attain?

2   What educational experiences can be provided that are likely to attain these purposes?

3   How can these educational experiences be effectively organised?

4   How can we determine whether these purposes are being attained?

These four basic questions have been translated into the objectives model in the following way:

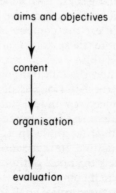

aims and objectives

content

organisation

evaluation

This simple linear translation may distort Tyler's four questions; it certainly results in a very naive and simplistic view of curriculum planning. Tyler, like other curriculum theorists, was motivated by the fact that many educational programmes were extremely ill-defined and incapable of evaluation. What began as a desire for clarity has been transformed into a curriculum theory, whereby the only valid educational objectives are those which describe pupil behaviour, not teacher behaviour. So objectives must specify how pupils are to behave at the end of a teaching sequence; and these behavioural changes must be measurable.

Despite many basic criticisms both of a theoretical and a practical kind, the objectives model has flourished, especially in the USA, and has been given additional credence by such theoretical devices as the 'taxonomy of educational objectives' produced by Benjamin Bloom and his colleagues in the 1950s. Generations of American teachers (and some in England) have worked at the various levels of the taxonomy, translating what they wanted to teach into terminology acceptable to curriculum planners of the behavioural objectives persuasion. Such efforts have inevitably generated criticism. Stenhouse in Britain, and Elliot Eisner in the United States, have been particularly vocal in their opposition to the behavioural objectives model.

Stenhouse (1975) claims that it is unreasonable to pre-specify objectives in, for example, teaching a Shakespearean play because to do so ignores the nature of studying English literature. It would be possible to specify the responses a teacher wanted and then to provide feedback to inform the pupils that these were the correct responses; but this would, according to Stenhouse (and others) be failing to realise that each individual's response to a work of art is unique. This kind of teaching situation is quite unlike teaching typewriting or simple arithmetic. Stenhouse argues that to use an output model for a process where the emphasis must essentially be on the input is totally unsatisfactory and unacceptable.

Eisner (1969) argues that in the expressive arts the purpose of the teaching/learning process is to encourage the child to produce his own response, not to pre-specify what response is regarded as appropriate. This is essentially the difference between instructional objectives and expressive objectives.

Arguments against the behavioural objectives model are not confined to the aesthetic subjects. Sockett (1976) has demonstrated that a behavioural objectives model is inappropriate for the teaching of science. In science, everything is, in principle, falsifiable. If a teacher pre-specifies the outcome of an experiment, then the experiment is no longer serious – it is rendered essentially unscientific, for the purpose of any experiment is to make refutation possible. Sockett goes further and asserts that the idea of basing a curriculum on behavioural objectives is impossible. He condemns this approach to curriculum design for the same reasons that Karl Popper condemns Plato and other Utopian social planners. Sockett suggests that a Utopian in curriculum design can be identified as 'someone who believes that a thorough and comprehensive analysis of all factors relevant to a curriculum can be marshalled and embodied in a master plan. This plan will contain fully detailed objectives organised in such a way as to promote the achievement of those aims derived from the rigorous analysis' (Sockett 1976 pp. 15–16). Human behaviour is far too complex to fit such a convenient model.

There are other more practical objections to the behavioural objectives approach. Even if it were desirable, it would be quite impossible to list all the behavioural objectives connected with any particular area of knowledge. If a teacher wanted children to develop 'respect for persons', for example, it would be impossible to work out in advance all the behavioural examples likely to occur in such a way that they could be tested and measured. The debate about the objectives model is not dead, but if the model is to survive in any useful way, it will need to be altered fundamentally, in order to move away from behavioural requirements.

The cultural analysis model
This model is also American in origin, although modified in its English versions. Smith *et al* (1957) and Broudy *et al* (1964) put forward a view of curriculum based on the idea of common culture and common curriculum. Similar ideas have developed in Britain, but not always by curriculum theorists or even educationists. In 1961 Raymond Williams, for example, published *The Long Revolution* which together with his earlier work (*Culture and Society*, 1958) has been extremely influential. Williams represents one strand of a debate about education which stems from teachers of English and English literature in schools and in universities. Others involved in this debate have included F.R. Leavis, Denys Thompson and Richard Hoggart.

Malcolm Skilbeck came to similar conclusions from a somewhat different starting point. He refers to his own scheme as situational analysis. His curriculum model is eclectic in that it includes some aspects of the objectives approach (but not behavioural objectives). According to Skilbeck, individual schools must come to terms with the social context of the school and plan a curriculum accordingly. Skilbeck outlines a sequence of stages:

1 situational analysis
2 goal formulation
3 programme building
4 interpretation and implementation
5 monitoring, feedback, assessment and reconstruction

In one sense, the whole of this model is an example of cultural analysis. In another, the specific cultural analysis is built into stage one of situational analysis. Skilbeck breaks down his cultural analysis into external and internal factors. The external factors of the cultural analysis include general cultural and social changes at a national and local level; the requirements of the educational system itself; changes of subject content; the potential contributions of support systems for teachers; general resources available to the school. The internal analysis consists of consideration of the pupils; the teachers; the ethos of the school and its political structure; material resources; shortcomings of the existing curriculum and other perceived problems.

Skilbeck also refers to his approach as 'cultural mapping'. He emphasises that the map is not a still life picture from the past, but a set of features and signposts concerning the present and the future. In general, Skilbeck sees the new curriculum as something quite different from 'subjects and subject matter'. He proposes a curriculum divided into two parts, one part common to all pupils, the other providing opportunity for choice and specialisation. The common curriculum would be based on a critical analysis of the main features of contemporary culture. These features will be perceived differently in particular situations, but they will include: typical work situations and modes of economic operation; social rules and patterns of social meanings including norms of conduct, value systems, and patterns of expectation; the major human symbolic systems of language, mathematics, scientific thinking, religion, the arts; leisure and recreational interests; institutional structures in both the public and private sectors; government and social policy; forms of inter-personal relationships and the management of tension and conflict; modes of individual expression and creativity.

Skilbeck has recently (1980) produced a 'core curriculum' for the Australian Curriculum Development Centre which successfully translates these principles into a document which can be understood and discussed by non-specialists.

My own approach to the curriculum is also radical rather than conservative. The curriculum is defined as 'a selection from the culture of a given society'. But who decides on the selection and by what principles? A simplified version of this approach, in a series of stages, is set out in Figure I overleaf:

STAGE I

There are at least two kind of question which are largely, but not exclusively, philosophical: first, epistemological questions about the structure of knowledge and how this relates to what should be taught in schools; second, questions about why some kinds of knowledge and experience are regarded as more worthwhile than others.

There is still a good deal of philosophical disputation about the structure of knowledge, but epistemologists tend to agree that it is necessary to sub-divide knowledge according to some kind of classification system. Kinds of knowledge can be distinguished by the concepts used; or the means by which concepts are built up into networks, or by different types of 'truth tests'. Most would agree, for example, that mathematics is different from science (although science makes use of mathematical concepts), and that both kinds of knowledge are in turn different from aesthetic and moral 'knowledge'.

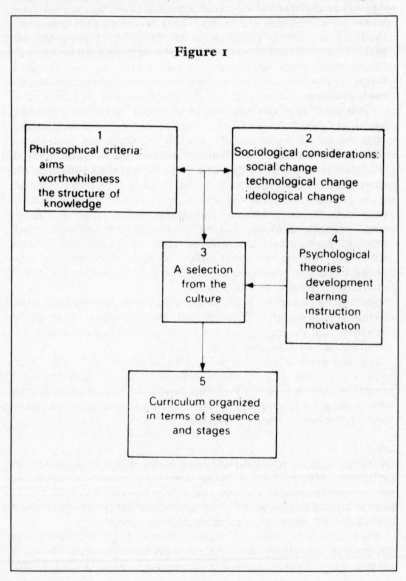

Figure 1

There are also good arguments to support the view that it is reasonable to regard knowledge about science as more important than knowledge about darts or cricket. This is not simply a matter of taste nor of bourgeois hegemony (see Lawton 1973, 1975).

STAGE 2

Apart from questions about the structure of knowledge and worthwhileness which would apply to any society, there are also questions of particular concern in our society at present: for example, we are a highly scientific, technological, industrial society; we also claim to be a democratic society. The first has some bearing on *what* should be taught; the second has some bearing on to *whom* knowledge should be made available.

Consideration of contemporary society will enable us to draw up a list of curricular priorities, but some reference back to Stage 1 will often be necessary: without the existence of a set of criteria which are of more general applicability than our own society's, education would become a mere reflection of particular social values. Stage 2 must interact with Stage 1 before we reach Stage 3.

STAGE 3

Once such questions as 'what are aims in education?', 'what do we mean by "worthwhile"?', 'what situations will pupils be faced with when they leave school?' have been clarified, we are in a better position to make a selection from the culture, based on criteria which can be made public even if total consensus is lacking. At this stage the selection is an 'ideal' selection in the sense that it does not have to take into account the limitations of individual schools (resources and teachers).

STAGE 4

This stage brings into operation such psychological theories as those of Piaget on children's development, of Bruner's views on 'instruction' as well as theories of learning and motivation. Considerations of these factors would lead to the final stage of curriculum planning.

STAGE 5

A curriculum based on an analysis of contemporary culture, but bearing in mind certain cultural and educational 'universals', would be very different from what is generally offered to most young people in primary and secondary schools today. For example, most schools provide some kind of curriculum in science, but offer little which would help young people to understand technology (or even the social implications of technology); similarly, most schools offer some kind of history and geography, but the majority of young people leave school almost totally ignorant of the political and economic structure of their own society.

One of the aims of the cultural analysis approach is to establish the range of knowledge and educational experience that all children should have access to. I would argue, for example, not only that there is a kind of knowledge called science which is different in important respects from other kinds of knowledge (Stage 1), but that this knowledge is of particular relevance in understanding and participating in our technological and industrial society (Stage 2). This establishes a case for giving high priority to science at Stages 3 and 5. But all knowledge is not scientific: the same process of cultural analysis would give high priority also to humanities and social science, for example, and to those kinds of experience which would help an individual to develop aesthetically and morally. An important part of this argument is that a major purpose of education is to help the young to understand and participate in their own society: cultural analysis attempts to map out the areas of knowledge and experience which are necessary for this purpose, and to identify major concepts and skills within each area as a minimum basis for understanding self and the environment. It follows that if any important 'area' is missing from a pupil's curriculum, then that individual has been inadequately educated. There is some evidence to suggest that this approach has influenced, directly or indirectly, the thinking of Her Majesty's Inspectors on the curriculum. Much of the HMI document *Curriculum 11–16* (1977) is based on the principles of cultural analysis, and there are many assumptions in the HMI Secondary School Survey (DES 1979c) which show the same approach: for example, an assumption that all children have a right of access to important areas of experience in a common curriculum.

I shall want to return later in this chapter to the HMI approach in *Curriculum 11–16*, but before doing so, it is necessary to examine some of the concepts connected with the problems of curriculum content.

The first problem concerns coverage: a well-planned curriculum should cover all the kinds of knowledge, skills and desirable experiences defined as educational. This includes the task of bringing a curriculum up to date by including technology as well as science, politics and economics as well as history.

The second concerns the desire for a balanced curriculum, including the avoidance of premature specialisation. (Premature specialisation is defined as any concentration on some 'areas' which might impede adequate development across the whole curriculum.)

The third problem is that of achieving a good formula for what is made compulsory and what can be left as optional choice.

The concepts of common curriculum and core curriculum are also involved in each of these three major problem areas. It may be useful to distinguish between these two concepts at this preliminary stage. Core curriculum is a weak concept associated with the notion that there are certain basic subjects which ought to be included in all pupils' curriculum at all levels. The HMI *Secondary School Survey* (1979) showed that, while nearly all head teachers subscribed to the idea of a core curriculum, in practice, the core amounted in most schools to no more than mathematics and English. The 1980 *A Framework for the School Curriculum* attempts merely to extend this core to mathematics, English, science, modern languages for two years, together with some attempt to cater for preparation for the adult world of industry. The danger of a core is that it may become the whole curriculum or is regarded as the most important aspect of the curriculum. The idea has also been criticised inasmuch as it tends to focus on subjects rather than on more fundamental purposes or areas. In other words, it is concerned with means rather than ends, or perhaps treats means as though they were ends in themselves.

The common curriculum concept is much more ambitious and wide-ranging in scope. It is a logical extension of the idea of comprehensive education or a common secondary education for all. During the sixties it began to be argued that comprehensive schools represented very little advance on the tripartite system unless they became more than three schools under one roof. It was argued that comprehensive schools should not simply be concerned with providing an education for all pupils up to the age of 16, but should be concerned with transmitting a common culture to all pupils by means of a common curriculum. Designing a common curriculum is, therefore, concerned with establishing those kinds of knowledge and areas of experience to which it is assumed all pupils ought to have access up to the age of 16. Such a curriculum is in no sense uniform, since although 'areas' are specified as necessary for all pupils, it is not suggested that everyone should reach the same levels of attainment. Not only would that be undesirable, it would also be impossible to achieve. The common curriculum implies, however, that all pupils have access to science, for example, and that it would not be satisfactory for some to be studying physics and chemistry whilst others would be having a walk around the gasworks (unless this represented a genuine introduction to scientific concepts and understanding).

This brings us back to the first of our problems – that of *coverage*. Despite the popular concern that the basic areas of the curriculum – especially mathematics and English – are not being taught adequately, the evidence from both primary and secondary HMI surveys would seem to indicate that *too much* attention is being paid to the basic subjects and not enough to other very necessary aspects of knowledge, skills and educational experiences. In the case of the Secondary Survey, schools were again criticised for allowing pupils too narrow a range of subject matter. This was partly a criticism of the options systems (see below) but also implies that schools were not ensuring that important areas of experience were available. The examination system was also blamed for cutting out, for example, important areas of aesthetic experience.

Another difficulty is that of 'curriculum inertia'. It is often suggested that schools continue with a curriculum which might have been suited to society a generation or a century ago, but has failed to keep up to date. Thus until recently Latin and Greek tended to dominate the curriculum in many schools whilst science was comparatively neglected. More recently it has been suggested that technology should feature much more prominently in the curriculum. There is also a good deal of evidence to show that most young people leave school at 16 or 18 almost completely ignorant of the political and economic aspects of their own society. Most schools have failed to incorporate these kinds of knowledge and experience into the subject-based curriculum.

A related problem to that of coverage is the question of *balance*. Can balance be left to pupils' choice, or should it be subject to strict control by curriculum planners either at a national or a school level? One contemporary view is that, after experiencing a common, balanced curriculum up to the age of about 14, it is then appropriate for pupils to choose their own curriculum. Unfortunately, this has not worked out well in practice. The evidence of research is that pupils choose their subjects in option systems for a variety of reasons which can hardly be described as rational; most self-chosen timetables do not amount to a balanced curriculum. Evidence suggests that pupils drop subjects if they feel they are not very good at them, irrespective of whether they need them or not, or that they choose subjects because they like the teacher in charge. The option-system is the most common method of curriculum planning (or non-planning) in secondary schools in the fourth and fifth years. This tendency has been encouraged by the single subject GCE and CSE examinations which do not specify any compulsory subjects or any desirable balance. The option system has been severely criticised by HMI in 1977 (*Curriculum 11–16*) and, more recently, in the *Secondary School Survey* (1979) and *A View of the Curriculum* (1980). The discussion document *Curriculum 11–16* is the most outspoken condemnation of the 'cafeteria' curriculum, and makes a strong appeal for 75 per cent of the timetable to be devoted to a common curriculum. The Inspectors suggest that the curriculum should be thought of in terms of 'areas of experience' rather than subjects. No pupil's curriculum can be considered satisfactory unless it provides adequate coverage of the following areas of experience:

the aesthetic and creative

the ethical

the linguistic

the mathematical

the physical

the scientific

the social and political

the spiritual

The trend away from free choice and a 'cafeteria' curriculum to more restraint and guidance within a common curriculum, has come about for a variety of reasons.

The first is a reaction against the exaggerated child-centred views which were very common in the optimistic days of the fifties and sixties, and reached a climax in the Plowden Report. The prevailing view seemed to be that children given 'freedom' naturally made wise choices adequately guided by their own needs and interests. This view of the child and of the curriculum has been questioned and criticised. The paradox here is that if we want adults to be free it does not necessarily follow that we achieve this by making children totally free: the young and the immature need to be assisted towards the achievement of autonomy.

A related argument is that if the state compels children to go to school for at least ten years, thus restricting their freedom for this time, then it has a corresponding duty to set out the advantages gained by that amount of schooling. In the optimistic fifties and sixties it was sufficient to assume that schooling was an obvious benefit. This has ceased to be the case. It is now necessary to spell out the benefits of education in terms of what children should have learned by the age of 11 or 16. This need not necessarily lead us into the direction of behavioural objectives, or of a competency-based approach to curriculum planning, but it does mean that teachers should be much clearer about what they are offering, and what advantages they hope will be gained by their pupils from these educational experiences.

Recognition of this would now seem to be common ground between DES, HMI, LEAs and the teaching profession. What remains to be sorted out is the kind of 'framework' or common curriculum which can be approved nationally for implementation locally. It is not an easy task – the 1980 *A Framework for the School Curriculum* was a very poor effort – but it had to be attempted.

Conclusion

In England the debate during the next few years is likely to be about practicalities of curriculum planning rather than theories and models. But it is interesting to note that some of the rival curriculum proposals make assumptions which are identifiable either with the behavioural objectives model or with the cultural analysis approach.

The HMI document *Curriculum 11–16*, based on the idea of access to a common culture by means of a common curriculum, is firmly based, whether the Inspectors realise it or not, in the cultural analysis approach. The 1980 DES document on a curriculum framework, however, is based on the idea of a core curriculum, minimum competency, output rather than input, and testing. In this respect, the core curriculum and *A Framework for the School Curriculum (1980)* have values much in common with those of the Assessment of Performance Unit set up by the DES in 1975. Officially, the APU has nothing to do with curriculum planning or the framework for a core curriculum. The tests are there to monitor standards and not to exercise any control on the curriculum. APU officers have been careful to say that they want to minimise the backwash effect of monitoring standards by the tests which will be used. But any official test will inevitably encourage 'teaching to the test' and it is difficult to see how the APU can possibly avoid this kind of backwash. It has additionally been promised that the APU will not indulge in 'blanket testing' but work on the basis of light sampling: it will be impossible to identify individual children, classes or even schools. Perhaps a more serious danger is that the APU exercise will legitimise blanket testing by local education authorities where there will be less control over the publication of results. This would have an even greater effect on the curriculum taught in schools.

The cultural analysis ('areas of experience') approach represented by the HMI documents *Curriculum 11–16, A View of the Curriculum*, and the primary and secondary school surveys is fundamentally different from the assumptions underlying the APU methodology. Areas of experience are associated with an *input* model – that is, deciding what is sufficiently worthwhile for inclusion in every child's curriculum, whereas 'kinds of development' are associated with pre-specified norms of development which can be tested – that is, an *output* model closer to the behavioural objectives approach. Many objections have been raised about the APU, such as the use of item banking and the Rasch model, but the real danger is that testing will dominate the curriculum and eventually result in curriculum planning by behavioural objectives. Many criticisms could also be raised about the document *Curriculum 11–16*, such as its unexamined assumptions about the structure of knowledge or the omission of technology, but much more important is the fact that this document is in the humane tradition of cultural analysis. The alternative approach would take us in the direction of the worst practices of evaluation in the USA in recent years.

This chapter started with the suggestion that there are three aspects of the curriculum debate: control, content and the choice of theoretical models. It will now be apparent that these have converged to become a single debate about the curriculum. On the question of control, there is still much discussion about a partnership between DES, LEAs and teachers; but in reality, the metaphor has changed from partnership to accountability, and the DES is closer to real control of the curriculum than it has been for many years. But will the control be exercised through a flexible framework for a common curriculum or through a more rigid testing machine? Will the content of the curriculum be specified in detail, not overtly but covertly, by means of test items? The answers to these questions will depend on which theoretical model emerges as the more acceptable. Curriculum planning by behavioural objectives will take us in the direction of a core of subjects (narrowly based) backed by powerful testing; a common curriculum based on cultural analysis and an input model would take us in the direction of an improved version of the Inspectors' document *Curriculum 11–16*. There can be little argument as to which of these models teachers and educationists generally would favour.

7
Why no Pedagogy in England?

Brian Simon*

The term 'pedagogy' is used here in the sense of the 'science of teaching' (OED). The title of the chapter is meant to imply that no such science exists in England; the fact that the term is generally shunned implies that such a science is either undesirable or impossible of achievement. And such, it is argued, is the situation.

The contrast here with other European countries, both west and east, is striking. In the educational tradition of the Continent, the term 'pedagogy' has an honoured place, stemming perhaps particularly from the work and thinking of Comenius in the seventeenth century, but developed and elaborated in the nineteenth century through the work of Pestalozzi, Herbart and others. The concept of teaching as a science has strong roots in this tradition.

Not so in England. It is now one hundred years since Alexander Bain published *Education as a Science* (1879). Since then, less and less has been heard of this claim. The most striking aspect of current thinking and discussion about education is its eclectic character, reflecting deep confusion of thought, and of aims and purposes, relating to learning and teaching – to pedagogy.

As an example we may look briefly at the work of the Schools Council, which, since its establishment in 1962, has had the task of stimulating change in the curriculum in an attempt to bring it up to date in the light of modern knowledge and of social and economic change. But the key feature of this effort has been the atheoretical, pragmatic approach adopted (together with the implicit acceptance of the status quo in organisational or administrative terms). The technique used has been the funding of teams of teachers and others with the brief of producing 'curriculum reform' plans, syllabuses and packages. These have worked out their own ideas based on 'good practice' implying an emphasis on grass roots experiences, on cur-

* The author wishes to thank Dr T.G. Whiston, of the Science Policy Research Unit, University of Sussex, for extremely helpful and stimulating discussions on this issue, as also for commenting on an early draft of this chapter. Thanks are also due to Professors E. Stones and J.F. Eggleston for very useful comments on an early draft.

riculum reform from below as compared to reform from above as in the United States and the USSR. Thus some proejcts have focused on the teaching of individual subjects at various levels, others on the integration of subject matter, yet others on 'the whole curriculum'. Some have focused (like the early Nuffield Science Projects) on 'top ability' pupils; others specifically on curricula considered appropriate for 'the young school leaver'. The overall approach can hardly be called systematic, and certainly has not been informed by any generally accepted (or publicly formulated) ideas or theories about the nature of the child or the learning/teaching process – by any 'science of teaching' or 'pedagogy'. In particular there has been an almost total failure to provide psychological underpinning for the new program- mes proposed.[1] In general the Schools Council approach has reflected a pluralism run wild – a mass of disparate projects. In these circumstances, there is, perhaps, little wonder that the 'take up' in the schools seems to have been vestigial.

This is not intended as a criticism of the Schools Council. No other outcome could have been expected; not so much because of the make- up and constitution of that body itself (revised in 1979) but more because the concept of 'pedagogy' – of a science of teaching embodying both curriculum and methodology – is alien to our experience and way of thinking. There are, no doubt, many reasons why this is so; among them wide acceptance of the unresolved dichotomies between 'pro- gressive' and 'traditional' approaches, between 'child-centred' and 'subject-centred' approaches, or, more generally, between the 'in- formal' and 'formal'. Such crude, generalised categories are basically meaningless but expressed in this form deflect attention from the real problems of teaching and learning. Indeed so disparate are the views expressed that to resuscitate the concept of a science of teaching which underlies that of 'pedagogy' may seem to be crying for the moon. I hope to indicate that it is, in fact, a realistic proposition; that the knowledge base for a science of teaching does exist, and that circumstances urgently demand that the matter warrants serious and close attention.

But first, it may be useful to advance an interpretation as to why the concept of 'pedagogy' has been shunned in England, and why instead our approach to educational theory and practice has tended to be amateurish, and highly pragmatic in character.[2] Relevant here is the practice and approach of our most prestigious educational institutions (historically speaking), the ancient universities and leading public schools. Until recently, and even perhaps today, these have been dominant, both socially and in terms of the formation of the climate of opinion. It is symptomatic that the public schools, in general, have until recently contemptuously rejected the idea that a professional training is in any sense relevant to the job of a public school master.

Why no pedagogy in England?

Although toying with the idea in the late nineteenth century, the Headmasters Conference has never adopted a positive attitude to such training, which traditionally has been seen as perhaps relevant and important for an elementary school teacher, but certainly not to someone taking up the gentlemanly profession of teaching in a public school. This was seen, perhaps, not so much as a job anyone from the middle or upper middle class could do, but as something those who wished to teach, having the appropriate social origins including a degree at Oxford or Cambridge, could learn, through experience, on the job. Certainly no special training was necessary.[3]

The reasons for this are not far to seek. The public schools developed as a cohesive system from the mid- to late 1860s serving the new Victorian upper middle class; indeed they played a major role in the symbiosis of aristocracy and bourgeoisie which characterised the late nineteenth century. As Honey makes clear, these schools were centrally concerned with the socialisation of these classes which could not be effectively undertaken in the home. This, he argues, is why, in spite of the epidemics, outrageous bullying, sexual dangers and insanitary conditions to which their pupils were exposed (and all of which took their toll), the popularity of these schools mounted irresistibly at this time (Honey 1977).

Socialisation, as the major function of these schools at this time, involved little emphasis on intellectual (or cognitive) development. More important, especially in conditions of developing imperialism, was the formation of character, specifically of the qualities embodied in the concept of 'manliness' which, in its late nineteenth century form, involved the religion of games. This is not to argue that intellectual development was totally neglected. The tradition of classical teaching was, in fact, reinvigorated at this period, both at Oxford and Cambridge and in the schools. But the area of studies was limited and a major effort in this direction confined to a small number of schools which had a tradition of success in winning scholarships at Oxford and Cambridge (for instance, Shrewsbury, and later, Winchester). The burden of the interpretation by modern scholarship of the evolution of the public schools in the nineteenth century focuses on the transition from the Arnoldian ideal of 'Godliness and Good Learning' in the early part of the century to the cult of manliness and games towards the end, the transition having been effected with the aid of 'muscular Christianity' personified by Hughes (*Tom Brown's Schooldays*) and Charles Kingsley.[4]

This is a world far removed from pedagogy – the science of teaching – and from its concerns. Bourdieu's analysis may be relevant here (Bourdieu and Passeron 1977). Teachers and pupils at the public schools, and in general also at the university, came from similar backgrounds and shared a common culture. They talked the same language and were interested in the same things. The schools, in an important sense, were extensions of the home, largely financed by the parents themselves (though the value of endowments should not be underestimated), the products of a close collaboration between parents and teachers. The teacher's pastoral responsibility – in terms of upbringing – was as important, or more so, than his intellectual (teaching) responsibility. In this situation upper middle class culture and attitudes were 'naturally' assimilated and reinforced – the process did not require the application of specifically 'pedagogical' means. Approaches to teaching were traditional, handed down from generation to generation, though here there were exceptions, and certain schools (and teachers) did contribute to new thinking and practice relating, perhaps particularly, to science (Rugby). Again, as far as pedagogy is concerned, one public school head stands out in the late nineteenth, another in the early twentieth century: Thring of Uppingham, who was particularly concerned with the development, mental and moral, of the normal or 'average' boy; and Sanderson of Oundle whose innovations in the area of science, crafts and technology are of outstanding interest. Of course there were others, but these are exceptions; the general picture is as described.

The (historical) denigration of the value of professional training by the public schools, then, falls into place; it simply did not appear as relevant to the schoolmaster's profession, as defined in terms of public school objectives and practice. And this, of course, implies disdain for the concept of pedagogy – or of a science of teaching – since the function of professional training is, in theory, to lay the basis in science of the practice or art of teaching. At no time over the last hundred years (the period of existence of public schools in their modern form as a system) have the public schools, as such, expressed more than a remote, or distant, interest in or concern with this process. While the proportion of public schoolmasters who have been trained has risen over the last twenty to thirty years, the amateur still reigns supreme (Kalton, 1966, pp. 50–53)[5].

The situation is precisely reflected in Oxford and Cambridge, which, of course, have had the closest links with the public school system over the last century. Neither of these universities has, until perhaps recently, contributed to any serious extent to the study of education or to the development of educational theory and practice. This may seem an extraordinary thing to say; nevertheless it is the case. Cambridge, admittedly, made a start in 1879–80 when a delegacy was formed concerning teacher training, and lectures given covering the history, psychology and the practice of teaching. But this initiative did not prosper, and Cambridge was, in fact, among the last of all British universities to appoint a Professor of Education (in 1948) though, even here, it is ahead of Oxford which still does not recognise the subject in terms of establishing a Chair. Although departments of education have existed at both Universities for several decades now, these have been undistinguished and little regarded, both inside and outside the respective Universities. The low prestige of education as a subject of study, the few resources devoted to it, and the lack of serious experimental or scholarly studies undertaken, all these (and other factors) reflect general attitudes.[6]

The result has been that education, as a subject of enquiry and study, still less as a 'science', has, historically, had little prestige in this country, having been to all intents and purposes ignored in the most prestigious educational institutions. As Matthew Arnold tirelessly pointed out over one hundred years ago, in France, Prussia and elsewhere the problems of education for the middle class were taken really seriously. In Britain, on the other hand, everything was neglected; a laissez-faire pragmatism predominated.[7] This situation has, to some extent, been perpetuated. The dominant educational institutions of this country have had no concern with theory, its relation to practice, with pedagogy. This is the first point to establish.

But this, of course, is only part of the picture, if an important one. For while the public schools expressed, at least in their practice, a total disregard for pedagogy, in fact a systematic, rational approach was being developed elsewhere – as an indigenous growth within the system of elementary education, and specifically in the last decade of the nineteenth century, just as this system 'became of age', as it were, after its establishment in 1870. This is an interesting and relevant phenomenon, and worth serious attention for its lessons today.

The context of what was, in fact, a serious attempt to integrate theoretical knowledge with the practice of education is to be found in the work of the advanced School Boards in the main industrial cities at this time. Described as 'citadels of radicalism' by Elie Halévy, the French historian, these, with their higher grade schools, pupil-teacher centres, and technical institutions of various kinds (some of which supported, or merged with local universities) were now, in cooperation with the Technical Education Boards established after 1888, deliberately developing cohesive systems of education with an organic relation between the various stages, having the perspective of covering the whole field from infant school to university. This potential development was sharply cut off and circumscribed by a series of administrative and legislative measures brought in by a deeply Conservative government in the period 1899–1904.[8] But through the 1890s, such a perspective appeared realisable. Now at last the mass of the children had been brought into the schools; buildings erected (some of them massive), teaching developing as a profession. The so-called 'extravagance' of the School Boards, as seen by such as Sir John Gorst (and the Tories generally), had some basis in fact. The outlook was optimistic. This was the context of the quite sudden, and apparently rapid, development of educational theory and practice – of positive, all-embracing, pedagogical means.

The social context of this development has been outlined; its theoretical context is equally important. This is personified – or crystallised – in Alexander Bain's *Education as a Science*, published in 1879, reprinted six times in the 1880s, and a further ten times before 1900. Examination of a number of student-teacher manuals, which proliferated in the 1890s, indicates their indebtedness to Bain's approach – or the extent to which they shared common interpretations both of theoretical issues relating to education, and of the practice of teaching.

Bain, Professor of Logic at Aberdeen, author of two large treatises on psychology (*The Senses and the Intellect*, 1855, *The Emotions and the Will*, 1859), biographer (and to some extent disciple) of James Mill and friend of John Stuart Mill, is perhaps best known, at least to historians of psychology, as the last of the classic line of associationists (stretching from John Locke, through David Hartley, Joseph Priestley, James and John Stuart Mill, to Bain's near contemporary, Spencer).[9] It was among the early associationists, in particular Joseph Priestley and Richard Edgeworth, that the concept that education might be a science, or at least could adopt scientific procedures, originally developed.[10] It is worth noting that Bain's book was published in Kegan Paul's International Scientific Series (comprising 54 volumes) alongside books by Tyndall, T.H. Huxley, and others. In this book, Bain firmly adhered to the view that education should be considered as a science.

The crucial basis for this approach lay in the theory, announced by Bain as fact, that the formation of associations of ideas in the mind was accompanied (or was the resultant of) new connections, linkages, or 'paths' formed in the substance of the brain. The process of education, since it consisted in the planned ordering of the child's experiences, must therefore have a necessary effect (as Priestly had argued one hundred years earlier), and this, of course, had been the basis of the theory of human perfectibility characteristic of the Enlightenment. This approach not only posited the educability of the normal child, it stressed the 'plasticity', as Bain put it, of brain functioning and processes. Education, then, as again Bain defined it, was concerned with *acquired* capacities and functions. It was about human change and development.

Empirical support for the theory of the formation of new connections in the brain as underlying the acquisition of new associations was available to Bain particularly from the work of his contemporary, the neuro-physiologist Henry Maudesley. Every sense impression resulting in a 'current of molecular activity' from one part of the brain to another, Maudesley wrote, 'leaves behind it . . . some after-effect' or 'modification of the nerve elements concerned in its function'. This physiological process, he claimed, 'is the physical basis of memory', the 'foundation of our mental functions'.[11]

It followed from this approach that, to order education aright in terms of the acquisition of knowledge, two things were necessary. First, to obtain a psychological (and physiological) understanding of the growth of human powers through infancy, childhood and youth; and second, to analyse the content of subject matter in terms of its own inner logic. Together these underlay the determination of the curriculum. But Bain was also closely concerned with motivation, discipline, teacher-pupil relationships, moral education, as well as with the mode of teaching the main curriculum areas. Seeing 'education' specifically as schooling, he covered in his book almost every relevant aspect of teaching, learning, and classroom organisation.

As suggested earlier, advances relating to pedagogy were an indigenous development from within the elementary school system. This is the case, in the sense that the many manuals for student-teachers published towards the end of the century were written by men working in the teacher-training institutions of the time, all of which prepared students specifically for the elementary schools.[12] The training colleges and pupil-teacher centres involved existed to serve the *elementary* system, or were outgrowths from it. To men working in this field, Bain clearly brought a wider view and deeper knowledge than they were likely to achieve themselves; and, without exception, these manuals reflected what might be called Bain's educational optimism. What is noticeable, particularly to the modern reader, is the stress laid on the extent to which failure to develop positive attitudes, skills, and abilities in the child may be a product of the teacher's own behaviour, or lack of skills, knowledge and method. Later interpretations of failure as the inevitable function of innate disabilities *in the child* (e.g. 'lack of intelligence') do not figure. It can be argued, with Joseph Priestley, that the theory which underlies these manuals – that educational actions have a necessary effect (even if this is not always identifiable) – also underlies the science of education; that is, pedagogy.

Of course the theories, and the practices, advocated by Bain and the authors of these manuals, had their limitations as well as theoretical weaknesses. That goes without saying. But, in the 1890s, the approach was serious, systematic, all-embracing. The pedagogy of this specific decade pointed the way to universal education, and was seen as such by its progenitors. What happened? Why was this embryo pedagogy not systematically developed? What went wrong?

First, the social and political context underwent an abrupt change, as indicated earlier. The development referred to took place within the *elementary* system, but one having for a short period a realistic perspective of organic growth. This was the backcloth, the crucial feature, of this movement as a whole. The administrative and legislative events of 1899 to 1904, almost traumatic in their effects, put a stopper on this, and apart from abolishing the School Boards, confined elementary education within precise limits, setting up a system of 'secondary' schooling parallel to, but quite separate from, the elementary system.

This created a new situation. A positive pedagogy based on scientific procedures and understanding and relevant for *all* was no longer seen as appropriate, or required. Intellectual development in the elementary schools was now at a discount (in parallel with the public schools, but for different reasons). The social-disciplinary ('containment') function of elementary education was now especially emphasised. The soil required to nurture a science of education no longer existed.

However, with the demise of the elementary school as the ground of pedagogy, there now emerged the new local authority-controlled systems of secondary education; it seems to have been into these new systems that the most advanced local authorities put their main efforts. These new systems, although strictly contained in their development by the central authority (the Board of Education), and designed specifically for what can best be described as the lower middle class (all such schools had to charge fees), were the only growth points permitted in the new dispensation. The more advanced local authorities, determined to extend educational provision, approached this new field with energy and developed a considerable pride in the school systems so created.[13]

It was the establishment, and rapid development of this new system of secondary schools which underlay new developments in the theory and practice of education. This system insistently required a pedagogy – the development of effective pedagogical means. Thus we find, in the period 1900–1914, a renewed concern to develop a relevant pedagogy and it is this that lies behind the great interest in, almost the discovery of, the work of Herbart, and of the Prussian educators who had developed Herbartianism into a system – itself a phenomenon of some interest.

Herbart himself, a philosopher with special interests in psychology and education, in fact published his works, including his *Science of Education*, early in the nineteenth century.[14] Once again basing himself on associationism in his theory of the 'apperception mass', Herbart set out to explain the process of human acquirements, seeing them as the resultant of education, of teaching and learning. His ideas were developed and their practical application modified and refined in the work of Rein at the University of Jena and of other educators, and found expression in the German schools and thinking from the 1860s.[15]

It was not until the turn of the century, however, that Herbart's ideas began to make a serious impact in Britain; selections from his writings were first made widely available with the translation and publication of *The Science of Education* in 1892. By the first decade of the twentieth century most existing universities were developing and expanding their departments of education and a number of chairs in the subject now existed. Several of the new professors of education, for instance, J.J. Findlay, John Adams, J.W. Adamson, pronounced themselves as Herbartians. These and others wrote a number of books for teachers either explaining and interpreting Herbart, or elaborating on his work.[16] Here, if perhaps rather narrowly circumscribed in its context, was a new attempt, at a new level, to establish a science of education – a pedagogy. There was, then, a brief new flowering of pedagogy – a serious concern with the theory and practice of education. But this new, and to some extent hopeful, development was in effect only partial (concerned with secondary schools, and related to their upthrust); and, in the circumstances that developed following World War I, did not, and could not, persist.

The reasons for this are complex, and relate both to the structure and nature of the system that developed in the inter-war years and after, and to the movement of ideas and their relation to that system. Briefly, selectivity became the central focus of the whole system, the classification of pupils and their categorisation became a main principle of school organisation. That system urgently required a rationale – legitimisation in the eyes of parents, teachers, pupils and the public generally. Such legitimisation was, by the mid-1920s, at hand in the theories (and the practice) of mental measurement, particularly intelligence testing.

Until now, the rational foundation for pedagogical theories – for the concept of education as a science – had lain in associationist psychological theories concerning learning. These were espoused by Bain, as we have seen, and underlay his whole approach; as also by Herbart and his protagonists (or elaborators). So it was theory and practice based on these ideas which gave rise both to the positive, or optimistic, pedagogics of the 1890s relating to elementary education, and to those of the period 1900–1920 relating to the new system of secondary education. But it was just at this period that new approaches came to predominate in the field of psychology which either relegated associationism to the background, or denied its significance altogether.

The two major influences leading to the demise of associationism as a major determinant of pedagogy were, on the one hand, the rise of philosophic idealism which denied the material basis of mind and decisively rejected the model of human formation of the strict materialists of the late eighteenth century (with its emphasis on man as the passive product of external stimuli); and, on the other hand, the triumph of Darwinism with its emphasis on heredity (Murphy, 1938, pp. 109–113). With the latter is linked Galton's work (*Hereditary Genius* was published as early as 1869), the rise of the eugenics movement with its associated theories (the Eugenics Education Society was found in 1908), and the work of the Galton Laboratory at University College, London, associated with the names of Pearson, Spearman, and later Cyril Burt. 'No request is more frequently made to the psychologist', wrote Burt in 1921, when he was educational psychologist to the London County Council, 'than the demand for a simple mental footrule' (Burt, 1921, p. 1). It was precisely this that the psychologists were now ready to supply.

The demands of the system and the movement of ideas now coincided. In the field of educational theory psychometry (or mental testing) now established its hegemony which lasted over forty years from the 1920s. The triumph of psychometry tied in with a new stress on individualism after World War I and a kind of reductionist biologism, both of which are central to the thinking of Sir Percy Nunn whose *Education, its Data and First Principles* was the central student manual of the interwar years.[17] For reasons which will be discussed later, this spelt the end of pedagogy – its actual death. If education cannot promote cognitive growth, as the psychometrists seemed to aver, its whole purpose or direction was lost. 'Othello's occupation gone', as Hayward, an LCC Inspector, once put it.

This, I suggest, is the background to our present discontents. For a combination of social, political and ideological reasons pedagogy – a scientific basis to the theory and practice of education – has never taken root and flourished in Britain. For a single decade in the late nineteenth century in the field of elementary education; for a similar short period early this century in secondary education, pedagogic approaches and analyses flowered – though never in the most socially prestigious system of the public schools and ancient Universities. Each 'system', largely self-contained, developed its own specific educational approach, each within its narrowly defined field, and each 'appropriate' to its specific social function. In these circumstances the conditions did not, and could not, exist for the development of an all-embracing, universalised, scientific theory of education relating to the practice of teaching. Nor is it an accident that, in these circumstances, fatalistic ideas preaching the limitation of human powers were in the ascendant.

Education and the technological revolution

The main objective of this paper is to argue first, that we can no longer afford to go on in the old way, muddling through on a largely pragmatic, or historically institutionalised basis, tinkering with this and that, but that a really serious effort can and should now be made to clear up current confusions and dichotomies. Second, in spite of what must surely be temporary setbacks in the provision of educational facilities, the conditions now exist for a major breakthrough in terms of pedagogy. This statement is made on the basis of two contemporary developments, the one structural, the other theoretical. Of major importance here is the insistent tendency towards unification of the historically determined separate systems of schooling through the transition to comprehensive secondary education. This has been accompanied, in the realm of ideas or theory, by a shift in the concern of educators and psychologists from static concepts of the child (derived from intelligence testing) towards dynamic and complex theories of child development. Both open new perspectives relating to the grounding of educational theory and practice on science (or on scientific procedures).

It is a commonplace that Britain now faces a deep economic crisis the especial severity of which arises from the relative obsolescence of British industry, as also from long-standing production and managerial inefficiencies (Pavitt 1980). Of particular importance, then, to the survival of this country in an increasingly competitive, and capitalised world, is the micro-processor revolution. It is argued authoritatively, by those making a special study of the matter, that, due to the cheapness, reliability and safety of the new technology it is quite certain to be applied whatever the situation and the consequences (Freeman, 1978, 1980). It is these that deserve consideration.

Experts are agreed that, although without further research and experience much remains unpredictable (especially in a society that rejects planning), the micro-processor revolution may itself have a twofold, dichotomous effect on human skills. First, the demand for people with high level skills and knowledge will increase greatly as production and other processes become both more complex, and subject to highly skilled control. Second, as has been the case with much technological advance, the mass of 'ordinary' jobs in manufacturing and industry generally may be subject to a de-skilling effect depending upon the form and degree of mechanisation that is introduced. Finally, in addition to this contradictory effect on skills, the introduction of micro-processors may well lead to massive 'labour-shedding' in some industries and service sectors. The extent to which this introduces a new element of structural unemployment will depend, of course, upon the extent to which alternative industries and growth-demand can compensate.

There is, however, a further possibility to be taken into account – the implementation on a large scale of automation. The importance of this in terms of education lies in the possibility automation holds out of systematically eradicating jobs which are essentially routine – specifically involving relatively simple forms of visual-motor co-ordination.

Automation has now reached a stage where such functions, by which the worker relates one particular movement to the visual inspection of the object in process of manufacture, can be performed more economically by machinery (through the development, in particular, of robotics). It is estimated that jobs on this level today constitute some 40 per cent of all; it is their essentially monotonous (and alienating) nature and comparative simplicity (many occupations can be learnt with very little training – in some cases a few days or even hours) that accounts, in part at least, for the disparity between the knowledge/skills demands of industry, and human potential, released partially through improved education, a standpoint interestingly developed by T.G. Whiston in a series of publications. To bring the two into a closer relation Whiston regards as a major objective in terms of human values, arguing that the relevant techniques regarding automation are now – or are becoming – available, though their implementation requires the thrust of deliberate policy. In this connection it is important to recognise that there is already today a great national shortage of highly skilled labour in many industries.[18]

It seems, then, that at the extremes, two opposite policy options are available. One is to allow the application of micro-processors to be determined entirely through the operation of laissez-faire (apparently the dominant trend in contemporary Conservative politics), relying on market forces alone to determine outcomes. In this case possible developments include mass structural unemployment as a permanent feature; domination by an expanded technocratic élite, accompanied by massive de-skilling for the majority of those remaining in employment – that is, the actual enhancement of the present bi-modal distribution of the knowledge/skills component of work. The second option is deliberately devised to exclude or counter such effects, and requires foresight, judgement and planning, no doubt of a highly sophisticated character and covering both short and long term objectives. By this option, the potential de-skilling effect of micro-processor applications may be countered by an active policy of automation (in mechanised industry), with the specific aim of achieving an all-round raising of the skill levels of employment, so, apart from other effects, both rendering work intrinsically more satisfying and overcoming (in the long run) the bi-modal distribution of the knowledge/skills demands of work.

Such a policy itself counters the establishment of a technocratic élite, since it implies that all, or the great majority of the work force is capable, given extended and relevant education, of work at the level now required, and that the nature of work itself in industry will generally, over time, approximate to that level. In addition, a deliberate policy of diffusing responsibility and control both through the extension of participation and decision-making at all levels in industry, and through regional and local organisations (as well as national) becomes a possible, and, indeed, a necessary means of democratic development, itself requiring the diffusion, or, better, formation of knowledge and skills covering a wide area among the population as a whole. Finally, this policy option requires the deliberate expansion of labour-intensive employment across a wide range of social and community services – that is, particularly, the areas of health, education, the 'caring' professions generally, the leisure industry, and so forth. Such measures, which raise the 'civilisation' aspect of any society – or which enhance the quality of life – provide the means, and the only ones, where new employment, on a mass scale, can be provided, given the consistent, long-term reduction in the labour demands not only of the primary sector (agriculture, mining, quarrying, etc.), but also of manufacture and indeed certain sections of the tertiary sector itself, for instance, clerical work where microprocessors have many applications. Such a policy involves a deliberate shift of employment through the rationalisation of production (and the office service sectors) towards expansion in human and socially satisfying areas.

This is not the place to argue the options. It will be assumed here, as axiomatic, that the second is the only one of the two which can be acceptable as a perspective for an advanced industrial society such as Britain. In what follows, the *intention* to implement policy on these lines is assumed.

Such a perspective has important educational implications. It posits the development of high level human skills and knowledge across the entire population, and, it is important to recognise, not only technological and scientific skills, but also those required to support responsible democratic decision-making and those underlying a massive expansion of employment in tertiary industries and services, such as education. In this context, limited, pragmatic measures to cope with the micro-processor revolution simply by expanding, and making more specialised, higher education alone (and perhaps technical education) will be entirely inadequate – such measures relate directly to the first option, not the second. To develop a population with the qualities and knowledge base required involves raising educational sights at all levels, primary and secondary, as well as tertiary. And this involves rendering the process of education more effective, once again right across the board. Hence the urgent requirement now to begin, quite consciously and deliberately, to develop effective pedagogic means.

As already indicated, the establishment of comprehensive secondary education, while no panacea in itself, does provide the conditions in which the target of high level mass secondary education appropriate for all becomes a possibility. This was excluded under the divided system of the past, which now appears as a simple reflection of the bimodal distribution of job requirements. The comprehensive school, on the other hand, can be seen as one condition for overcoming this bimodality, and to reflect, in its organisational form, a situation where the skills and knowledge requirements not only of industry but also of social and political life generally may be greatly raised as compared with the past. In this sense a base is coming into being from which a major advance may be made. The virtual elimination of streaming in the primary schools – a product of the last ten to fifteen years – is another reflection of the same approach. In a sense, educational change has taken the lead, and created new conditions appropriate to current and future requirements. The agony of the transition, and the nature and significance of educational developments in the 1950s and 1960s can now be more fairly assessed for what they are. It is true that the independent schools still remain as a separate system, with their own goals and objectives – and functions. Indeed recent legislation has strengthened their position. If these could be brought functionally within the publicly maintained system of education, this dichotomy would be overcome. However it can be argued that these schools no longer have the same over-riding importance and position, relative to the public system, that they had in the past, and are no longer as influential in determining the climate of thought or practice in education as they were a century ago.

Finally, and most important, there is the shift towards dynamic concepts of child development and learning, referred to earlier. This represents a new situation in terms of educational studies – of, to use Bain's term, 'systematic (educational) knowledge'. As a result the prospect exists of reinstating pedagogy as the basis for educational practice in the period that lies ahead – one which provides a perspective, as Harold Entwistle makes clear in his chapter, of a more satisfying humanised life for all. Provided social changes, where necessary, can be made, education has the opportunity now to come into its own, as one – *the?* – essential component of the society of the future.

A revitalised pedagogy?

What, then, are the requirements for a renewal of scientific approaches to the practice of teaching – for a revitalised pedagogy?

First, we can identify two essential conditions without which there can be no pedagogy having a generalised significance or application. The first is recognition of the human capacity for learning. It may seem unnecessary, even ridiculous, to single this out in this connection, but in practice this is not the case. Fundamentally, psychometric theory, as elaborated in the 1930s to 1950s, denied the lability of learning capacity, seeing each individual as endowed, as it were, with an engine of a given horse-power which is fixed, unchangeable and measurable in each particular case, irrevocably setting precise and definable limits to achievement (or learning).[19] It was not until this view had been discredited in the eyes of psychologists that serious attention could be given to the analysis and interpretation of the *process* of human learning.

The second condition has been effectively defined by Professor Stones in his helpful and relevant book *Psychopedagogy*, sub-titled 'Psychological Theory and the Practice of Teaching' (1979). It is the recognition that, in general terms, the process of learning among human beings is similar across the human species as a whole. The view on which Stones's book is based is that 'except in pathological cases, learning capability among individuals is similar', so that 'it is possible to envisage a body of general principles of teaching' that are relevant for 'most individual pupils'. The determination, or identification, of such general principles must comprise the objectives of pedagogical study and research (Stones 1979 p. 453).

One further point may be made at the start. The term 'pedagogy' itself implies structure. It implies the elaboration or definition of specific means adapted to produce the desired effect – such-and-such learning on the part of the child. From the start of the use of the term, pedagogy has been concerned to relate the process of teaching to that of learning on the part of the child. It was this approach that characterised the work of Comenius, Pestalozzi and Herbart, and that, for instance, of Joseph Priestley and the associationist tradition generally.[20]

Both the conditions defined above are today very widely accepted among leading psychologists directly concerned with education and with research into human cognitive development. When Bruner claimed, in a striking and well-known statement, that 'any subject can be taught to anybody at any age in some form that is both interesting and honest', he was basing himself on a positive assessment of human capacity for learning, and deliberately pointing to the need to link psychology with pedagogy. In an essay aimed at persuading American psychologists of the need to concern themselves with education – to provide assistance in elucidating the learning process for practising educators – he stressed his central point, 'that developmental psychology without a theory of pedagogy was as empty an enterprise as a theory of pedagogy that ignored the nature of growth'. 'Man is not a naked ape', writes Bruner, 'but a culture clothed human being, hopelessly ineffective without the prosthesis provided by culture'. Education itself can be a powerful cultural influence, and educational experiences ordered and structured to enable people more fully to realise their humanity and powers, to bring about social change – and so create a world according to their felt and recognised objectives. The major problem humanity faces is not the general development of skill and intelligence, but 'devising a society that can use it wisely' (Bruner 1972 pp. 18, 131, 158).

When writing this, Bruner was clearly concerned with social change, and with the contribution that pedagogical means might make to this, as we must be in Britain in face of the dramatic social challenge that technological change now presents. And in considering the power of education, rightly ordered, to play a central part in this, it may be as well to recall that, while the simplified and certainly over-mechanist interpretations of the associationist psychologists of the nineteenth century are no longer acceptable in the form, for instance, expressed by Alexander Bain (and his predecessors), yet the concept of learning as a process involving the formation of new connections in the brain and higher nervous systems has in fact not only retained its force, but been highly developed by neuro-physiologists and psychologists specifically concerned to investigate learning. Among these, perhaps the greatest contribution has been made by A.R. Luria in a series of works relevant to teaching, education and human development generally; but perhaps particularly in his work on the role of language in mental development, and in his theory of the formation of what he calls 'complex functional systems' underlying learning (Luria 1962).

It is now generally accepted that in the process of mental development there takes place a profound qualitative reorganisation of human mental activity, and that the basic characteristic of this reorganisation is that elementary, direct activity is replaced by complex functional systems, formed on the basis of the child's communication with adults in the process of learning. These functional systems are of complex construction, and are developed with the close participation of language, which as the basic means of communication with people is simultaneously one of the basic tools in the formation of human mental activity and in the regulation of behaviour. It is through these complex forms of mental activity . . . that new features are acquired and begin to develop according to new laws which displace many of the laws which govern the formation of elementary conditioned reflexes in animals.

The work and thinking of both Luria and Bruner (as representative of their respective traditions) point in a similar direction – towards a renewed understanding both of the power of education to effect human change and especially cognitive development, and of the need for the systematisation and structuring of the child's experiences in the process of learning. And it is precisely from this standpoint that a critique is necessary of certain contemporary standpoints, dichotomies and ideologies, and, in particular, of the whole trend towards so-called 'child-centred' theories, which have dominated this area in Britain basically since the early 1920s, to reach its apotheosis in what is best called the 'pedagogic romanticism' of the Plowden Report, its most recent, and semi-official expression.

It may be unfashionable, among educationists, to direct attention specifically to this point, more particularly because a critique of 'progressivism' was central to the outlook expressed in the Black Papers in the late sixties and early seventies; but to make such a critique does not imply identification with the essentially philistine and a-theoretical standpoint of the Black Paperites, as I hope to establish. Indeed the dichotomies which these and other critics sought to establish, for instance between progressive and traditional approaches, between the 'formal' and 'informal', do not reflect the options now available, nor even contemporary practice as it really is.

The basic tenets of child-centred education derive in particular from the work of Froebel who held that children are endowed with certain characteristics or qualities which will mature or flower given the appropriate environment. The child develops best in a 'rich' environment. The teacher should not interfere with this process of maturation, but act as a 'guide'. The function of early education, according to Froebel, is 'to make the inner outer' (Froebel 1912 p. 94). Hence the emphasis on spontaneity, as also on stages of development, and the concomitant concept of 'readiness' – the child will learn specific skills and mental operations only when he is 'ready'.

That there is a fundamental convergence between this view and the theories (or assumptions) embodied in Intelligence Testing has been overlooked; nevertheless it is the close similarity between both sets of views as to the nature of the child which made it possible for both to flourish together in the period following World War I and after. Intelligence Testing also embodied the view that the child is endowed with certain innate characteristics; in this case a brain and higher nervous system of a given power or force – Spearman's 'Mental Energy or Noegenetics' (Spearman 1927), and that the process of education is concerned to actualise the given potential, that is, to activate and realise the 'inner' (in Froebel's sense). Both views in fact deny the creative function of education, the formative power of differential educational (or life) experiences. The two trends come together strikingly, for instance, in the work of Susan Issacs who, on the one hand, firmly believed in the scientific truth of the doctrines of Intelligence Testing, and, on the other, forcefully propagated Froebelian approaches, which she considered particularly appropriate for advanced (middle-class) children with high 'intelligence' (Isaacs 1932 pp. 25, 28–29; 1963 pp. 41–42).

The theoretical, or pedagogical stance of the Plowden Report represents an extension of these ideas. In their re-interpretation of the conclusions derived from psychometry they reject the concept of total hereditary, or genetic, determination. Development is seen as an interactional process, in which the child's encounters with the environment are crucial. Yet Plowden takes the child-centred approach to its logical limits, insisting on the principle of the complete individualisation of the teaching/learning process as the ideal (even though, from a pedagogic standpoint, this is not a practical possibility in any realistic sense). In their analysis the hereditary/environmental interactional process is interpreted as exacerbating initial differences so greatly that each child must be seen to be unique, and be treated as such. The matter is rendered even more complex by their insistence that each individual child develops at different rates across three parameters, intellectual, emotional and physical; and that in determining her approach to each individual child each of these must be taken into account by the teacher. The result is that the task set the teacher, with an average of 35 children per class when Plowden reported, is, in the words of the report itself, 'frighteningly high' (Plowden 1967 I paras 75, 875).

I want to suggest that, by focusing on the individual child ('at the heart of the educational process lies the child'), and in developing the analysis from this point, the Plowden Committee created a situation from which it was impossible to derive an effective pedagogy (or effective pedagogical means). If each child is unique, and each requires a specific pedagogical approach appropriate to him or her and to no other, the construction of an all-embracing pedagogy, or general principles of teaching becomes an impossibility. And indeed research has shown that primary school teachers who have taken the priority of individualisation to heart, find it difficult to do more than ensure that each child is in fact engaged on the series of tasks which the teacher sets up for the child; the complex management problem which then arises takes the teacher's full energies. Hence the approach of teachers who endeavour to implement these prescripts is necessarily primarily didactic ('telling') since it becomes literally impossible to stimulate enquiry, or to 'lead from behind', as Plowden held the teacher should operate in the classroom. Even with a lower average of 30 children per class, this is far too complex and time-consuming a role for the teacher to perform.[21]

The main thrust of the argument of this chapter is this: that to start from the standpoint of individual differences is to start from the wrong position. To develop effective pedagogic means involves starting from the opposite standpoint, from what children have in common as members of the human species; to establish the general principles of teaching and, in the light of these, to determine what modifications of practice are necessary to meet specific individual needs. If all children are to be assisted to learn, to master increasingly complex cognitive tasks, to develop increasingly complex skills and abilities or mental operations, then this is an objective that schools must have in common; their task becomes the deliberate development of such skills and abilities in all their children. And this involves importing a definite structure into the teaching, and so into the learning experiences provided for the pupils. Individual differences only become important, in this context, if the pedagogical means elaborated are found not to be appropriate to particular children (or groups of children) because of one or other aspect of their individual development or character. In this situation the requirement becomes that of modifying the pedagogical means so that they become appropriate for all; that is, of applying general principles in specific instances.

What is suggested here is that the starting point for constructing the curriculum, or children's activities in school, insofar as we are concerned with cognitive development (the schools may reasonably have other aims as well) lies in definition of the objectives of teaching, which forms the ground base from which pedagogical means are defined and established, means or principles which underlie specific methodological (or experiential) approaches. It may well be that these include the use of co-operative group work as well as individualised activities – but these are carefully designed and structured in relation to the achievement of overall objectives. This approach, I am arguing, is the opposite of basing the educational process on the child, on his immediate interests and spontaneous activity, and providing, in theory, for a total differentiation of the learning process in the case of each individual child. This latter approach is not only undesirable in principle, it is impossible of achievement in practice.[22]

In a striking phrase Lev Vigotski summed up his outlook on teaching and learning. Pedagogy, he wrote, 'must be oriented not towards the yesterday of development but towards its tomorrow'. Teaching, education, pedagogic means, must always take the child forward, be concerned with the formation of new concepts and hierarchies of concepts, with the next stage in the development of a particular ability, with ever more complex forms of mental operations. 'What the child can do today with adult help', he said, 'he will be able to do independently tomorrow'. This concept, that of the 'zone of next (or "potential") development' implies in the educator a clear concept of the progression of learning, of a consistent challenge, of the mastery by the child of increasingly complex forms – of never standing still or going backwards. 'The only good teaching is that which outpaces development', insisted Vigotski.[23] Whether the area is that of language development, of concepts of number and mathematics – symbolic systems that underlie all further learning – or whether it covers scientific and technological concepts and skills as well as those related to the social sciences and humanities, appropriate pedagogical means can and should be defined, perhaps particularly in areas having their own inner logical structures. In this sense, psychological knowledge combined with logical analysis forms the ground base from which pedagogical principles can be established, given, of course, effective research and experiment.

This chapter has been strictly concerned with cognitive development, since it is here that technological/scientific and social changes will make their greatest impact and demands. But for successful implementation of rational procedures and planning, in the face of the micro-processor revolution, more than this needs consideration. There is also the question, for instance, of the individual's enhanced responsibility for his own activities; the development of autonomy, of initiative, creativity, critical awareness; the need on the part of the mass of the population for access to knowledge and culture, the arts and literature, to mention only some aspects of human development. The means of promoting such human qualities and characteristics cannot simply be left to individual teachers, on the grounds that each individual child is unique so that the development of a pedagogy is both impracticable and superfluous. The existing teaching force of half a million have, no doubt, many talents, but they need assistance in the pursuit of their common objective – the education of new generations of pupils. The new pedagogy requires carefully defined goals, structure, and adult guidance. Without this a high proportion of children, whose concepts are formed as a result of their everyday experiences, and, as a result, are often distorted and incorrectly reflect reality, will never even reach the stage where the development of higher cognitive forms of activity becomes a possibility. And this implies a massive cognitive failure in terms of involvement and control (responsible participation) in the new social forms and activities which the future may bring.

Notes

1 An attempt in 1962 by Nuffield Science project teams to gain assistance from psychologists was entirely negative. At a meeting convened to discuss possible research on the intellectual development of children in areas relevant to the projects, leading psychologists held that little advice was possible since 'so little research had, as yet, been undertaken with British children' on teaching and learning (Waring 1979 p. 133).

2 The English failure to take pedagogy seriously is stressed in an article on the subject in an educational encyclopedia of a century ago. Interest in pedagogy 'is not held in much honour among us English'. The lack of a professional approach to teaching means that 'pedagogy is with us at a discount'. This, it is held, 'is unquestionably a most grievous national loss . . . Without something like scientific discussion on educational subjects, without pedagogy, we shall never obtain a body of organised opinion on education.' (Fletcher 1889 pp. 257–258).

3 An exception here was R.H. Quick, author of *Essays on Educational Reformers* (1869), a public schoolmaster himself who fought hard for professional training and who appears to have been largely instrumental in setting up the Cambridge

Syndicate which organised (prematurely) the first systematic set of lectures on education in an English university; those delivered at Cambridge in 1879–1880 (see Storr 1889 pp. 349–388). For a young teacher's experience of 'learning on the job' in the 1930s, Worsley 1967, Chapter 1.

4   See Newsome (1961), especially chapter 4; Simon and Bradley 1975, especially chapter 7 by Norman Vance, 'The Ideal of Manliness', and chapter 9 by J.A. Mangan, 'Athleticism: a Case Study of the Evolution of an Educational Ideology'.

5   An unusual, but very sharp, critique of public school attitudes to this question was made by A.A. David, headmaster of Rugby and Clifton and later Bishop of Liverpool, in the early 1930s (David 1932 pp. 64ff).

6   It is symptomatic that the most recent (and internal) examination of studies at Oxford ignores the topic altogether, *Report of Commission of Inquiry* (the Franks report), 2 vols., 1966.

7   See, for instance, Arnold 1874, which devotes a lengthy chapter to the professional training of schoolmasters for the *gymnasia* and *realschule* in Prussia (chapter 5).

8   I have analysed developments in this period in detail in Simon 1965.

9   Bain developed his associationist theory most notably in his *Mental and Moral Science* (1868).

10 Priestley held that 'Education is as much an art (founded, as all arts are, upon science) as husbandry, architecture, shipbuilding'. Just as there are laws covering mechanics, chemistry, physics, so there are laws governing the functioning of mind – whether physical or moral. It is, therefore, possible to establish the causes (which must exist) by which the mind 'is truly and properly influenced – producing certain definite effects in certain circumstances'. It follows that there are laws governing education, discoverable by observation and experiment.

11 Quoted in Fitch 1898 p. 129. The full quotation from Maudsley given by Fitch, who is explaining association, reads as follows: 'That which has existed with any completeness in consciousness leaves behind it, after its disappearance therefrom, in the mind or brain, a functional disposition to its reproduction or reappearance in consciousness at some future time. Of no mental act can we say that it is "writ in water". Something remains from it whereby its recurrence is facilitated. Every impression of sense upon the brain, every current of molecular activity from one to another part of the brain, every cerebral reaction which passes into movement, leaves behind it some modification of the nerve-elements concerned in its function, some after-effect, or, so to speak, memory of itself in them, which renders its reproduction an easier matter, the more easy the more often it has been repeated, and makes it impossible to say that, however trivial, it shall not in some circumstances recur. Let the excitation take place in one of two nerve-cells lying side by side, and between which there was not originally any specific difference, there will be ever afterwards a difference between them. This physiological process, whatever be its nature, is the physical basis of memory, and it is the foundation of our mental functions'.

12 For instance, A.H. Garlick, 'Headmaster' of the Woolwich Pupil–Teacher Centre (Garlick 1896); David Salmon, Principal of Swansea Training College (Salmon 1898); Joseph Landon, Vice-Principal and 'Later Master of Method' of Saltley Training College (Landon 1894); and many others.

13 See especially Legge (1929) on Liverpool, and Gosden and Sharp (1978 pp. 77ff) on the West Riding.

14 J.F. Herbart (1776–1841) published a work on Pestalozzi in 1804 and his *Universal Pedagogy* (*Allgemeine Pädagogik*, later translated as *Science of Education*) in 1806. In 1841 he published *Plan of Lectures on Pedagogy*. His works in philosophy and education were collected and published in twelve volumes in 1850–1852 by Hartenstein.

15 Harbartian associations were formed in many parts of Germany in the late nineteenth century, first, in the Rhine and Westphalia with over 400 members; later

in East Germany, Bavaria, Wurtemberg, Saxony and Thuringia. The first meeting of the latter, in 1892, attracted over 2,000 educationists, Professor Rein of the University of Jena being elected President (Felkin 1895 p. 3).

16 For instance, the London County Council Inspectors, F.H. Hayward and P.B. Ballard, both of whom were prolific writers on education.

17 Percy Nunn was Principal of the University of London Institute of Education from 1922 to 1936. His textbook went through over 20 reprintings between its publication in 1920 and 1940; it was required reading for many graduates training as teachers. For an acute critique of Nunn's biologism, see Gordon and White 1979 pp. 207–213.

18 This standpoint is argued in a series of papers by T.G. Whiston, Science Policy Research Unit, University of Sussex. These include 'Technical Change, Occupational Skill and Retraining Issues' unpublished paper given at a seminar on Employment and Technical Change, November 1978 and 'Technical Change, Employment and Education Policy', SPRU mimeo, July 1979; 'The Development of Education: Its Technological and Social Dimensions' in *The Future of Education and the Education of the Future*, ed. R.M. Avakov UNESCO, Paris 1980 pp. 319–360; 'Education and Training for the less academic young person in relation to ongoing social and technological change' in *Report of the Conference on Provision to meet the Needs of less Academic Students between the ages 16–19*. Southern Regional Council for Further Education, Wokingham, Berks, June 1979; 'La prevision au niveau gouvernemental: orientation normative', *Conference of International Institute d'Administration Publique*, Paris 1979 pp. 9–19. See also 'Population Forecasting: Social and Educational Policy', Chapter 7 in *The Uses and Abuses of Forecasting*, ed. T.G. Whiston 1979 pp. 143–181.

19 This position is concisely reflected in a statement by Cyril Burt in 1950: 'Obviously, in an ideal community, our aim should be to discover what ration of intelligence nature has given to each individual child at birth, then to provide him with an appropriate education, and finally to guide him into the career for which he seems to have been marked out' (Burt 1950).

20 This point was clearly and emphatically made by James Ward in the first of his Cambridge lectures in 1879–80 (but only published in 1926). Entitled 'The Possibility and Value of a Theory of Education', this starts by saying that a science of education 'is theoretically possible', and that such a science 'must be based on psychology and the cognate sciences'. He goes on, 'To show this we have, indeed, only to consider that the educator works, or rather ought to work, upon a growing mind, *with a definite purpose of attaining an end in view.* For unless we maintain that the growth of mind follows no law; or, to put it otherwise, unless it be maintained that systematic observation of the growth of (say) a hundred minds would disclose no uniformities; and unless, further, it can be maintained that for the attainment of a definite end there are no definite means, we must allow that *if the teacher knows what he wants to do there must be a scientific way of doing it.* Not only so. We must allow not merely the possibility of a scientific exposition of the means the educator should employ to attain his end, but we must allow also the possibility of a scientific exposition of the end at which he ought to aim, unless again it be contended that it is impossible by reasoning to make manifest that one form of life and character is preferable to another' (Ward 1926 p. 1, my italics).

21 These points are argued in detail, supported by empirical evidence derived from systematic classroom observation, in Galton, Simon and Croll 1980.

22 For a critique of this approach by a psychologist who has worked closely with Piaget (regarded as the authority for individualisation, for instance, in the Plowden Report), see Duckworth 1979.

23 See Vigotski 1963; see also Vigotski 1962, 1967. For Vigotski's views on education, 'Teaching and Development: a Soviet Investigation', Special Issue of *Soviet Education*. Vol, 19, Nos. 4–6, 1977.

8
Accountability and Evaluation

Michael Eraut

This chapter sets out to achieve three main purposes: (1) to make conceptual distinctions that clarify the range of meanings associated with the term accountability; (2) to examine accountability as a political phenomenon that came to prominence in Britain in the mid-1970s; and (3) to analyse the accountability procedures currently used in British education together with some of the new procedures which have been recently suggested. The process of conceptual clarification will be interwoven with more practical considerations, and relevant empirical evidence will be presented when available. I will begin with the personal accountability of those who work in education, and the role of accountability in national politics. A discussion of information flow, judgement and evaluative transaction then precedes an analysis of current and newly proposed accountability procedures.

Throughout the discussion accountability will be seen to depend on evaluation in two distinct ways. First, as a matter of practical politics, accountability has to relate to how people *do* evaluate a teacher, a school or an educational system, regardless of how ill-informed or prejudicial their judgements. Second, as a matter of morality, account-ability has to relate to how people *should* evaluate, taking into account principles of justice, fairness and truth. The events of the late seventies have shown that there is a considerable danger of these principles being ignored in practice. The challenge for the eighties and nineties is to find forms of accountability that are both practical and moral.

Personal accountability: moral, contractual and professional

The first distinction I wish to make is that between moral account-ability and legal or contractual accountability. Apart from his oblig-ation as a citizen to obey the law of the land, a teacher is legally accountable only to his head and the local education authority which employs him. Though much responsibility is delegated to him, he is still accountable to the head and the authority for his transactions with pupils and their parents; and, if parents wish to complain formally about his conduct, it is the head or the authority whom they must normally approach. A teacher has no contractual relationship with pupils and parents, but he does have a moral obligation towards them. Indeed, we are all morally accountable to those who are affected by our actions. This moral obligation to pupils will often impinge more strongly on a teacher's mind than any contractual obligation because he is in daily contact with his pupils. Contact with his head is usually much less frequent, and that with the authority so rare that teachers seldom mention it when talking about accountability. Another reason for the lesser attention given to contractual accountability is that it seldom creates problems. Contractual obligations are usually met by conforming to professional norms and local traditions, and thus get taken for granted or subsumed within professional accountability (see below).

The same distinction can be applied to a head or even to a chief education officer. A head is legally accountable both to his governing body and to the authority, and morally accountable to his teachers, pupils and parents. A CEO is legally accountable to his authority through its Education Committee for the quality of education in the schools under his care, and morally accountable to those schools for his advice to his Committee and his executive actions. The authority itself can be regarded as contractually accountable to the electorate and as morally accountable to its teachers above and beyond its legal obligations as their employer. Thus schools are right to observe that their accountability relationship with their authority involves mutual obligations, but should not conclude that the relationship is symmetrical by confusing legal with moral accountability.

A third form of accountability is introduced by teachers' claims to be professionals. This claim is complicated by an often deliberate confusion between personal accountability – for adherence to personal standards and values – and collegial accountability – for adherence to the standards and values of the professional group. The arguments for professional accountability are essentially as follows:

1   The teaching profession has developed forms of practice that work well; and responds to changing circumstances or unusual local conditions by modifying this practice to an appropriate degree, being responsive to but not overdetermined by temporary fashion or minority pressure groups.

2   Only members of the teaching profession are trained to understand and implement these practices.

3   Teachers are accountable to their colleagues for maintaining the standards and values of the profession.

4 Individual teachers have considerable freedom to select and adopt from the range of approved practices those that are best suited to their own particular context.

5 In so far as teachers make autonomous decisions they are accountable to themselves for seeing that the effects of those decisions accord with their personal standards and values.

6 Provided that these personal standards and values are within the domain of those approved by the profession as a whole, a teacher's accountability to his profession can be subsumed within his personal accountability.

7 In so far as colleagues in a school are interdependent, they are accountable to one another. However this relationship may be contractual, if determined by the head; or moral, if based on mutual consideration. It only becomes professional if there is a deliberate attempt to develop a common policy.

We shall return later to the important issue of the extent to which teachers emphasise personal or collegial accountability, as opposed to moral or contractual accountability.

Meanwhile, it is proper to note that these claims have not gone unchallenged. Teachers do not have a professional code of practice, and there seems to be little consensus about what competent teaching involves. In so far as there is a consensus about incompetence, little appears to be done about any but the most extreme cases. As the proportion of the public with sixth form education and higher qualifications increases, the subject knowledge possessed by teachers becomes commoner. Thus there will be pressure to make knowledge about teaching rather than subject knowledge the distinguishing hallmark of the profession; and this will be accentuated by the separation of sixth form and tertiary colleges from secondary education. So far teaching appears to lack the kind of technical knowledge base that could protect it from external criticism by ordinary laymen. The teacher's favourite expression 'at the chalkface' conjures up images of mining rather than law or medicine, which may be good for salaries but belies the claim to professional status.

Accountability as a political phenomenon

The term 'accountability' began to be used in Britain in about 1975, having been prominent in the United States since before 1970. However, it is difficult to estimate how much the accountability debate in Britain has been influenced by earlier American developments. The important issues can be traced back to the early seventies when little American influence was apparent, yet reference to American practice has now become increasingly common. Maclure (1978) has identified four main features of the British debate and traced their political origins. These are: standards of attainment, curriculum content, parental participation and managerial responsibility. I shall discuss each in turn, focusing on political debate rather than detailed accountability procedures; and only referring to the American experience where it is directly relevant.

STANDARDS OF ATTAINMENT

The irrational nature of much political debate is clearly exposed when the topic under discussion is standards of attainment. I shall discuss how judgements are made about schools in a later section, but here it is important to note that they are seldom based on any rational consideration of all the available evidence. Opinions are formed from fragments of personal experience, from sharing views with others, and from eulogistic reflection on the past; and they can be affected by accounts of individual incidents without any evidence of context, frequency or typicality being presented. Moreover, the interpretation of evidence is strongly influenced by lay theories of education which incorporate ideas like a fixed pool of talent, the benefits of rote learning or the early appearance of giftedness; and these theories can be invoked at a tacit level without exposing them to counter-arguments or revealing some of their internal contradictions. Thus the assertions of the Black Papers have gradually gained popularity through frequency of repetition and support from the press in spite of their misuse of evidence and fallacious argument. The eagerness of the press to report the problems of newly-formed comprehensive schools has encouraged the public to believe that all such schools are chaotic and inefficient. Incidents such as the William Tyndale Inquiry have strengthened a growing conviction that primary schools have largely abandoned the three Rs; and the total refutation of this belief by the HMI Primary Survey has had little political impact. A prominent industrialist who declares on the basis of scanty evidence that his new intake of apprentices lacks mathematical competence can gain more attention than a report showing an increase in the number of 'O' level passes. The industrialist is right because he says what is believed to be true, but the report can be dismissed as showing that statistics can be fixed. If more people are passing 'O' levels then surely, it is argued, the standard of 'O' level must have declined. The argument survives counterattack both because people are suspicious of numbers and because there is an implicit appeal to the fixed pool of talent theory.

Perhaps the most controversial aspect of the recent debate has been the proposal to use standardised attainment tests as a form of accountability. For most lay people such testing has a triple significance. First, testing is seen by many as the only technique by which standards can be measured; and hence, by association, concern with testing is readily identified as concern with standards. Second, testing is a symbol of traditional as opposed to progressive education. Then, third, testing is seen as an instrument for improving the efficiency of schools and for asserting greater control over what they do. All three connotations combine to give testing considerable political appeal in the current climate, regardless of the educational arguments. Hence the symbolic role of testing makes it impossible to separate the proper discussion of educational policy from a similar consideration of public relations. On the one hand one can review the role of tests in obtaining evidence about standards of performance and argue about the proper use of such evidence, while on the other hand one has to consider how people with little understanding of such matters are likely to react and the way in which proposals for testing and reports of testing can be used to influence public opinion.

This uncertainty about the relationship between testing as research and testing as politics has been accentuated by the creation within the Department of Education and Science of an Assessment of Performance Unit (the APU). Its research purposes – developing new instruments of assessment and providing information on trends in achievement – are admirably clear (Kay 1975 pp. 11–18), though beset with technical hazards. Its political purposes are subject to considerable speculation (Becher and Maclure 1978), not least because its North American predecessor, the National Assessment of Education Progress, is commonly perceived to have had little influence on decision-making (W. Taylor 1978b). Some authors see the APU as part of a general move to gain more central control of the curriculum and to shift English education towards societal rather than individual or professional goals and values (House 1978). Others regard it as no more than an expensive exercise in public relations. However, this political speculation is often accompanied by a deeper educational concern. In spite of the modesty with which the Unit presents itself and its reassuring awareness at times of the limitations of its technology, its very existence helps to promote an image of education as an industrial process. To view education as an industry with precisely defined inputs and outputs, which can be improved by systems analysis, is not only to misconceive its goals but to misunderstand the way it actually operates (Levin 1974 pp. 363–391). Critics argue that testing technology is quite incapable of measuring the inputs and outputs of education with sufficient reliability or validity to meet even the simplest requirements of the industrial model (Macdonald 1978, Stake 1973); and that conducting a systems analysis on a system whose major variables are known to be external to it (Rosenshine and McGaw 1972 pp. 640–643) is patently absurd.

The important unknown factor in the situation may turn out to be not the direct effect of the APU but its influence on local education authorities and the testing policies which they develop during the 1980s. Hitherto LEA testing policies have been primarily concerned with screening – the early detection of slow readers – and with transfer to secondary school, where district-wide testing provides information to guide pupil allocation. However, some LEAs are now using similar tests to assess general standards of performance. In spite of its political attraction, the process has not been problem-free at the level of public relations. When one LEA got rather better results than had been expected, some of the councillors declared that the tests were too simple and that the whole exercise had been a 'whitewash' by the professionals. In two others there is considerable worry over good results because they give little scope for further improvement; and because they may be used to argue that cuts in educational expenditure have had little effect on standards. In America, where testing has had its greatest impact at state level, one of its foremost advocates has admitted that taxpayers have not had a 'reasonable return on their investment in educational assessment' because there is little evidence that the information gleaned has led to any significant educational decisions (Popham 1978 pp. 19–23). I shall return to the educational significance of testing in a later section but meanwhile it is worth noting the range of conclusions people can draw from test results, the failure in America to translate information from testing into constructive action, and the ultimately political nature of judgements about standards. A recent review of attempts by American state legislatures to establish performance standards for their schools concluded that 'educational movements supposedly based upon criterion-referenced testing are not founded on any genuine technological advance, but rather make appeals to technology to support other, more basic motives'; and these motives are 'clearly political' (Glass and Smith 1978 pp. 12–18). There remains the uneasy feeling amongst teachers that all schools will somehow be expected to be above average!

CURRICULUM CONTENT

This topic is more fully discussed elsewhere in this volume by Lawton and by Chanan so my treatment will be brief. The accountability debate has emphasised three aspects of the curriculum. (1) More attention to basic skills is demanded, and there is a threat that test-scores will be used to ensure that it is given. (2) Greater stress is being placed on examination results, and there are threats to publish league-tables. (3) There is pressure to introduce more science, to make the curriculum more vocational and to devote more time to links between schools and industry. The conflicts between these expectations, especially that between using examination results as an indicator of success and pursuing a curriculum that is relevant to living and earning in the future, are seldom acknowledged. The curriculum reform movement of the sixties and seventies failed to shift the curriculum very far towards either a more personal or a more technological education because the examination system and the power of established school subjects preserved the dominance of traditional academic values. The chances of further change in the eighties will be diminished still further by the new examination arrangements at 16 +, and, as Taylor shows in Chapter 1, the increased competitiveness and curriculum retrenchment that comes with falling rolls. There is some chance that links between schools and industry will improve mutual understanding, but one wonders for how long teachers and industrialists will afford to spend time in each other's company when incentives and career prospects lie elsewhere.

PARENT PARTICIPATION

The parent issue on the accountability agenda has three main dimensions – parent rights, parent involvement in school government, and parental choice of school. Though parent rights could be said to incorporate the other two dimensions, it is convenient to confine it to those principles that are now universally acknowledged: that parents have the right to be kept fully informed about what their children's school is doing and about their own child's progress; that there should be proper channels for them to ask questions and to express their worries and concerns; and that there should be clear complaints procedures. Within this agreed framework there are many practical issues, such as what is meant by 'fully informed' and whether parents should have access to records, which will continue to cause controversy.

Parent involvement in school government is quite a different issue, because it assumes that parents can be regarded as an interest group that is capable of being represented in some meaningful way. The findings of the Taylor Report are more fully discussed in Chapter 11 by Howell. Here I shall merely state that this may not be the best way to serve parent interests. Our research in Sussex has shown that parents see their relationship with schools in individual rather than collective terms, so it might be more relevant to improve school–parent communication and complaints procedures than to pursue their involvement in school government. Beattie (1978 pp. 41–48) suggests that in several European countries consultative and participation arrangements have been used to depoliticise issues by rerouting them into a defined area where confrontation is permitted but can be safely contained, while Bacon's (1978) research in Sheffield has shown that parent representatives have little influence on school board decisions. It is also difficult to see how the boards themselves can gain much power when they neither employ teachers nor determine a school's financial provision.

Though parent involvement in school government is often linked with community participation, where the problems of representation become even more acute, this line of thinking is incompatible with the notion of parental choice. Choice implies a lack of commitment to any individual school, and belongs with the market approach to accountability – the very opposite of a community approach. However, the issue is unlikely to disappear from the political arena because, ultimately, there is no way of reconciling what some parents believe to be best for their child with the general good of the community. While the education system continues to serve as a mechanism for distributing qualifications, the pursuit of those qualifications is bound to be a priority for individuals; and those that possess them have a vested interest in preserving their currency, irrespective of their relevance to individual development or social need (Dore 1976).

MANAGERIAL RESPONSIBILITY

To the insider the British educational system seems a reasonable compromise between interested parties, but to the outsider it appears to offer endless opportunities for passing the buck. The question of who is responsible for what has been frequently asked, yet it is often unclear whether the dispute is about the structure of governance or the way in which that structure is interpreted. I believe that, apart from the Taylor Report, the main issue has been whether managerial responsibility is being properly exercised; but the threat of changes in the power structure has remained in the wings as a hidden deterrent to any perceived lack of response. Since possible changes in the government of education are discussed by Howell in Chapter 11, I shall concentrate on managerial responsibilities within the existing framework and avoid the temptation to turn a discussion of accountability procedures into yet another debate about the power structure. For some politicians and pressure groups accountability is merely a pretext for attempting to increase external control, but for most it is about improving the responsiveness of all sections of the education system to external concerns and demands.

There are several reasons why the connection between possible changes in accountability procedures and changes in the power structure has been somewhat exaggerated. First, it is only the most extreme accountability proposals which seriously threaten the current balance of power. These are unlikely to be widely adopted, and many of them are quite impractical. Second, none of the existing limitations on the exercise of power is likely to be altered. In particular, the ultimate sanction of dismissal will remain unusable in all but the most exceptional circumstances. Third, though changes in accountability procedures may improve the flow of information, they do not extend the range of possible consequent action. They cannot provide any new mechanism for solving classroom problems. Fourth, increased centralisation of policy decisions will make central authorities more accountable for their decisions. Given the fate of many central initiatives in the last two decades, this is not necessarily a prospect they will relish. The DES in particular has much to gain from maintaining a position of influence without responsibility.

Nevertheless, suspicion about hidden agendas has given teachers a sense of insecurity; and it is only when the more extreme proposals have been removed from the political arena that many of them will be willing to approach the problem of accountability in a more constructive frame of mind. If teachers are forced to see accountability primarily in political terms, then we will have good cause to be worried about the future.

Information flow, judgement and evaluation transactions

Accountability can be formally defined in terms of the presentation, evaluation and discussion of accounts – information provision, judgement and response. But this tidy definition ignores the real world. Much of the information which flows across institutional boundaries is unplanned and haphazard. Judgements are not necessarily based on information that is formally provided. Evaluation can be incidental and irrational. Communication is imperfect and misinterpretation common.

Consider, for example, the information a parent may receive about a primary school. Some of it, such as pupil behaviour in the street, is beyond the school's control. Much of it is unintended. Children talk about school. So do dinner ladies and parent helpers. Then others talk about what they have heard and seen. Snippets of information get distorted yet gain credibility as they circulate round the 'grapevine'. Information intentionally provided by the school is only selectively received. While nearly all parents go to open evenings when they can discuss their child's progress with the teacher, attendance on other school occasions is usually much lower. Parents do not always find out what they want to know and many lack the confidence to take the initiative. Written information may be provided by formal reports on children's progress or by a school prospectus, but some schools issue neither. So much of the information received by parents is acquired fortuitously; and there is no reason to suppose that incidental information from the grapevine is accorded any lower priority than that deliberately provided by the school itself. The scope for misunderstanding is considerable, and our research in Sussex found many parents believing that their children were taught neither spelling nor tables, when this was not in fact true. The gap between what parents think is happening in schools and what actually happens is considerable, even when schools are devoting significant effort to home–school relations. Images created by the grapevine and the press thrive in conditions of anxiety and uncertainty. For it is not the information provided by schools but the information received by parents which determines their opinions.

Examining the content of information used to form judgements provides another perspective. The literature tends to focus on four categories – curriculum, teaching processes, individual pupil progress and general standards of performance. We have found two others to be equally significant: personnel, and milieu. The personality of the head has a major impact on how a school is regarded and individual teachers also acquire reputations on the grapevine. They may be judged on whether pupils get on with them, on whether they are thought to get good results, or on how they respond to queries and suggestions in informal conversation. The teacher unions are constantly urging the public to trust the teachers and let them get on with the job; and many evaluations depend on whether, as a result of personal acquaintance, the public are prepared to do just that. Milieu is another factor that figures prominently in both lay and professional comments about schools. It refers both to the physical appearance of a school and to the social-psychological environment. Though influenced by the buildings and by rules and regulations, the milieu is largely constructed from the daily transactions between teachers and pupils which give a school its life and meaning. Insiders and outsiders alike expect both moral and physical order and a friendly but industrious atmosphere, though they may interpret similar situations in very different ways.

Given these six categories of evidence and the lack of opportunity to collect more than a small quantity of information, outsiders have to rely on shortcuts to make evaluations. These involve either generalising from an inadequate sample within a given category, or making theoretical assumptions which allow evidence from one category to be applied to judgements in another. Such lay theories of education enable a parent who sees an unruly group of children rushing out of school to deduce that the three Rs are not being taught; or a teacher who talks about children's creativity to be understood as being soft on discipline. Professional observers also use shortcuts and often fail to recognise the assumptions that underpin them. Advisers sometimes use very short visits as a basis for making important judgements. Officers use indicators like test results, truancy rates and teacher absenteeism as evidence of a school's state of health. The use of shortcuts is inevitable, so can it be improved? But the limitations of such thinking will need to be properly recognised in formal accountability procedures if they are to conform to principles of fairness, truth and justice.

Another problem is that most people do not have to make conscious summary judgements about schools, so evaluations remain implicit and based on partial opinions. Some information can be immediately labelled 'good' or 'bad', but most evaluation involves some kind of comparison with norms and expectations. Such norms are not always readily available or clearly understood. Many parents are anxious because they do not know what standard to expect, and it is unusual for them to receive any professional guidance. So they are forced to give priority to simple numerical indicators and information they can evaluate with confidence – class rank, examination results, performance in basic skills, teacher responsiveness and pupil behaviour. Professionals do little better when they use the term 'good practice' to cover a tangle of norms and expectations, value judgements and empirical judgements which they are usually quite unprepared to unravel. Evaluations depend not only on the information received but also on the criteria that are readily available for judging it.

Finally, we need to examine how evaluations get discussed and what happens as a result. The tidy image of accountability collapses altogether, because there are very few occasions when an evaluation of a school, a department or a teacher gets formally transmitted. Yet many transactions within schools and between schools and outsiders can be construed as communicating evaluative messages. Questions imply areas of concern, suggestions imply dissatisfaction with the 'status quo', comments carry evaluation overtones, conversations reveal opinions. External views are communicated through numerous evaluative transactions; and it is this informal system of accountability which dominates, backed by concrete evidence of pupil recruitment and teacher promotion. The extent to which introducing a system of regular formal evaluations, such as annual staff interviews, departmental reviews or adviser reports on schools, will displace this informal system or merely give it a formal face must remain a matter for conjecture.

Response to external pressures is also likely to be complicated. An accumulation of messages can gradually cause subtle changes in climate, without their being recognised or attributed to any particular source. When there is no immediate change schools may appear less responsive than is actually the case. But if change is quickly agreed and not properly implemented, the opposite may be true. The appearance of responsiveness may be different from the reality. Judgements of responsiveness are often based on the attention given to external views and the extent to which there appears to be a genuine effort to understand them, not on whether changes in the classroom eventually occur. The relationship between evaluation and action needs to be much more closely studied before too many decisions get made about accountability policy.

Accountability procedures

The previous section described how people *do* evaluate schools and emphasised the relatively small influence of formal accountability procedures. Now we have to give equal attention to how people should evaluate schools. What are the implications of the principles of moral, professional and contractual accountability for the information that parents, managers and LEAs *should* receive? What opportunities for evaluative transaction *should* be made available? For convenience I have grouped accountability procedures under four main headings: accountability for individual pupils, accountability to parents, school-based accountability for policy and standards, and authority-based procedures.

ACCOUNTABILITY FOR INDIVIDUAL PUPILS

Judgements about the performance of individual pupils provide the base from which most evaluations develop. But this foundation is much less firm than commonly believed. Formal systems of testing and record-keeping tend to neglect the variable nature of human performance and the idiosyncratic pattern of individual learning. Teachers' assessments of pupils are not based on single incidents but on observing them at work over long periods in varying contexts and circumstances. Hence providing succinct reports is a frustrating process in which judgements lose meaning by being abstracted out of context. It is rather like trying to summarise a series of film clips by a single still photograph. It can be done, but what does it mean?

Evaluating a pupil's progress also involves assessing his potential, but on what evidence can this be based? On IQ or aptitude tests, by looking at his best work, or by observing his behaviour in class? Ideally, one needs some combination of the three; but there is a natural temptation to avoid this complex issue by taking shortcuts, either relying on 'track record' or concentrating on motivation and effort, thus appealing to the theory that a motivated hard-working child is *ipso facto* working to potential. However, the question of responsibility for motivation is also problematic. Is it the pupil who is responsible for working hard? Is it the home which is 'encouraging' or 'not encouraging'? Is it the teacher who has to 'get on' with the pupil, engage his interest and provide 'appropriate' work? Accountability is partly about reducing underachievement, but at the individual level this is difficult to assess and the responsibility for it is never clear-cut.

At school or departmental level, one has to find a balance between neglecting the need for some formal framework of reporting and wasting time on lengthy records which no-one ever reads. Given the limitations of records, it might be sensible to give more attention to regular discussions of pupil progress based on samples of work than to compiling and exchanging summary judgements. Moreover, some explicit consideration of alternative provision would also need to be included, as there is little point in trying to obtain a diagnosis that is more sophisticated than the treatment. Introducing new procedures will have little practical effect unless both the difficulties of evaluating pupils' progress and the need to associate such evaluations with possible adjustments to teaching are fully appreciated.

SCHOOL-PARENT RELATIONS
I suggested earlier that parent rights to be informed about their child's progress and the education he was receiving, and to ask questions about it, were now generally acknowledged. What was in dispute were the detailed procedures. Significantly the three most popular items in a recent survey of primary school parent preferences were those that our own interview-based research had identified as most important (Webb 1979 pp. 24–29).

1 An open evening with an interview with the class teacher.

2 A detailed school prospectus including accounts of the educational policy and teaching methods of the school.

3 A school report.

The first and third are complementary methods of reporting pupil progress and it is the combination of the two which probably works best. Parents like reports in spite of their limitations, because their formal status suggests they are receiving the 'official' view of their child and because they have time to reflect on written comments and discuss them. Many talked to us of listening to oral comments without taking them in, and being mesmerised by a web of teacher talk which they later found they couldn't remember. However, both parents and teachers feel that direct discussion offers the opportunity for elaboration and explanation, for question and response even if some parents lack the confidence to take advantage of it. When a written report is followed by an interview one or two weeks later, the report serves as a useful starting-point for discussion; and it is still possible for a teacher to correct a false impression that may have been gleaned from a necessarily brief report. The traditional practice of waiting for the summer term might also be reviewed. The process of compiling and discussing reports causes teachers to reflect on individual children, and it seems wasteful that this opportunity for evaluation should be postponed until it is too late in the year for consequent action to be taken.

Though popular with parents, both interviews and reports could be much improved by careful planning, in-service training and local experiment. Many parents do not get the information they want from interviews. Teachers are not trained in interviewing. At most open evenings interviews are rushed and semi-public when ideally they need to be leisurely and private. Parents stress that they want to be told the 'straight truth', while teachers talk of the need to 'dress it up'. Our research in Sussex also found that detailed accounts of individual areas of the curriculum are extremely popular with parents; and schools have much to gain from providing them because what they teach is closer to what parents want than many people realise. I would therefore recommend the gradual introduction of detailed school prospectuses, allowing time for experiment and for teachers to develop skills in writing them. Since I expect it will eventually become a legal requirement, why not proceed with small-scale experiments and try to do it properly?

General attitudes towards home-school relations are important, and schools need to recognise considerable differences among parents. Some parents have high expectations of teacher-parent contact and welcome social occasions and educational evenings. Others prefer not to be involved unless there is a problem. All expect to be treated with equal respect. Teachers also react defensively if they think their competence or judgement is being doubted, but they tend to interpret anxiety as hostility and questioning as criticism. While some parents like to rely on the teacher for information, others prefer to make independent judgements by looking around and seeing for themselves. This independent attitude is neutral rather than critical, but can become more critical if opportunities for acquiring information are denied. Naturally, it is their own child's work which parents primarily want to see and discuss; and one wonders if relations could not be improved by organising more parent-oriented activities at class level rather than school level. This section has emphasised parent needs for information for three main reasons. First, there is good empirical evidence for it. Second, it is the aspect of our research into accountability which always seemed to attract the greatest interest. Third, I have a strong hunch that parent uncertainty and anxiety provide much of the fuel that keeps the political controversy burning.

SCHOOL-BASED ACCOUNTABILITY FOR POLICY AND STANDARDS

One response to proposals that school performance should be more formally and regularly evaluated by external agencies has been to introduce the idea of internal school self-accounting. Some self-evaluation already takes place as a normal part of professional life; but it is now suggested that this could be developed into a formal framework and that school self-accounts could be reported to, and possibly audited by, outsiders. The main arguments in favour of this approach are as follows. (1) Test results are based on too narrow a range of evidence and cannot make proper allowance for school context and circumstances. (2) Inspection is too costly to be applied regularly to all schools. (3) School self-accounting is the logical consequence of the current system of delegating many decisions to individual schools. (4) Self-evaluation increases the probability of appropriate action, while external evaluations are resisted, misinterpreted or only partially accepted, with little consequent change. (5) Other forms of accountability will only increase external control over schools without being able to translate that control into improvements in the quality of teaching.

What then might such self-accounting involve? Clearly it would need to be more than improving arrangements for general monitoring, the spotting and diagnosis of incipient problems within the context of existing policies. The policies themselves would need to be periodically reviewed, together with general standards of performance. The proposal endorsed by the Taylor Report was for a three year or five year rolling programme of internal reviews, each of which would examine a particular aspect of a school's provision. This would carry greater credibility than just using a self-evaluation checklist, though the latter might serve a useful intermediate purpose. While some teachers in some schools now possess the necessary skills to conduct such reviews, it will take time for every school to develop this capability. Suitable procedures and techniques exist, but would benefit from further development as more teachers begin to acquire the necessary skills, attitudes and experience.

The two main arguments against school self-accounting are that teachers lack the necessary skills and attitudes, and that the whole approach lacks external credibility. While it is hoped that the former can be countered by a carefully phased introduction with appropriate in-service training, the main response to the credibility issue has been the idea of auditing. In addition to reviews being reported to governing bodies and officers of the local education authority, it is suggested that an independent comment be obtained from an auditor. Such an auditor might be an adviser, a lecturer, a teacher or even a visiting panel of teachers, and the role and conditions of appointment would be locally negotiated. The auditor would be expected to read the report, visit the school and add independent comments of his own to which the school would have the right of reply. The essential difference between auditing and inspection is that the former is based on the school's own account and has to relate to, if not agree with, the school's own situation analysis and evaluative criteria.

The effect of introducing such a system on the internal politics of a school, and on professional life in general, should not be underestimated. The contradiction between arguing for delegation to schools and arguing for teacher autonomy within schools is seldom appreciated. If a school has to describe and justify its policy in greater detail, its internal arrangements have to move towards rather more conformity, whether or not this is achieved by democratic means. Thus the implementation of school self-accounting depends on teachers developing an extended professional role which is both less individualistic and more self-critical. But it also offers the opportunity to demonstrate a technical knowledge base, on which teachers' claims to professional status may ultimately depend.

AUTHORITY-BASED ACCOUNTABILITY PROCEDURES

While many commentators have seen school-based and authority-based procedures as alternative approaches to accountability, I prefer to see them as complementary. Though some schools may be in competition at a time of falling rolls, they are equally dependent on the collective reputation of schools in general. If events at one school hit the headlines, the others also suffer. So at the level of public relations, all schools stand to gain from an authority's ability to make confident general statements about policy (e.g. all our schools teach maths for at least four hours a week) and from LEA monitoring procedures that prevent a William Tyndale-type eruption. One also needs to recognise that schools are contractually bound to their authority and their authority to its electorate. The authority is legally responsible for what happens to every pupil. Much of the responsibility is delegated, but to neglect it altogether would be to abandon our current system of democratic government. Moreover, in addition to maintaining and reviewing their own accountability procedures, LEAs have a crucial role to play in the development of school-based accountability. Their support is needed for developing schools' capabilities for self-evaluation, and for establishing the appropriate attitudes. Then a formal framework will need to be negotiated which ensures that all schools fulfil their self-accounting obligations.

Authority-based procedures have two main functions: the detection and diagnosis of problems, and the maintenance and improvement of standards. The first is concerned with general monitoring, the second with institutional or policy reviews. Monitoring includes making short visits to schools, watching out for signs of trouble like parent complaints, listening to the grapevine and using quantitative indicators such as examination results and truancy rates. All these methods are clear rather than thorough, so it is important that possible problems are further investigated before definite conclusions are drawn. However, there is much to be said for insisting on such simple scanning procedures as a systematic roster of visits and a careful analysis of test results in addition to the usual rather random opportunities for observation and informal communication. It is eminently sensible to have warning lights on the instrument panel, provided one does not attempt to use them for regular navigation.

An inspection is a common response to the identification of a major institutional problem, the ultimate in problem diagnosis. But some authorities are considering inspection as a form of regular institutional review. Since few LEAs have the staff to inspect a school more than once in ten years, it looks as though inspection policy will be difficult to determine. In spite of the anxiety they cause, inspections are more acceptable to teachers than other forms of external accountability because they take local circumstances into account and use a broad range of evidence. However, being confidential, inspection reports do not get publicly discussed. Their methodology cannot be criticised like that of other accountability procedures, and they are of no value to schools other than the one inspected.

Policy reviews on the other hand can be published without specific reference to individual teachers or schools. These present a general picture of policies and standards across an LEA in one curriculum area, incorporating evidence from tests and examinations into its proper context. This approach is not widely used at local level but has the advantages of putting the public in the picture, giving scope for evaluative comment and serving as a springboard for constructive follow-up in individual schools. Confining this kind of review to the national level as in the Bullock Report and the HMI Primary and Secondary Surveys may be taking it too far away from the scene of the action.

Another possibility is to publish inspection reports, but this proposal would need to be very carefully considered. Anxiety might be greatly enhanced, attempts to deceive the inspectors might increase, criticism might become too muted to be useful, and a general atmosphere of hostility might make constructive follow-up almost impossible. Advocates of such policies seem to assume either that public disgrace improves performance or that teachers can be sacked.

Finally, an LEA can alter its accountability stance by specifying its policies in greater detail. Curriculum guidelines, for example, are being developed by several LEAs; and the assumption is that deviations will not be forbidden but will need to be convincingly justified. Hitherto most guidelines have not been very specific, but they still offer some protection to schools who may wish to assert that their policies have LEA approval. Most authorities have formal policies for tests and records, and they may wish to consider whether certain forms of reporting to parents or school-based self-review should not also be mandatory. Changes of this kind would involve some slight reduction in the freedom that schools currently possess, but could hardly be regarded as a major shift in the power structure. No doubt these and other new accountability procedures will continue to be matters for debate.

9
Educational Research and Educational Practice

John Nisbet

The other chapters in this book identify issues which are likely to prove important for education in the years ahead. It is often assumed that such issues, once identified, should become priority topics for research so that future policy and practice can be based firmly on empirical evidence and experiment. Research is thus a common contemporary response to the identification of a 'problem', and government investment in educational research is based on the optimistic belief that research will resolve issues. The recent track record of educational researchers set to work on policy-oriented studies has come in for severe criticism, and consequently the future of educational research is itself one of the issues for the eighties. What is the function of research in education? Can research provide definitive answers to problems, and if not, what use is it? Who should decide research priorities, which topics should be investigated and which topics should be funded? Research is a growth point for educational practice, and therefore the control of research is a key element in controlling the direction in which the educational system will develop. The argument of this chapter is that the instrumental view of research commonly adopted by policy makers and practitioners is naive: it has some validity for limited purposes, but the impact of research on policy and practice in education is a much more complex process. A clearer understanding of the function of research is necessary if it is to make an effective contribution to educational practice.

The instrumental view looks to research to perform at least four kinds of service in education. Research provides an information base for politicians and administrators, who can then add the necessary value judgements and thus legitimize their policies on a sound basis. Implementing policy decisions raises a further set of tasks for research. A third way in which research can make itself useful is by working out the implications of new 'inventions', such as the micro-processor or computer-assisted learning or a new approach to the teaching of French or physics. Fourth is evaluation, checking the effectiveness of innovations and intervention programmes and monitoring educational standards, for which research techniques and trained personnel are needed. The second and third of these are sometimes described as 'development' rather than research; the first three are commonly referred to as 'educational R & D'. All four fall in the category of 'policy-oriented research', in contrast to 'conclusion-oriented research' which is concerned with theories and ideas. Policy-oriented research is favoured by those responsible for the funding of educational research, who seem to believe that educational researchers are inclined to neglect it, preferring to direct their energies towards more academic conclusion-oriented studies which are remote from practical problems and are therefore generally useless. The Permanent Secretary of the Department of Education and Science declared to a House of Commons Select Committee:

> I have to say, of course, that the great thing about educational research is that a part of it is rubbish and another part (I will not be specific about the proportions) leads nowhere and is really indifferent; it is, I am afraid, exceptional to find a piece of research that really hits the nail on the head and tells you pretty clearly what is wrong or what is happening or what should be done. (Pile 1976)

There are two lines of argument to meet the serious criticism which Pile makes. The first is that research has influenced policy and practice in education, though not in the way that policy makers and teachers expect, not even perhaps in the way that researchers themselves expect. The second is that Pile is assuming a linear model for the impact of research, and this model is sadly inadequate as an explanation of how research exercises its influence. The linear model is caricatured by Weiss (1977): 'A problem exists; information or understanding is lacking; research provides the missing knowledge; a solution is reached.' There are gaps and distortions at every stage: the definition of the problem predetermines the nature of the information likely to be sought; and the findings of research are accepted selectively according to the predispositions of those who ask the questions. The linear model has come under increasing criticism in recent years, and in its place an interactive model has been suggested as a more adequate way of understanding the impact of research.

The first of these lines of argument is developed by Travers in the preface to the latest edition of *An Introduction to Educational Research* (1978):

> Research has had a vital impact on education. Those who cannot see this impact are generally looking for cookbook solutions to problems, and cookbook solutions do not emerge from research in most

fields . . . Although research cannot provide specific remedies, it can provide general principles that will help the teacher cope effectively with many problems and aid the curriculum developer to produce more useful materials.

Halsey, in the 1972 report *Educational Priority*, summarises the point:

> (Research) is unlikely ever to yield neat and definite prescriptions from field-tested plans . . . Research brings relevant information rather than uniquely exclusive conditions . . . What it offers is an aid to intelligent decision-making, not a substitute for it.

Travers's argument is that if we can stand back sufficiently to see developments in perspective, the influence of research is plain and obvious. In Part Two of *An Introduction to Educational Research* he outlines the aspects of education where research has had greatest impact: reading materials, the design of textbooks, vocabulary studies; individual differences, age-placement, the sequencing of subject matter to fit pupils' stages of thinking, studies of learning and the psychology of elementary school subjects; tests and examinations, remedial education, screening, diagnostic testing, academic and vocational guidance; evaluation; the education of handicapped children (especially the deaf), learning a second language and others. What these have in common is that they are all relatively non-controversial areas. In topics where there is a general consensus on values, research findings seem to be particularly effective: they are readily incorporated into policy or action. But when basic assumptions are challenged, then research seems to lose its relevance, or at least is not readily accepted. If there is no consensus on values, research is treated merely as one more pressure group with vested interests. The example of testing and selection, the 11 plus examination and the selective secondary school, illustrates this point: research was widely used to improve the selection procedure, and it did this well; but with the introduction of comprehensive schools this research was discarded (although it still had much to contribute), because it was based on a system which no longer commanded widespread support.

There is a second line of argument in answer to the criticism that research in education is useless. This rejects the linear model in which the impact of research is seen as a simple utilisation of findings. 'Knowledge is presented; behaviour is changed accordingly': this is not how things happen. Instead, the main influence of research on policy and practice is seen as indirect and long-term. Research shapes people's perceptions. They become aware of aspects previously unnoticed; they interpret situations differently because of research findings; they adopt different methods of tackling problems; and they have different expectations of what is feasible and what is accepted as unchangeable. Research thus influences practice indirectly, but practice also influences research: events in the practical field similarly affect the perceptions, interpretations, methods and aspirations of researchers. This is an interactive model for the impact of research, and it is a much more adequate description of the relation of research and practice in education. It is not, however, a model which readily fits the pragmatic style of the administrator.

This interpretation of research impact was well described in the 4th Annual Report of the American National Council on Educational Research in 1978. That report reviewed the issue of the impact of research on educational practice, and summarised its conclusions with four 'spheres of influence' of research on practice. Research gives to teachers, first, a *view of reality*. It interprets the world of the school to the teachers, and gives them a language for understanding it. Thus it influences perceptions. Second, research gives a *vision of the achievable*. It influences expectations, shows 'what might be'. 'Each new advance . . . has the potential of altering educational vision'. Thus research influences *aspirations*. Third, research is concerned with *know-how*, the *techniques* of instruction. This aspect is often over-emphasised by those who see research as concerned essentially with improving instructional methods. Fourth, research strengthens the *commitment to act*. It sustains the professional attitude that the action is worthwhile. Many factors influence this, and salaries and working conditions are important. But 'if the practice of education were motivated by nothing more than the need to make a living, the whole enterprise would falter'. Thus, research influences *motivation*.

A view of reality, influencing perceptions; a vision of the achievable, influencing aspirations; know-how, the improvement of techniques; and a commitment to act, supporting motivation through professional understanding. Thus, the report argues, the potential of research is to

alter teachers' views of reality,
change their conceptions of what is educationally possible,
offer them better ways of working, and
deepen their commitment to their work.

All these are part of what the report calls 'the glacial advance of human understanding': more people in full-time education, more varied curriculum, college-work now taught at high school, enriched materials, the disappearance of the dunce's cap, rote memorisation and parroting of answers half-understood – in their place, more human attitudes and a readiness to treat each learner with greater dignity.

The interactive model is developed by Weiss (1977) in *Using Social Research in Public Policy Making*. Her view is that research is

. . . only one part of a complicated process that also uses experience, political insight, pressure, social technologies and judgement (in policy making) . . . The process is not one of linear order from research to decision, but a disorderly set of interconnections and back-and-forthness that defies neat diagrams.

This particular contribution of research, according to Weiss, is 'conceptualisation', a process of defining issues (or redefining them), creating an awareness of problems and altering our perceptions of them. Thus research tends to prepare for decisions rather than to make them. Its contribution to education is more often in establishing appropriate questions to be asked by those who have to decide and act, than in providing them with ready-made answers. This is no slight contribution. To quote Einstein (1947):

The formulation of a problem is often more essential than its solution, which may be merely a matter of mathematical or experimental skill. To raise new questions, new possibilities, to regard old questions from a new angle, requires imagination and marks real advance in science.

Social science also provides a common language of discourse for the discussion of ideas, and the existence of this language directs attention to selected aspects: 'The vocabulary tells us which items out of the buzzing blooming confusion to pay attention to . . . These are the going generalisations.'

This view of the function of educational research was expressed earlier by W. Taylor (1973):

For the most part the influence of research has been to *sensitise*. It has indicated the importance of certain problems and the danger of the unselfconscious use of certain procedures, without necessarily providing clear cut calculations of advantages or a firm foundation for decision. . . Such a sensitising effect, an awareness that there is a problem which needs to be thought about, can result merely from the existence of a particular piece of research, independently of its conclusions. Not all research is like this, but there is more of it than we would like to admit . . .

Research influences the climate of opinion: it builds up 'a prevailing view' (Cronbach and Suppes 1969), 'ideas in good currency' (Schon 1971), or 'a gradual accumulation of research results which can lead to serious and far-reaching changes in the way people and governments address their problems' (Weiss 1977). Schon (in Weiss 1977) writes of research as 'problem setting' rather than 'problem solving', that is, formulating problems and setting them in appropriate frameworks, which highlight certain aspects, select out others and bind the salient features in a coherent pattern. One important influence of research, according to Travers (see Nisbet and Broadfoot 1980), has been to develop a philosophy of education which embodies a conception of human nature; and though this affects the way people see educational issues, it is not easy to fit into an administrative context.

Paradoxically, research appears to have most obvious influence when it fits the prevailing view. This is what was implied in the statement earlier in this chapter that the direct impact of research is seen in those areas where there is a consensus of values. Research which fits the accepted framework of thought and meets conventional demands for relevance and applicability, clearly is likely to have more immediate impact, being more readily incorporated in practice, but its impact may be short-term. Conversely, the research which is most influential in the long term is likely initially to be neglected or even rejected, because it does not readily fit our preconceived notions. As long ago as 1762, Rousseau in *Emile* protested: 'People are always telling me to make practical suggestions. You might as well tell me to suggest improvements which can be incorporated with the wrong methods at present in use.'

Thus research is not always a force for change: it also operates as a stabilising factor, or even as a restrictive or reactionary influence. Topics which are seen as problems within the accepted framework of thought become priorities for investigation, and the fact that they are investigated and discussed reinforces the accepted framework. From time to time, however, evidence accumulates to produce a paradigmatic shift of the kind described by Kuhn (1962) in the natural sciences. How and why such fundamental changes of attitude occur, and what is their phasing, are topics which deserve study and analysis. The example of interventionist studies in the 1960s suggests a ten-year cycle: after a long period of incubation, the new idea takes about two years to emerge, two years to take shape in new policies, two years for implementation, two years for evaluation, and two years for challenge to build up. But this is an over-simple explanation, for the influential factors include changes in society as a whole and changes in public concern. In the natural sciences, a Kuhnian revolution occurs relatively infrequently, so that in the interim there is time for much incremental work to be done. In education, major changes of paradigm occur too frequently for comfort. Forsyth and Dockrell (1979) explain this in terms of an 'oscillation model', which bears resemblance to 'catastrophe theory' in mathematics. According to this theory, because of the contradictions inherent in any educational context, the decision-maker is faced with a choice between two (or more) conflicting 'right' lines of action, each right in its own terms. He adopts one, and countervailing pressure builds up. When this pressure reaches the critical point, the pendulum swings and the new alternative priorities are in favour. In such a process, research performs both a stabilising and a revolutionary influence, often simultaneously, to the frustration of those who have to make practical decisions.

Concern over the gap between educational research and practice dates back long before the seventies. As early as 1934, Bagley, one of the pioneers of educational research, 'looked back on the expectations he had had in 1900 . . . and was surprised at the small effect educational science had had on the schools'. In 1950, Kandel, reviewing the *Encyclopaedia of Educational Research*, said he was 'doubtful whether the mountain of material . . . would lead to the improvement of educational practice'. In 1965, Westman wrote: 'Despite a minimal estimate of 20,000 articles and books devoted to reading retardation, there is still little consensus on either the prevalence of reading retardation or its correlates', and Bereiter (quoted in Clifford 1973) complained: 'One looks in vain for discoveries that have had any impact on the enterprise which educational research was intended to serve'. Lamke, in 1955, wrote that if research over the past three years in medicine, agriculture, physics or chemistry were wiped out 'our life would be changed materially; but if research on teacher personnel over the same three years were to vanish, educators and education would continue much as usual'. There are many examples of such criticisms: Clifford (1973) quotes Charters 1948, Hoyt 1953, Beach 1954, Corey 1954, Ahrens 1956, Stanley 1957, Amatora 1957 and Ross 1958; Bloom (1966 pp. 211–221) and Nisbet and Broadfoot (1980) provide a selection of more recent examples, and these are only a few from a steady flow of complaint. Towards the end of the sixties the flow increased. One reason was the greatly increased investment in educational research and development. Between 1964 and 1969, expenditure on educational research and development in Britain increased ten-fold, and this growth raised high hopes and aspirations. When these hopes were not immediately realised, a sense of frustration passed readily into criticisms of 'failure'.

Before 1960, almost all educational research in the United Kingdom was done on a voluntary basis by graduate students and by university teachers in their spare time without funds or on minute budgets. In 1960, the total budget of the National Foundation for Educational Research in England and Wales was £34,000, and the budget of the Scottish Council for Research in Education (then in its thirty-first year) was £8,388, covering salaries of the tiny staff (part-time director and secretary), accommodation, materials and all running costs. Expenditure on research in Britain now is of the order of five or six million pounds annually. In the USA, the growth of research expenditure has been even more dramatic. A recent article in

Educational Researcher (Sharp and Frankel 1979 pp. 6–11) presented results from a national survey of expenditure in the fiscal year 1976–77: the organisations which provided data for the survey reported spending 734 million dollars on educational research, development, dissemination and evaluation, and employed 22,300 full-time professional staff primarily in these activities. Are schools any better, or even any different, for all this outlay? Is there evidence of sounder decisions being made in educational policy? Such questions are not easily answered, and in the absence of evidence to the contrary it is commonly assumed that the research effort is failing to produce the results which would justify this level of investment.

Each side tends to blame the other for the limited effect of research. Researchers criticise teachers for failing to keep up with research. Teachers criticize researchers for isolation (ivory tower, priorities wrong, more concerned with academic audiences and promotion than with being useful) and poor communication (jargon, indifference about dissemination or reporting back to schools). Each blame the administrator (not enough funds for research, nor time for teachers to read and study), while administrators blame researchers and teachers, seeing the solution in developing a properly organised research programme. The conclusion reached by those who control funds was that, since research could not give direction to policy, the solution was to reverse influence and give to policy-makers the control of research, allowing policy priorities to determine and influence the choice, design, methodology and reporting of research. This was the decision of Mrs Thatcher in 1970, when she was Secretary of State for Education and Science: she declared her intention that the Department's research policy should be 'the active initiation of work by the Department on problems of its own choosing, within a procedure and timetable which were relevant to its needs'. The same point was made more recently by the Senior Chief Inspector:

> It is a sad fact that educational research does not seem to have the place in the system reason tells one it should have. To be honest I don't think this is all the system's fault. But the Department is currently attempting to create strong links between educational research and policy making. The general approach is to select areas of high importance such as, in the schools field, education in a multicultural society, management issues, education for special needs and the challenge of 16–19. The idea is that the Department should take greater initiative in defining the questions to be answered and in seeking out researchers to attack them. (Browne 1979)

In 1971, government policy on research funding was set out in the Rothschild report, which proposed to 'solve' the issue by the crude formula: 'The customer says what he wants; the contractor does it (if he can); and the customer pays.' This customer-contractor formula has been applied to all government-funded research, but its application to education has been less restrictive than in some other fields. This is partly because research funding in education is small compared with science, medicine and agriculture and is therefore of lesser importance to those concerned with finance, and partly because of the emergence of a procedure of 'negotiated research' in preference to a customer merely specifying his requirements. The 1975 Annual Report of the Scottish Council for Research in Education describes the procedures:

> The customer does not simply present us with a problem and tell us to go ahead and find the answer. Instead, the first step in the process is that Council staff are invited to a meeting where officials or teachers outline their concerns. There is a general discussion, and a second meeting is held where the staff explain the contribution which they think research can offer. On this occasion, there is a fairly lengthy discussion in which misapprehensions are cleared up and alternatives are explored, and the customers either agree that research would be useful to them or decide that it would not help to solve their problems. If they agree, there is a third meeting in which a costed project is presented for discussion, and sometimes further meetings are required until agreement is reached. Decisions on research projects are thus based on negotiation between researchers and customers, each accepting and respecting the other's contribution to the proposal.

Even within this modified procedure, the criterion of utilisation remains a main consideration in determining the priorities for research funding.

The idea that good educational research is research which can be *used* to answer questions is one which has a long history. The growth of educational research in the first 40 years of this century was dominated by the aspiration to establish a science of education. The notion can be traced back earlier, to Alexander Bain's *Education as a Science* (1879) and to William James and John Dewey. A science of education would provide an organised body of empirical evidence, from which would be derived theories and principles refined and tested by experiment. From such a science of education, it would be possible to derive answers to problems, or at least to develop methods to obtain answers. The 'scientific movement' in educational research reflected a positivist philosophy, in that it assumed that there were 'best methods' of teaching and 'correct answers' to educational problems which were capable of being discovered by systematic enquiry. Hence, experiments were conducted to decide the optimum time to be devoted to spelling, and whether in subtraction the method of 'decomposition' was better than the method of 'equal addition'. The hey-day of this movement was the 1930s: the 1938 Yearbook of the National Society for the Study of Education was entitled *The Scientific Movement in Education*, and in 1935 the American Educational Research Association published an influential book entitled *The Application of Research Findings to Current Educational Practice*. The influence of the scientific movement is seen in the dominant position of educational psychology in the development of educational research, and in the emphasis placed on empirical studies, research design and statistics in training courses for educational researchers.

The achievements of the scientific approach to educational problems should not be underrated, and there is still a contribution to be made by research in this direct way. In addition to the positive effects listed earlier in this chapter, it has helped to establish a more sophisticated approach to curriculum development, in which new materials are pre-tested in 'pilot schools' and modified in the light of experiment, and to evaluation, particularly the evaluation of innovatory programmes which has become almost a new industry in the USA. Also, it must be acknowledged that the demand for useful results and for evidence of impact has had some good effects – for example, in greater attention to dissemination, in increased resources for research and in the beginnings of a collaborative partnership of researchers with teachers and administrators.

Dissemination has been sadly neglected by researchers. In the research world, the number of publications has tended to count for more towards academic status than the quality of the research, or the size of the readership. The mere recording of a conclusion in a thesis or a journal article has been considered an adequate act of publication, and over-zealous efforts to gain publicity are liable to be regarded with disdain. Most serious is the use of technical language in reporting, a convention which safeguards against misinterpretation but which too often restricts understanding to a select group of fellow researchers. The pressure towards utilisation has produced, from some projects at least, a variety of forms of reporting directed at different audiences, and a readiness to follow up by discussion with practitioners. Provision for dissemination is now a legitimate addition to an application for research funding.

Resources for research have increased because of the implicit promise of a return for investment, and the overall standard of research work is undoubtedly much higher now than 20 years ago as a result. The regional laboratories in the USA, the national institutes for educational research in other countries, local centres, advisory services, specialist organisations for testing and computer facilities, training programmes and recruitment have all benefited from the flow of funds.

Research itself has benefited from the discovery that it has much to gain from closer collaboration with practitioners. The Ontario Institute for Studies in Education, to take only one of the many examples, has set up nine field centres which 'link teachers, educators and local agencies to the specialised skills and services offered by Institute staff, and help provide OISE researchers and teachers with knowledge of local conditions' (OISE pamphlet). In collaborative research, objectives are defined by participants and modified in the course of experiments, leading to small but incremental changes in practice. These 'field development studies' are based on a philosophy which 'rejects the mechanistic notion of research as something which is invented in one place and applied somewhere else'. A similar development in evaluation can be illustrated by Patton's book, *Utilization-Focused Evaluation* (1980), which reviewed case studies of 20 projects. His conclusion was:

> The power of evaluation varies directly with the degree to which the findings reduce the uncertainty of action for specific decision-makers . . . (The key to success was that) the guy who was asking the question was the guy who was going to make use of the answer.

All these trends demonstrate the increasing emphasis on the instrumental function of educational research. There is a danger that in a period of economic stringency research funding will be limited to projects which offer an immediate and direct pay-off. If direct impact and acceptance of findings become the criteria for deciding which research is to be supported, we come dangerously close to the situation in which the only research encouraged is that which is compatible with established policy and with popularly accepted assumptions. It is already difficult enough to swim against the tide. Access to schools is unlikely to be granted for projects which are not seen as relevant. Problems are defined in terms of generally accepted perceptions. Results are taken up selectively by the media – and even by journal editors – if they accord with what are seen as current issues. Methodologies which have not been given the formal approval of the research fraternity will have difficulty even in finding a way into the literature. Dalin (1976), reviewing the implementation of educational innovations, suggests that certain factors favour implementation:

> consonance – the degree of fit between the goals of the innovation and the accepted goals of the institution;
> support – the backing given by those in authority;

divisibility – can the innovation be introduced in part?
compatibility – can it be combined with established practice?

while other factors operate against:

centrality – the attempt to change the central norms of the
institution, the displacement caused by the innovation;
complexity – the extent to which changes are far-reaching or the
number of groups affected;
competition – interference from other aspects of the institution;
feasibility – the availability of resources needed.

It is not only in Orwell's 1984 that we should be prepared to question
the growing powers of central authority and special interest groups to
determine our priorities.

Clearly there is a place for both kinds of research in education: the
practically oriented work which elaborates and refines established
policy, and which may indeed, by testing, challenge and modify
accepted practice; and the research which explores alternative frameworks and though not immediately usable may prove to have a greater
or more fundamental impact. It is necessary, however, to recognise
that the impact of research is not necessarily beneficial to educational
practice. For example, the social Darwinism of the early decades of
this century encouraged the view that the lower socio-economic
groups in the population were genetically inferior, and research gave a
degree of credibility and legitimation to the idea. The complexity of
the matter is evident if we review the changes of attitude to learning
and failure to learn over the past hundred years. In the nineteenth
century, a pupil's failure to learn was seen as a moral lapse – due to
failure to put enough into it, to pay attention and to try hard. Research
into educational psychology destroyed that mode of thinking, and
substituted what we can call 'Mode 2'. In the period 1920–1950, a
pupil's failure to learn was explained as due to lack of ability, and
intelligence was a central concept, usually regarded as a fixed quality in
the individual, whether inherited or not. The 'Mode 2' explanation
was not such a substantial step forward as was thought 30 years ago,
for it still saw defects as located in the learner. Research in the 1950s
introduced a 'Mode 3', which explained learning problems in terms of
the social environment of the learner, in terms of deprivation or the
inadequacies of the family or the sub-culture – any source other than
the actual teaching. All these explanations reflect an overemphasis on
'predestination': they are explanations which direct attention away
from the individuals directly concerned in the process, the teacher and
the learner. More recently, research has moved to a 'Mode 4', which
looks for an explanation in the actual teaching, or the context in which

the learning has been arranged, a rather obvious point, most teachers would say, surprisingly neglected, and a more challenging diagnosis of failure to learn. Focus on the actual teaching, both content and method, on the social interactions, and on the process of learning, is a more productive way of thinking about it and of explaining success and failure in learning. This is a reflection of the research of the past decade, which has been concerned more with classroom observation, interaction analysis, cognitive psychology, information processing, memory and a number of related studies which fit together in a promising way to clarify the whole process of teaching and learning.

If this illustration provides a valid analysis, it suggests that research in education stands to gain from a close association with educational practice. Two worlds of educational research may be distinguished, the practical and the theoretical, pure and applied; but we are more likely to maintain a balanced attitude if we can have a foot in both worlds.*

* Parts of this chapter are developed from an address given by the author to the Northern Ireland Council for Educational Research in Belfast in November 1979. The topic is considered more fully in J. Nisbet and P. Broadfoot, *The Impact of Research on Policy and Practice in Education*, Aberdeen University Press, 1980.

10
Political Education and School Organisation

Pat White

In 1979 Michael Rutter and his colleagues introduced a new term into educational discussion – or rather they revived one which had largely dropped out of our active vocabulary: that term is 'ethos'. In the report of their research into the effects of secondary schools on their pupils, *Fifteen Thousand Hours*, ethos is described as a 'set of values, attitudes and behaviours which (are) characteristic of the school as a whole' (Rutter *et al* 1979 p. 179). It is, in other words, what most of us would recognise, particularly when visiting schools, as the 'general feel' or the 'atmosphere' or the 'climate' of a school. But not only does the report by its use of the term confirm us in the belief that it makes sense to talk in this way about institutions having different general atmospheres, it also alerts us to the importance of ethos for academic standards. It is important to note at this point that *Fifteen Thousand Hours* embodies a very particular concept of ethos and a particular measure of academic standards, namely achievements in public examinations, which not everyone would share. One could, therefore, profitably spend some time considering these notions as used by Michael Rutter *et al* and attempting to refine them. For my immediate purposes, however, this is unnecessary. Instead, I want to focus on what I think would be generally agreed to be *one* element prominent in embodying and creating the values, attitudes and behaviour which constitute the ethos of a school, namely its internal organisation, its decision-making arrangements and its style of leadership. I want to explore the relationship of *this* element of school ethos to certain specific educational standards, namely those in political education. The question I am concerned with is: what is the relationship, if any, between the organisation of a school and the quality of political education achieved in that school?

Can the work of Michael Rutter and his colleagues help here? Did the team discover that particular kinds of school organisation were associated with any particular educational outcomes? Unfortunately here we draw a blank. The report says: 'We did not look in any detail at the particular styles of management and leadership which worked best; this is an issue which it is now important to investigate.' (Rutter *et al* 1979 p. 203). So, what does this mean? Must we simply sit and wait for more empirical investigations, perhaps *Rutter Revisited*, before we can pursue the connection between school organisation and the political education of pupils? Undoubtedly more empirical investigation in this area is needed but it could not be sufficient to answer our question. Let me make this point concretely. It seems clear to me that we are not simply interested in the school organisation that produces certain educational results *regardless* of the form that organisation takes. For instance, if we found a school all of whose 15-year-old pupils could converse intelligently about the policies of current cabinet ministers, the recent activities of various pressure groups and the background to the troubles in Northern Ireland – all those things, in other words, which the Hansard Society report tells us a large percentage of 15-year-olds cannot do (Stradling 1977) our initial view of these impressive achievements might be changed if we knew how they had been brought about. If we learned, for instance, that the head publicly pilloried in a suitably ceremonial fashion at end of term assemblies – perhaps on occasion employing stocks made in woodwork classes – those form teachers whose pupils' knowledge of political matters fell below a certain level, then despite the impressive achievements, we might not approve of the organisation which produced them. This is because we make the judgment – independent of any surveys of school organisation – that the organisation of a school must itself come up to certain standards, standards which are not established by empirical investigation but reflect what we think is *desirable* in terms of school organisation.

What might these standards be? If we are to arrive at an intellectually and morally defensible set of standards, we shall need to consider, amongst other things, the important question of what kinds of organisation are appropriate to institutions in a *democratic society*. This will not provide us with an exhaustive account of *all* the standards to which school organisation should ideally conform (e.g. perhaps, standards of efficiency) but it will establish an important set of standards within the whole. To do this, however, will involve coming to some understanding of what might be meant by 'a democratic society'. This is not an easy task but it cannot be avoided if we are to determine what kind of organisation is related to the achievement of high standards in political education.

What is meant then by a 'democratic society'? There is a notion of democracy – what one might call the pessimistic view – that sets out from the premise that most people are either unable or unwilling to participate responsibly in the political decisions in their society. People who take this view point, for instance, to low turn-out at election time and the fact that electors seem to be swayed by clever-clever propaganda techniques rather than coherent argument for or against policies. According to such theorists democracy is purely and simply a *method* for arriving at political decisions. As Schumpeter, perhaps the most well-known exponent of this point of view, puts it, the democratic method is 'that institutional arrangement for arriving at political decisions in which individuals acquire the power to decide by means of a competitive struggle for the people's vote' (Schumpeter 1943 p. 269). In other words, the characteristic of democracy is a *competition for leadership*. There is no role for citizens to participate in *decision-making* at any level, because Schumpeter holds that 'the electoral mass is incapable of action other than a stampede'. The only role for citizens is to vote, when required, and so keep the leadership competition going. It is a system, therefore, which can comfortably accommodate a large amount of political apathy and/or ignorance amongst its citizens.

This, however, is a curious argument for democracy which attempts to argue from an alleged *fact* about the political interest and abilities of citizens in particular societies to the *value judgment* that therefore such dismal political creatures should have a certain kind of arrangement for making political decisions. Suppose, however, interest can be aroused and abilities sharpened by education, what kind of political set-up would be appropriate then? I would say a *democratic* one, but clearly in saying this I am relying on a *different* conception of democracy and one which, I would argue, is more soundly based than Schumpeter's.

Let me outline this alternative conception. We can start with the so-called democratic method, or the machinery of democracy – universal suffrage, majority voting, periodic elections, official opposition, etc. Machinery is by definition a means (e.g. a washing machine is one way of washing clothes) and democratic machinery is in fact no exception, it is a means to certain ends. The ends in this case are certain values which the machinery is designed to institutionalise. For instance, universal suffrage is a familiar piece of democratic machinery and it attempts to enshrine the values of justice, consideration of interests and the ideal of moral agency. The rationale for universal suffrage in terms of these values is that everyone's interests matter and matter equally and as a moral agent each must have the same opportunity to bring his point of view to the decision-makers' attention. Periodic elections and limited terms of office and a legal opposition are further pieces of machinery to attempt to ensure that all interests are conscientiously regarded and to enable the individual to act as a responsible moral agent and call the government to account for acts done with his authority.

Here we have then an altogether different conception of democratic government which sees it as intelligible only as the embodiment of certain moral values. An autonomous moral agent who accepts the need for some political authority can only accept one which recognises the autonomy of himself and his fellow-citizens as moral agents and embodies in its institutions the moral principles to which he and they are committed. This conception of democracy, through its institutional machinery, attempts to take moral autonomy seriously. It is in this way that a society of people aspiring to be morally autonomous agents must order their political life.

Two concluding points should be made regarding this alternative conception of democracy. First, the empirical democracies of the real world as they exist about us – even the best of them – will not of course perfectly embody in their machinery the moral principles which underlie them. This is for a variety of reasons. For a start devising or adapting machinery to enshrine certain values is no easy matter (What *is* the best system, first-past-the-post or PR?) and secondly, moral agents have their weak moments and do not always act within the spirit of the institutions. Secondly, and very importantly, this conception of democracy puts demands for *participation* and *power-sharing* into perspective. On this view the current interest in grass-roots participation in all kinds of political, social and economic set-ups is not to be dismissed as a fad, the latest trendy Sunday supplement thing. 'Industrial democracy', for instance, is not, on this view, a frill, an optional extra, it is an integral part of the understanding of what it is for a society to be a democracy. Just as moral principles cannot be hived off only for use amongst friends and relatives, equally they cannot be restricted in their application only to governmental institutions. They must get application in the authority structures of the work-place too. On this view, with its moral insistence that authority structures must be accommodated to the conception of the individual as an autonomous moral agent, the *presumption* must be in favour of direct participation in decision-making in *any* organisation unless good reasons can be given as to why that would be inappropriate, unworkable, etc. Such reasons, if operative, must always be kept under review, lest conditions should change in such a way as to make them inapplicable.

The Schumpeter conception of democracy, which gives citizens the chance to play a minimal part in the periodic selection of leaders, does not make intellectual or moral sense – the criticisms which can be made of it have only been very briefly indicated here.[1] The only conception of democracy which is rationally defensible is the conception which sees it as the kind of political arrangement which autonomous moral agents can find tolerable. It is the implications of this conception of democracy which I wish to pursue for school organisation and for political education.

School organisation as it affects non-pupils

First, let me say something about the implications of school organisation as its affects non-pupils, e.g. head, staff, helpers, dinner
supervisors, etc. This may seem remote from the question of the pupils'
political education but there is an important connection which I will
develop in a moment.

Clearly, given the conception of democracy I have just outlined, the
organisation of the school must be of such a sort that it recognises in its
decision-making arrangements the moral autonomy of those employed
in it. In saying this I am not arguing of course for a mini-parliament
with voting, opposition parties and so on. As I have been stressing,
democratic machinery is to be seen as a means of institutionalising
moral values. What machinery is appropriate will be different for
different contexts. All that is concretely implied by saying, in my
sense, that the organisation should be democratic is that all those
employed in school – head, teaching staff, secretaries, dinner supervisors, caretakers, helpers, etc. – should participate in decisions which
affect their work and should be accountable to other members of the
institution for their delegated responsibilities in the running of the
institution. I am not of course presupposing here that all decisions
affecting the running of the school should be made by those within the
institution. In a properly democratic society decisions about the shape
and structure of the curriculum will be made by democratic bodies
outside the school on behalf of the community. To argue this through
in detail now would take me too far away from the topic in hand[2]. But,
briefly, the reasons for locating overall control of the curriculum with
such bodies is that curricular decisions ultimately affect the nature of a
society. To see the force of this point compare, on the one hand, a
society in which there is a common curriculum to 16, say, with a
society where there is one curriculum for an elite selected at an early
age and another, quite different one, for the rest of the population.
They are likely to be societies of a very different character. This
illustrates the point that curricular decisions are moral and political
decisions about the kind of society those making them judge ought to
develop. This being the case, they are not the sorts of decisions which
can be made by professional experts, but the kind of decisions which
all members of a community, as moral agents, have a right and a
responsibility to make. This is not to say that such bodies should lay
down syllabus details to be followed in every particular in every school
in the land but only that it is their responsibility to determine the broad
shape and scope of the curriculum. However, when this division
between what is to be decided within the institution and what outside
has itself been democratically made, then the internal decision should
be made democratically, i.e. with due regard to the moral autonomy of
all members of the institution.

The *general* reason for this should be clear. I have argued already that if a society is to be a through-and-through democracy rather than simply a society with a democratically elected government then authority structures in the work-place too must take account of the moral autonomy of their employees. There is, however, a *particular* reason why authority structures in schools must be democratic in this sense. This is connected with certain educational standards which in a democratic society we must be helping our pupils to achieve. What I have in mind are the standards involved in *political education*.

The enterprise of political education in a democratic society needs little in the way of elaborate justification. If one accepts that democracy is a desirable form of government – either because it embodies a conception of the individual as a moral agent or for some other reason – and if one accepts too that democrats are not born but made, then it follows that one of our aims in bringing up our children must be to prepare them to live as democrats in a democratic society. That said, of course, there still remains the question of what part of the task of political education, if any, should be undertaken by the *school*. Clearly, educational aims can be realised by agencies other than the school. Should that be the case with political education? Should it be left to other agencies – the media, political parties, etc? Here I would accept that there may be some room for debate over what precise parts of political education should be the responsibility of the school. There is however one aspect of political education about which we have no choice. Any school must have *some* kind of organisation, some procedures for making decisions among its employees. (For instance, some things may be decided at staff meetings, some may be decided by the head, some decisions may be left to individuals.) A fair proportion of these decision-making procedures, in turn, are bound to be known to most pupils. There is no way in which all the procedures could be secret or confidential. Indeed it would not cross anyone's mind in most schools to attempt to keep them so. It follows, therefore, that as well as learning their French, maths, environmental studies and so on, pupils are also learning how their particular school is run. They are developing conceptions of authority, power, what it is to be responsible for something, what are considered appropriate decision-making procedures and so on. What I am suggesting is that if we are to provide children with a political education of an appropriate standard, we have to be sure that we can defend our decision-making procedures and the roles and statuses we assign to different members of the institution as the ones most suitable for a school in a democratic society. In this connection, for instance, we may need radically to revise a common British conception of the school head. Is it appropriate for the head of an educational institution to be the (often) unchallengeable determiner of both major educational policies within the school as well as the details of the dress of its members? Could the role of head, as often presently conceived, be replaced by administrators covering some of his functions and, say, a school's council covering others?

If you feel inclined to doubt what I have said about the pupils' knowledge of the school organisation, you might like to find ways of asking pupils about the organisation of their school and who decides what, etc. In my experience even infants' school children give a pretty accurate picture of the way things are organisationally. That being so, obviously the important thing is that it should be a defensible picture. In so far as pupils are getting a picture of an indefensible authoritarianism they are being faced with a worrying inconsistency. There is *talk* of democratic ideals, practices, etc. but they *see* that important institutions in society are actually being run on anti-democratic lines. A political education which involves these unexplained contradictions and inconsistencies is clearly falling short. It is not coming up to the necessary standards.

It is important not to underestimate the educative influence of a well-run democratically organised school. The point here is essentially that made by R.B. Haldane about the Civil Service in 1923 in his Presidential address to the Institute of Public Administration. There he says:

> It is not only by rendering highly skilled service to the public in dealing with administrative problems and questions, even of policy, that the civil servant of the future may serve the public. The Civil Service, if itself highly educated, may become one of the greatest educative influences in the general community. It may set a high example and may teach lessons which will have far-reaching influence. I believe in its own interests, not less than in those of the State, it is well that it should set this ideal before itself as one which is of immense practical importance in its tendency to raise the standards in business and in life generally of those with whom it will have to be dealing constantly.[3]

The same might be said of the day-to-day dealings of all the staff – teachers, secretaries, dinner supervisors, caretakers – in a school.

Pupil participation in school organisation

There are various ways of viewing participation by pupils in the organisation of their schools. One could argue for it on instrumental grounds – if pupils are involved in their school organisation, it improves their school work – or one might argue for it on grounds of children's rights. In contrast, I would argue for participation as a necessary part of children's political education in a society like ours which aspires to be a through-and-through democracy. Of course, even if you accept that experience in the running of democratic institutions is a necessary part of political education – and I shall give reasons in a moment for thinking that it is – you might argue that children could get it elsewhere, in voluntary organisations like youth clubs, sports clubs, Scouts, Guides and so on. There is room for debate over precisely what aspects of political education should be the responsibility of the school. Indeed, it could well be the case in a society rather differently organised from our own that children would get this experience in voluntary organisations. However, in our society, where education is compulsory up to 16 – two years before people are expected to participate responsibly in national politics – but where not every child belongs to a voluntary organisation, there is a strong case for pupils getting their experience of participation in running an institution, in school.

Now, if one accepts that one important place for such participation is the *school*, this still leaves the question: is participation in the running of democratic organisations a *necessary* part of political education? At this point it is important to recall again the conception of democracy developed earlier. Then I argued that the presumption in all authority structures must be in favour of direct participation in decision-making unless good reasons can be found to the contrary. From that it follows that political education must prepare people for such participation in later life. This gives us four reasons why the *experience* of participation is an essential part of political education.

1   The first is the crucial one. It relates to the acquisition of political attitudes, like for instance attitudes to authorities, power, working with others and so on. The point about attitudes – familiar from discussion about moral attitudes – is that people do not acquire them overnight. Attitudes develop, they build up. None of us were silly unreasonable children until some magic age at which we suddenly became reasonable, considerate, etc. It is the same with the kind of political attitudes we want to encourage in democratic citizens. People can acquire all sorts of knowledge *about* democracy. They can learn *that* citizens should be, for instance, appropriately critical of authorities, tolerant of other viewpoints, willing to have their mistakes pointed out and to rectify them especially if they are wielding power and so on, but they need political *experience* to *learn how* to do these things in context. For instance, were you to say to a 12-year-old before a meeting 'If we're going to get through all the agenda items before 1 p.m. I think you will need to be a fairly firm chairperson. Don't stand for any long, irrelevant contributions', she would be unable to take your advice, even if she wants to, unless she has had some experience of attending meetings, having her attention drawn to the way in which

they are chaired and having already had some experience of chairing meetings herself. She has to know *how* to be firm without being autocratic and actually be *able* to do it – judge the right moment to intervene in an overlong contribution and find the right form of words with which to do it on this particular occasion – and this, given human beings as they are, is unlikely to be possible unless she has had the opportunity to try, and been advised and corrected on the job. It is my claim that in our society it is the school par excellence which can provide such carefully guided practice in participation in decision-making, if it shapes its organisation with that end in mind. The remaining three points follow from this one.

2 This kind of experience of decision-making would provide a valuable model of small-scale political organisation, often lacking in the kind of political education which concentrates on national politics and thus gives people the impression that politics begins and ends with the activities of central government. Such school experience could be useful in connection with consumer groups, residents' associations, shop-floor committees, etc. making them more accessible to people who might otherwise see them as self-help associations for the informed and socially assured only. The aim of providing such experience in school would be to allow people to develop the abilities and social confidence to permit them to function in such groups when they judged this to be appropriate.

3 Guided experience of decision-making in school would also provide a yardstick against which to measure in due course the authority structure of the work-place and would enable people to make some contribution to the organisation of work-places on democratic lines (see White 1979).

4 Properly planned, school experience in decision-making, as an integral part of political education, should provide opportunities for everyone to feel that he can be politically effective, can contribute to decision-making. This would constitute a not insignificant contribution to the struggle against sexism and racism in our society. In addition it would concretely illustrate ways of life in business, public administration and so on which would give people some understanding of jobs which might otherwise remain closed books to them. Again, this would be an attempt, if only a small one, to even up the job opportunities for different sections of the population.

Three objections

The above arguments will by no means convince everyone. Let me try and deal with what seem to me to be three important objections. Before I consider these, however, there are two qualifications to be made without which there could be some misunderstanding of the position argued here. First, I am not concerned to determine precisely *what* children should and should not decide and at *what* ages. For reasons already explained, they will not be taking decisions about the shape and structure of the whole curriculum. Beyond that it is not possible to go further here than the general principle that the presumption must be in favour of direct participation in decision-making unless good reasons can be given as to why that is inappropriate. The detailed work on exactly how children can contribute to decision-making in their schools must necessarily be done by others, much of it in context to take into account the details of local conditions. Secondly, what I have outlined is certainly not to be taken as constituting the whole of political education. Elsewhere I have attempted to sketch what political education in general might cover, including, for instance, the explicit development of conceptual frameworks, the analysis of argument, understanding of relevant historical developments as well as some understanding of the different forms of knowledge (see White 1977). The kind of experience in decision-making argued for, therefore, is only one part, although an important part, of the whole task of political education. I am not saying that such necessary experience is sufficient for an adequate political education. Now the objections.

Firstly, it might be argued that this treatment neglects the obvious point that politics is about power, that '. . . political skills, whether exercised within a democratic framework or not, are predominantly those that enable one to impose one's own views on others, and get one's own policy or one as like it as possible – whether or not one regards it as in the best interests of all concerned – translated into corporate action. . . . The love of power, the competition of rival factions – surely these things are absolutely typical, indeed of the essence of any political activity'. Therefore, the argument goes on, democratic participation in schools is likely 'to prematurely whet the appetite for power and intrigue' (Dunlop 1979 pp. 45–46).

In one particular this is right. Any politics is about power in that the decisions made necessarily affect people's lives and interests, crucially or trivially. In this sense decision-makers may be said to exercise power over others, more obviously, for example, in compelling them to pay taxes, less obviously, perhaps, in determining what gets on to the political agenda.[4] This is a fundamental point which no-one involved in decision-making should lose sight of. Indeed, in the kind of experience of decision-making in schools I have been advocating the force of this point can be brought home to every single pupil since, if the organisation is planned intelligently, everyone will, at some point, be involved in decision-making and therefore in wielding power. Every pupil can therefore be made aware of the fact that he is morally responsible for the decisions to which he contributes. Far from neglecting the point that politics is about power, my argument in favour of experience in decision-making actually *emphasises* that point and its necessarily moral implications.

On the other hand, I would reject the view expressed above that political skills in a democracy must necessarily be exercised with the purpose of imposing one's views on others. Of course in organisations which claim to be democratic this can happen – no institution is proof against human frailty – but there is no reason to regard it as a *necessary* part of political life. One of the functions of the school experience of decision-making would be to help pupils to make judgments about the nature of sectional interests and the common interest and their mutual relationship. These distinctions and judgments are among the most difficult in politics but there is no reason why a pupil should not slowly build up some understanding in this area over time so that at least he is not limited to the simplistic view that politics can be no more than a sophisticated means of getting your own way. Rather, he is able both to consider and aspire to a conception of politics which sees its task as attempting to order people's lives together so as to allow individuals to flourish in a fair and fraternal society. Furthermore, the experience of participation can help him to acquire the habits of working within the conception of politics to which he aspires. Thus the educative force of the school ethos can help him to acquire habits and intellectual conceptions *pari passu*. My point is, very emphatically, that there is no reason why the school ethos should necessarily emphasise power-seeking, thus whetting the appetite for power, rather than a concern to do what is right in the context of the whole community.

The second worry about pupils' participation in school organisation is that it may constitute a form of indoctrination or, at least, an undesirable kind of moulding. In other words, there may be openness at the level of formal political education – all kinds of possible forms of political organisation may be discussed – but the structure of the school will carry a determinate message: *this* is how an institution should be organised.

This is undeniably how things must be. As I have argued elsewhere (White 1979), however, one can escape the charge of moulding pupils' views of democracy through the structure of the school by encouraging them to appreciate this very problem. As part of pupils' political education one must ensure that they appreciate that the school has to have some decision-making structure. They must then come to understand the particular one which has been devised for their school, whatever form it takes, and finally they must grasp that as a democratic structure it is not fixed for all time. It can be changed in all kinds of ways.

A third kind of objection might be levelled at the proposals here, not in principle but as a practical possibility. It might be argued that although it would be desirable to have schools run democratically it is not possible because teachers, never mind dinner supervisors, caretakers and so on, would not be able to cope with the demands it would make on them. Teachers, as well as non-teaching staff, might find it difficult to cope with the experience of being questioned by children, having to justify school policies and so on. They might also find it hard to give pupils responsibilities for which the pupils would be accountable. Something of this sort might well be true and in the short-term at least this has two interesting implications. First, it suggests that people seeking employment in schools, in any capacity, might have to give evidence of their willingness and ability to work within such a democratic system. In other words, if we are to take these proposals seriously, superb teaching qualifications or fast typing speeds and efficient office practice will not be sufficient for someone who seeks employment as a teacher or a secretary in a school. How the evidence of willingness to work within a democratic system is to be obtained raises questions, but if such a system is to be introduced this is one problem which will have to be tackled. Secondly, there could be training schemes for school staffs,[5] probably of a fairly practical workshop nature, although – and this goes back to the first point – for a person to be considered for such a scheme he would have to want to work within a democratic framework. These are stringent demands but necessary ones if the school is fully to realise its potential influence in creating an ethos which will foster democratic habits in its pupils.

Let me turn finally from objections to something – and something particularly relevant to the theme of this book – on which there seems to be general agreement. I have not argued that children should 'decide everything' as part of their political education in schools and neither do other writers in this area, who express similar views to those here.[6] Equally, neither do critics of these views suggest that children should decide nothing:

> I should not like to leave the impression that I consider all kinds of pupil participation in decision-making undesirable in schools. There are in any case . . . various *ways* of involving pupils and various *degrees* to which they can be involved (Dunlop 1979 p. 53).

I will not engage in futurology and predict what those concerned with political education will be doing in the 1980s and 1990s. I only urge that what we ought to be doing is determining in a non-arbitrary, rationally defensible way how we ought to be using the organisation of the school as part of political education. Given that there is general agreement that we can and should do so to some *degree* and in *some* areas, let us give some priority to determining *how* and to *what* degree and in *what* areas.

Notes

1 For fuller critical discussion see Pateman (1970).
2 For a more detailed exposition of this view see White (1976).
3 Quoted by Thomas (1978 p. 159).
4 For a full discussion of the nature of political power, see Lukes (1974).
5 I have previously argued that all teachers need some preparation for their work in political education (White 1977). It now seems to me that all school staff may need the opportunity for some kind of training for their responsibilities in developing and maintaining the democratic framework of their instutitions.
6 See, e.g., Bridges (1978).

11
Problems of School Government

D.A. Howell

'Who should control the schools?' has been a question for debate ever since the emergence of a publicly provided system of education over a century ago. Consideration of the rights and responsibilities of central government and local education authorities, the teachers, children and their parents, and other beneficiaries in the control of the education system, raises questions of great philosophical, political and educational importance, which would need a book or more to do them justice. In this essay we discuss the government of schools within the context of the system as it is, and take more or less for granted the current distribution of responsibilities as between the Department of Education and Science and the Local Education Authorities, while trying to appreciate those developments which appear to be of increasing and long term significance. Several developments, to be noticed below, have steadily widened the area of debate about school government, so that it must be considered now in a context which would have appeared unfamiliar, and possibly alien, ten years ago.

The most obvious of these developments has been the challenge mounted to traditional concepts of teacher accountability by those concerned (with what degree of justice we do not say) to monitor performance throughout the education system and within the schools, and to ensure the maintenance of standards acceptable in the outside world. Challenges, not always compatible with each other, have been pressed for example by parental interests, by employers, by community groups and self-proclaimed guardians of the public interest and educational standards. The argument about the limits of teacher autonomy and the nature of their accountability clearly has a long way to run yet, not least because of the emergence of a more political perspective in thinking about school government.

Until fairly recently, questions relating to school government had been considered in traditional administrative terms, with existing political institutions and relationships taken for granted. The basic precepts of the 1944 Education Act went unchallenged. Debate, whether on the composition or functions of governing bodies, was presented in terms of marginal adjustment, such as the appropriate number of places to be allocated to local councillors, or the precise nature of governors' share in the appointment of teaching staff. Areas of greater controversy were left in comfortable obscurity, on the arguments that the system doesn't matter, it's the personalities that count; that there was no real conflict of interest between parties of goodwill; and that current practices and attitudes were flexible enough to accommodate all the strains to which they might be subject.

Nevertheless, a more political approach to school government has made itself felt at several levels. At one level, the study of educational administration deriving ultimately from systems analysis is concerned with the survival and adaptability of political systems and sub-systems, among which LEAs are certainly to be included. The activities of school governing bodies may well be susceptible of analysis in similar terms, as constituents of the larger system. The identification of sources of power, its exercise and distribution are other relevant concepts although they do not figure overmuch in most studies of local government or educational administrators: nor, it must be said, do processes for the resolution of conflict. New ideas about participation in local government have led to an interest in the possibility of community-based services, more open recruitment to controlling bodies, and greater responsiveness to local groups, among whom previous assumptions about consensus and commitment can no longer be taken for granted.

Demands for a greater and more detailed lay oversight of curriculum can no longer be dismissed as tiresome irrelevance or outrageous invasions of professional autonomy; and however vague the concept of teacher accountability may be, the debate stimulated by the Taylor Report *A New Partnership for our Schools* still has to run its course. In a very real sense then, questions about the functions or composition of school governing bodies have to be answered with direct reference to the basic question 'Who should control the schools?' In this chapter we cannot even hope to refer to all the broader educational, philosophical or sociological implications; we suggest rather how, in the light of emerging preoccupations and our own analysis, it might be helpful for all those concerned, whether as practitioners, students or recipients, to approach the question of school government. We also indicate a number of ambiguities and dilemmas which are a necessary, if at times irritating, feature of any dynamic political system. Before doing this, however, some time must be given to an account of the development of the present system; if only to indicate the great influence which the provisions of the 1944 Act still have on current attitudes and practices.

The scheme of 1944

The formal system remains in essentials that prescribed by the 1944

Education Act. The modifications made in the 1980 Education Act,* while compelling some LEAs to modify their existing practice, do not signify any great change in official thought about school government. The relevant provisions of the 1944 Act attracted relatively little attention and less opposition during their passage through Parliament.[1] In essentials, every primary or secondary school, whether county or voluntary, should have a body of managers or governors respectively. The local authority was to draw up rules of management for primary schools, and articles of government for secondary schools;[2] rules and articles for voluntary schools[3] were to be approved by the Ministry. An attempt was made to secure a place for parents on managing and governing bodies; but the government, although sympathetic to the idea, thought that this was a matter best left for the local education authorities.

The functions to be exercised by governors were discussed in a Command Paper, and then amplified in model articles subsequently issued for the guidance of LEAs by the Ministry. In financial matters, governors were to prepare estimates on the school's expenditure and submit them to the LEA. Jointly with the LEA, governors were responsible for the appointment of heads. Appointments of assistant staff should be made by governors in consultation with the head, subject to confirmation by the LEA. Teaching staff could be dismissed on the initiative either of the governors or the LEA, but the latter must always have the last word. Non-teaching staff should be appointed in practice by the governors on the advice of the head. In the section dealing with governors' oversight of the school the LEA was given the right to settle the general educational character of the school and its place in the local system; subject thereto, the governors were to have the general direction of conduct and curriculum, while the head was to control the internal organisation, management and discipline of the school, and also to have the power of suspending pupils, subject to a report being made forthwith to the governors and the authority.

All proposals and reports affecting the conduct and curriculum of the school should be made available to the governing body as long as possible beforehand. The head should be entitled to attend throughout all governors' meetings except for good cause. There should be full consultation at all times between the head and the chairman of governors; free co-operation and consultation between the head and chief education officer (CEO) on matters affecting the welfare of the school; and suitable arrangements for the teaching staff to submit their

---

* These prescribed that each governing body should have at least two parent governors and – except in the smallest schools – at least two teacher governors; that the head should be a governor except when he elects otherwise; and that if LEAs proposed to group more than one school under one governing body they must seek the Secretary of State's approval except when they proposed to group two primary schools.

proposals to the governing body through the head. The articles, which were in every case to be approved by the Minister, had the specific object of determining the functions to be exercised by the LEA, the governors and the head. However the instrument of government, which specified the composition and the treatment of the governing body, and the number of schools (if any) to be grouped, were entirely at the discretion of the authority.

Parity of esteem, one of the main aims of the 1944 Act (Barnard 1969 pp. 301–303) was to be secured by a variety of expedients, some of which may now strike us as faintly comic; W. Taylor's study *The Secondary Modern School* refers *inter alia* to 'school uniforms, caps and blazers . . . good carriage and tidy appearance' as being seen as contributory to such parity.[4] Others saw the establishment of a separate governing body for each secondary modern school, along the lines of the bodies established for county secondary (grammar) schools after the 1902 Education Act, as further tangible evidence of such parity of esteem. Several speakers in the House of Commons debate saw the establishment of governing bodies as helping to bridge the gap between independent and publicly provided schools, by making available on a wider scale the most desirable features found in the government of the former, and thus insulating to some extent the publicly provided schools from the alleged disadvantages of direct public control or interference (Baron and Howell 1974 p. 32).

LEAs and the operation of the 1944 scheme

In practice, LEAs had a completely free hand in devising their schemes of school government, in spite of the Ministry's need to approve the articles for county secondary schools and all voluntary schools.

By no means all LEAs were enthusiastic about governing bodies and the roles they might play. In many urban authorities, particularly those usually under Labour control, there was a suspicion that they might take politically embarrassing decisions for the majority party, and that they detracted from the primacy of the elected member in decision-making. They were held to be administratively expensive and time-wasting. There was alleged to be a shortage of suitable people to serve as governors; untutored interference by a lay body in the running of schools was a very real danger. To some extent these criticisms stemmed from deeply rooted political attitudes; equally strong traditions of active school management by lay bodies led other urban authorities (including the largest of all, the London County Council and its successor, the Inner London Education Authority) to develop what they claimed to be a vigorous and effective system. In some urban authorities, the existence of a large voluntary sector, where each Anglican or Roman Catholic school had its own statutory managing or governing body, stimulated the argument that county schools were entitled to a similar degree of esteem and administrative quasi-independence. In the shire counties generally, as in a minority of the former county boroughs, the potential, and indeed the actual, effectiveness of a separate governing body for each school was more or less taken for granted. (Many of those authorities were under the perpetual control of Conservatives or Independents, who generally had a more relaxed attitude to independent and possibly awkward action by governing bodies. The sheer size of the authority made it plausible to maintain that governing bodies had a real job to do.)

To judge by the results of a national enquiry carried out in the late 1960s, heads generally gave qualified approval to governing bodies (Baron and Howell 1974 pp. 84–94, 131–136). Those in LEAs where the Education Committee acted as the governing body for all schools, or where several schools were grouped under one body, thought they would benefit from having their own. Those with their own governors were on the whole glad to have them. The main drawbacks to be found were that the composition was too politically based, with members turned out after each election, irrespective of their contribution, and that the LEA did not consult governors or listen to them enough. However, if heads made an attempt to educate their governors, they could be very useful allies, and do a lot to help the school in relation to the authority. In spite of misgivings about the calibre or objectivity of parents, heads thought they were at least positively committed to the school, and they were often the youngest members of the governing body. Teacher representation was almost unheard of, heads regarded themselves as entirely adequate spokesmen for their staff, while the very idea of pupil participation would have seemed bizarre, if not outrageous.

An assessment of the 1944 scheme

The conventional wisdom on governing bodies could be summed up as follows. They had a useful part in the administration of education by providing a body of support and advice to the school (which heads were prone to identify with support for themselves); they were interested but did not interfere in the curriculum; they could exert influence on the LEA on behalf of the school, particularly if one or more councillors were found among their ranks; and they could develop a link between school and the community it served. These activities were more important than the traditional 'managerial' functions, which could be classified as (a) crucial but occasional, such as the appointment of a head, or being involved in the suspension of a pupil or the dismissal of a member of staff, (b) minor administrative activity, often superseded by a more centralised LEA practice, such as preparing an annual estimate of expenditure, or appointing assistant staff or a schoolkeeper, and (c) inspectorial activities often deriving explicitly from the very early days of the LEA or even its forerunner, the School Board – inspecting the fabric of the building, checking the punishment book, 'seeing that the schoolkeeper exercises due economy in the use of fuel and cleaning materials'. In the performance of all their varied roles, political, psychological or managerial, governors were implicitly working as one with the LEA and the head for the good of the school.

Sceptics doubted whether there was any real justification for schemes of government which could be expensive, time-consuming, irritating and essentially fruitless (Byrne 1974 p. 178). There was a sense in which the governors were a fifth wheel on the coach. They were essentially reactive bodies (and quite often reactionary) in relation to initiatives which were taken on behalf of the school either by the head or the LEA. Their direct influence on the LEA was hard to identify, and schools anyway had their own well-developed channels of communication with the authority. Where a CEO claimed to be able to get to any of his schools within 20 minutes, there was no need for intervention by a third party. The political subordination in many areas of governing bodies to the education committee and to the party line made them unlikely to speak out against established policy. They could not be regarded as significant partners in the local educational system.

Reappraising school government – a political approach

As long as debate about governing bodies was conducted on the above lines, with a general assumption that they functioned almost entirely as agents of routine administration or resolvers of minor crises, and should be assessed in that same context, the champions of governing bodies had a hard job showing sceptics that the system was all worth while. It was hardly enough, for example, to point out that tens of thousands of lay people were brought into the local administration of education, if their involvement was as intermittent and peripheral as some critics claimed. However, several general developments and specific issues in recent years have brought home the need to consider governing bodies in an altogether broader context. These features have led to a major reappraisal of governing bodies, the implications of which cannot be ignored in any discussion of the central question 'Who should control our schools?'

Several political scientists and administrative theorists have used a systems analysis approach for the study of local government, and have developed a view of local authorities as miniature political systems, able to make authoritative allocations of value within their society, and operating within, and adapting to, an environment comprising the main political system[5]. How far local authorities operate as open or closed systems does not concern us here; whether open, half-open or closed, they undoubtedly meet the requirements of political systems, with a substantial degree of autonomy in their operations (Dearlove 1973 p. 231, Jennings 1977 ch. 7, Stanyer 1976 pp. 59–64). Within the local authority the education service can be envisaged as a major political sub-system, of which schools are individual constituents. Schools receive demands from other sub-systems, such as other schools, examining boards, or the local community. These demands are reduced and converted into outputs in a fashion which enables schools to maintain themselves successfully as organisations while adapting themselves to these outside pressures. The schools' outputs, which comprise the intended consequences and the less intended but equally important outcomes, generate positive or negative feedback, which produces fresh stresses on the schools, or on occasion reinforces them, through the mechanism of feedback response.

Where, on this interpretation, do governing bodies fit it?[6] They can be seen as an important element in the feedback response mechanism, generating positive or negative feedback, and either producing support for the school, or by threatening to withdraw support, causing it to make some modification. Governors' claims to act as a source of feedback are reinforced by their connection with other sub-systems which interact with the schools and which form part of their total environment. Governors can also act as demand regulators, protecting schools from excessive or unwanted stress. There is no reason why schools should feel compelled to adapt themselves to every instance of negative feedback; to argue that they need to show themselves responsive is a long way from claiming that they should simply cave in. If feedback is to be positive rather than negative, and transmitted effectively in the form of external demands acceptable to schools, then it has to be managed. Governors can help to transform feedback so as to produce the most favourable interaction with the school's environment.

Governing bodies and the exercise of power

When discussing LEAs as political systems or sub-systems, one must ask where effective power lies, and how it is exercised. What powers do governing bodies possess in relation to schools and the LEA? What evidence is there that governing bodies have their own areas of political operation, and that their exercise of formal powers influences the subsequent course of events? The legal provisions, in indicating the general duties and responsibilities of LEAs, governors and schools leave a number of important issues unresolved, not least because so few cases involving governors' duties or powers have been the subject of legal scrutiny.[7] These legal provisions, moreover, do not give any specific guidance on disputed issues. The LEA has the overriding responsibility for providing an efficient education service; and governors discharge their responsibilities subject to those of the LEA, and, at least in the model articles, heads discharge their subjects to those of the governors. Many LEAs, however, have regarded this degree of formal teacher subjection as unacceptable, and have reduced or eliminated it from their schemes of government. LEAs also appoint directly a majority of governors, and are free not to reappoint at the end of the normal period of office. During their normal four-year period, governors can be removed only for non-attendance or for falling under one of the statutory provisions against holding public office, such as bankruptcy or mental illness.

Conventionally, governing bodies are regarded as partners in the local education system, working with the LEA and the head for the good of the school. As partners, governing bodies 'know their place'; they subscribe to the dominant consensus within the LEA, even when they feel compelled to intervene forcefully against either the LEA or the school. For their part, LEAs urge heads to cultivate their governors and to exploit such talent as they may possess for the benefit of their school. LEAs also treat governors as full partners when they apply the doctrine of anticipated reactions, consulting or informing governors about forthcoming policy or administrative issues. Such conduct tends to diminish conflict and reinforce support for the local system; and if LEAs take governing bodies seriously, and try to accommodate their views, then spectacular examples of successful intervention by unsatisfied governing bodies will be relatively uncommon. However, one would not be justified in concluding that in these circumstances governors' intervention is irrelevant, and will make no real difference.[8] Governors remain a potential source of conflict with the LEA or the school. Their established period of office is sufficient to make them more than a temporary nuisance. Their political links enable local dissatisfaction to be brought to the notice of the controllers of the system, and for controversial issues to be resolved at the highest levels, as the following cases show.

1 *William Tyndale School.* The most celebrated instance of governors using their full powers in relation to both the head and the LEA is the affair of the William Tyndale Junior School in North London, during 1973/75.[9] The governors became increasingly dissatisfied with the educational regime followed by most of the teaching staff; they found the teachers completely unresponsive, and the LEA indifferent. For their part, the teachers regarded the governors' concern as an impertinent intrusion on their own sphere of autonomy. Conflict became open, and the governors resorted to unorthodox measures to force the LEA to intervene. After arguing for a long time that the differences between governors and teachers were none of its business,

but that a school regime was essentially a matter for the head, the LEA intervened officially by holding a partial inspection of both the junior and the infant school (which was separately housed but on the same premises). The junior school teachers refused to co-operate and walked out on strike. Finally, the LEA appointed a lawyer to carry out an independent enquiry into the teaching, organisation and management of both junior and infant schools.

His report, which was published in July 1976, showed – although its findings do not carry the weight of a formal judicial pronouncement – that LEAs have an overriding power to give general directions about the running of the school, and that governors' general oversight of the school necessarily involves scrutinising and enquiring about the curriculum. The central issue was not about the merits or demerits of the school regime, but about the limitations of teacher autonomy, the legitimacy of governors' intervention, and the duties of the LEA – in short the control of education. For the record, the report allocated responsibility and blame in an even-handed fashion, acknowledging that the governors, acting in the interests of the children, had some excuse for acting unconstitutionally. Eventually the striking teachers were dismissed for indiscipline (the head and senior teacher being also technically demoted for inefficiency). The two schools were re-organised as one, under the headship of the former Infants School head; a new governing body was constituted for the reorganised school, most of the existing governors resigning in the interests of giving the school a fresh start.

2 *The Headship of Highbury Grove*.[10] Two further examples illustrate, if in a less dramatic way, what happens when governors dig their heels in. In 1974 the staunchly traditionalist head of Highbury Grove School in North London resigned on election to Parliament. The governors had strong ideas as to the kind of head they wished to see appointed, namely someone who could be guaranteed to carry on the traditions of his predecessor. So, too, did the LEA, who apparently favoured someone who would do precisely the reverse. The procedure was for the chairman of governors to prepare a short list together with the LEA's officers. The governors would interview the short-listed candidates (with a senior officer from the LEA present as adviser) and submit the names of not less than three candidates, with a possible recommendation for appointment, to the LEA. The final selection would be made by a panel of LEA members, the chairman of governors being present but not voting.

There were several opportunities for conflict, all of which were exploited. The governors did not like some of the names proposed for short-list, and pressed the claims of an internal candidate with limited experience of senior management in school. The LEA insisted on the original short-list. The governors refused to interview the candidates who had already been called to the school. A fresh short-list was then compiled, with the one internal candidate added. The governors put forward his name alone to the authority, suspecting that the authority would prefer to appoint one of the rivals if three names were put forward. The authority refused to accept the governors' proposal, and apparently contemplated making the appointment without the co-operation of the governors. The governors protested that such a step would invalidate the procedure, and that they would have no confidence in an appointment thus made. Eventually, the LEA gave way, and the governors' internal candidate was appointed by the usual procedure, having by now (several months later) gained sufficient senior experience.

The argument which tipped the balance among LEA members was that if governors as representatives of the local community thought that the school needed a certain kind of head, and adhered to this view under sustained pressure, it was not right for the authority to over-ride them. It should be noted that most LEAs give their governors a greater share in the appointment of heads, either by making them equal partners with LEA members in both short-listing and final selection, or giving members the majority at short-listing but leaving the selection entirely in the hands of governors.

3   *Walderslade School.* At Walderslade School in Kent, in 1979, the head had been the subject of complaints and a campaign directed at the alleged severity of the school's regime.[11] The governors investigated these complaints, as required by the articles of government, pronounced them virtually groundless, and expressed their full confidence in the head. Meanwhile the LEA, as it was fully entitled to do, had conducted its own enquiry into the same complaints, concluded that they were justified, and resolved to dismiss the head. The head, through his union, sought an injunction to quash the LEA's decision on the grounds that it was against natural justice for the LEA to dismiss him on grounds where the governors had found him blameless. The injunction was granted, and the LEA had to reinstate the head.

Termination of appointment is reserved to the LEA. If governors are dissatisfied with the head, they can recommend dismissal to the LEA, but the authority is not bound to accept the recommendation. The LEA can take its own initiative to dismiss a head, and is not bound to consult the governors – even though the governors' views will be an important factor in the final decision, and such consultation will almost always be a wise move. If the head is in breach of contract with the LEA, then the LEA's power to dismiss is clear-cut. If the alleged grounds for dismissal do not amount to breach of contract, the

LEA will need a report, generally on the basis of some kind of investigation. The LEA cannot stop governors from carrying out their own investigations to establish whether the head deserves their continuing confidence; so if the governors effectively pre-empt the LEA by holding an earlier investigation, the LEA will have to find some different grounds for dismissing the head.

These three examples suggest that governors play an independent and irreducible role in the local education system, i.e. they are a genuine source of power. Although they cannot take politically binding decisions in respect of their schools, they can take political initiatives and compel the authority to respond; and they can limit the authority's role by withholding consent to a proposed course of action. Does this mean, then, that under certain conditions governing bodies might become the focal point for some kind of community-based control of schools? This argument demands some attention.

Governing bodies, lay participation and open government

The main stimulus for this argument was the debate current in the late sixties and early seventies about the benefits of increased lay participation both in the policy-making process and in the running of publicly-provided institutions. Such participation, it was held, tended to make systems and institutions more responsive to local demands, and harnessed a greater measure of local support (Pateman 1970, Hill 1974). It thus created a more open system of government, generally accepted as a political good. Whether it would generally lead to a better class of decision is a separate issue. A more open system would involve recruiting as governors various categories of people other than councillors or active members of political parties, particularly representatives of teachers, parents and community groups. Some critics argued that governing bodies which were not subordinated to the LEA might be potent sources of educational innovation, and be in a position to challenge the so-called educational establishment of LEA members and senior officers and teachers. They could function as organs of a more participatory democracy (Locke 1974, Bacon 1978).

There are several difficulties in accepting this group of arguments. One can accept that traditional representational theories give an inadequate account of a healthy democracy, and need to be supplemented by elements of pluralist and participatory theories, so as to ensure that more weight is given to the claims of interested parties, client and consumer groups, and the public at large (cf Pateman 1970 pp. 105–108). Yet one needs to distinguish between the full sense of participation, in which all interested parties take an equal share in strategic decision-making and enjoy a substantial opportunity to influence all outcomes, from interaction and consultation. By itself, the occasional nature of governors' involvement with their school (one statutory meeting per term) would seem to preclude any regular collective interaction with the school, let alone anything approaching a system of industrial democracy based on syndicalist ideas of worker participation. So it is hardly realistic to think of governing bodies as a continual independent source of power in the local educational system. They can exploit their access to the sources of power – mostly the head and the LEA – and develop their influence to the mutual benefit of school and community or clientele rather than mark out their own area, where decisions are not subject to review or challenge.

The arguments for more open recruitment of governors have been sufficiently rehearsed elsewhere, and need no elaboration (Bacon 1978 ch. 2, Bacon and Howell 1974 pp. 209–213, Taylor Report 1977 ch. 4). With all the benefits accruing from a greater public involvement in education, a number of reservations can be expressed. Will governing bodies recruited in equal numbers from the LEA, teachers, parents and the community be more innovative? Will they speak out on behalf of the school more vigorously? Perhaps, but if there are four identifiable groups on the governing body, may they not be inclined to defend what each group sees as its own interest? Once governors are recruited as representatives rather than as individuals who possess certain talents, attributes or connections, they will be under pressure both to defend and report to their interest groups. Explicit attempts to innovate, by whatever interest, will be evaluated in relation to other established and possibly conflicting interest groups, with a greater likelihood of stalemate, or advance at the pace of the slowest. As their commitment to the idea of the school serving the community increases, so the interest may become increasingly parochial. Paradoxically enough, according to some critics, such governing bodies will reinforce the power of the head and the LEA (Bacon 1978 ch. 8). Teacher governors will be inhibited from speaking out if they are at variance with the head. Parent governors will lack the expertise to challenge the head or LEA, and may also suffer from doubts about their legitimacy. While parent governors may be welcome for their own sake, it is difficult to argue that they are in any sense representative if they have been appointed at a poorly-attended parent gathering, if they do not comprise a cross-section of parents as a whole, and if they are in no real sense accountable to the body which appointed them. Moreover, it has been questioned whether parents as such have any greater claim to representation than as citizens, or as members of the public at large (Bogdanov 1979 pp. 163–164); but parents do have a greater claim, as the guardians of the clients or immediate beneficiaries who are not able to speak in their own right.

The Taylor Report – its main conclusions

The Taylor Committee was set up in April 1975 'to review the arrangements for the management and government of maintained primary and secondary schools in England and Wales . . . and to make recommendations'. In its report, published in May 1977, the Committee endorsed the principle of wider recruitment of governing bodies, and argued, with one exception, that this would not produce a degree of operational freedom unacceptable to LEAs (Taylor Report pp. 30–34, 125–129). In its appraisal of the composition of governing bodies, and its review of specific responsibilities to be discharged, the committee was covering familiar ground, as it was in reviewing governors' concern with matters of discipline and crisis, and in their function as an appellate body. Their report was more catalytic in its treatment of control over the curriculum and teacher accountability. In recommending that governors should assume responsibility, subject to the general policy of the LEA, for setting the aims of the school, considering the means by which they are pursued, and reviewing the progress made thereto, Taylor was breaking new ground (ch. 6). His formulation of governors' responsibility went considerably further than simply spelling out an interpretation of 'the oversight of the school and curriculum'. The report indicated, in the convincing examples given in Appendix G (pp. 215–222), how the governors might take initiatives themselves or respond to those presented by teachers, on specific issues such as streaming or non-streaming, examination policy, pastoral care systems and so forth. No external curricular initiative, however forcefully presented, could come to anything without the support of the teaching staff who would alone have the expertise to evaluate it and the managerial skill to implement it.

The detailed programme of the school's aims would similarly rely heavily on the teaching staff, and its presentation by heads and teacher governors. A pluralist governing body would be most unlikely to impose aims repugnant to the teaching staff, and in any event, staff who felt threatened by ill-considered intervention could generally count, in the last resort, on the support of the LEA. For all that was heard in some teacher unions of Taylor being a 'busybodies' charter', it is noteworthy that the six teacher members of the committee did not share this view, or voice any professional reservations. A well-argued minority report against the Taylor proposals would have been a strong weapon for the defenders of professional autonomy against lay interference.

The presentation and consideration of a school's aims and objectives demand a high degree of sophistication from all concerned, one means of achieving this being through training programmes for governors and heads.[12] Without such programmes, governors may not appreciate the difficulties involved in measuring or assessing educational achievement. They may concentrate on the quantifiable at the expense of the rest; if they suggest curricular proposals themselves they may exert pressure on teachers to achieve quick and visible results, even when they may well be inappropriate.

Governors and teacher accountability

Within the last three years, there has been a noticeable quickening of public interest in the content of the school curriculum, educational attainment, and the monitoring of performance. This public interest has called into question previous assumptions about the professional autonomy of teachers, and the extent of their accountability to their professional peers, the controllers of local education systems, and their clients and beneficiaries. If governors, in exercising the general direction of the school and the curriculum, can expect to take initiatives and monitor progress and performance, this implies some kind of teacher accountability towards them. Now teacher account-ability can be justified on several grounds: accountability to one's professional peers and supervisors (i.e. colleagues, heads, the CEO and his staff) by virtue of their specialist expertise; accountability to the elected representatives of the public (the LEAs) by virtue of their statutory obligation to provide resources and develop services, and their authority to make binding political decisions; and accountability to governing bodies, by virtue of the legitimacy conferred on them through the LEA schemes of government, and their function as articulating the more direct public interest in an individual school.

What do we mean by teacher accountability? It cannot be left wholly in a vaguely metaphorical sense, and it must have some literal basis. The main conditions for accountability are that the account rendered gives a fair and full picture, and that those to whom the account is rendered will be able to understand it, and use it as the basis for scrutiny and questioning. Professional peers and LEAs can apply effective sanctions, if they are not satisfied with the account given by heads and their colleagues, such as demotion, reprimand or dismissal. Similarly the LEA and the professionals can reward good perform-ance. What sanctions are open to governors? As we have seen, there are few final sanctions, but plenty of intermediate ones. Governors can refer back controversial or unwelcome proposals, or ask for a fuller explanation, or for regular reports. Heads will have to come to terms with governors' powers of scrutiny and approval, and they will be concerned to enlist their governors' support, so as to generate positive feedback. If dissatisfaction persists, governors can seek the interven-tion of the LEA; and since the determination of the William Tyndale affair LEAs can no longer claim that differences between heads and governors are none of their business. Normally, indeed in all but exceptional circumstances, the heads and governors operate on a basis of shared assumptions about their respective roles and their mutual relationships, so that governors aim to steer a course halfway between passive inactivity and over-zealous interference. Their prejudices generally tend to the former, so that the very mention of sanctions may seem out of place. But the consensus between teachers and governors cannot be taken for granted indefinitely; sanctions are available and they have been operated.

Ambiguities and dilemmas in school government

We have shown that in order to appreciate the part that governors play in the control of schools, it has been necessary to adopt a broad political perspective. We must conclude by mentioning other features of the administrative scene which have some bearing on the role of governors. Firstly, more LEAs are trying to build up the autonomy of their schools by devolving greater responsibility on to heads. The school allowance is made over to the school as a general grant; the school secretary becomes upgraded to administrative officer, and takes over many routine financial matters, and possibly acts as clerk to the governors. Heads can authorise minor repairs and purchases on their own initiative. However, such diffusion of responsibility makes for a more complex system rather than a simpler one. Problems of communication increase; heads may be unsure of the limits of their responsibility; the authority may insist that some issues are matters of policy, and not of local administrative discretion. Similarly, the school becomes an increasingly complex organisation. Its links with other social agencies, all with their own priorities and their own autonomy of operation, become more demanding of time and skill. All these features add to the scope for governors' intervention, especially as a body of advice and support, but correspondingly they increase the areas of uncertainty within which governors operate.

Secondly, in spite of the clarification produced by the Taylor Report, it is not clear how governors will manage to meet and reconcile all the diverse and possibly conflicting demands being prescribed for them. One may ask how at one and the same time they can function as:

1 a body effectively linked to the LEA, and able to use those links on behalf of the school, and a free-standing source of community interest in a particular school

2 a semi-professional executive agency heavily involved in the school's decision-making, and a semi-detached largely lay body concerned more with the school's social objectives and its progress towards them

3 a body of advice and support to the school, and a monitor of teacher performance and a check on teacher autonomy

4   a body committed to the individuality of the school and the needs of the immediate neighbourhood, and one aware of the demands of the local education service as a whole.

Not all these dilemmas will be apparent at the same time, and many governing bodies will be able to coast along indefinitely without bothering about the direction they are taking. But those concerned with the control of education and the government of schools must be aware that these dilemmas exist, and could be of great significance in determining the role of governors.

Notes

1   A fuller account of the discussions relating to school management and government, and the passage of the relevant clauses of the 1944 Education Bill through Parliament is given in Baron and Howell (1974 pp. 19–36).

2   In the interests of simplicity, the terms 'school government' and 'governing bodies' have been used in relation to primary and secondary schools in accordance with the practice of some LEAs, the recommendations of the Taylor Committee on school government, and the Education Act of 1979.

3   For reasons of space, discussion in this chapter is confined to issues in school government common to wholly maintained and voluntary (i.e. religious denominational) schools. Issues peculiar to the latter are regretfully excluded, notwithstanding their importance.

4   Interestingly enough, neither W. Taylor (1963) nor Banks (1955) mentions governing bodies as a factor of any significance.

5   The classic statement of political systems analysis is still Easton (1965). For its application to the study of local government see Dearlove (1973), especially pp. 71–75; and Stanyer (1976), Pt. II. For its use in the context of social administration see Hall *et al* (1975) especially pp. 23–40, 483–486; and in the study of educational administration, Jennings (1977).

6   This question is discussed in more detail in Howell (1976), pp. 65–72.

7   e.g. Enfield Grammar School 1967: see Baron and Howell (1974) pp. 60–63; Buxton (1970) pp. 209–10; Kogan (1978) pp. 80–83; Walderslade School, Kent 1979, see, in temporary absence of *Times Educational Supplement*, *Daily Telegraph* 25 and 26 June 1979.

8   cf Byrne (1974); for another view, Richardson (1973) pp. 342–345.

9   See Auld Report (1976) and, Gretton and Jackson (1976). The author has to declare an interest as one who took an active part in the proceedings: he feels obliged therefore to mention Ellis *et al* (1977).

10   For reports on this issue see *Education* 14 June 1974 p. 696; *Times Educational Supplement* 31 May 1974, 14 June 1974 and 25 October 1974.

11   See *Daily Telegraph* 25 and 26 June 1979.

12   As argued for example in Taylor Report (1977) ch. 10.

12
The Need For Curricular Diversity

Gabriel Chanan

There can be no single best form of curriculum in a society which is in continual change. The best overall principle must be provision for basics plus diversity. There is some dispute as to how diverse existing curricular provision really is (see Reid 1979, Morgan 1980). That the British system allows for more diversity than continental systems is well established. But this relative licence seems rather to allow for a fuzzy fringe of experiment than to lead to vigorous variations in the nature of whole-school curricula.

There has been a clear trend in the last few years towards greater centralisation of control over curricula. The diversity we have so far known, whatever its extent, is under threat.

My aim here is to defend the principle, and argue the need to extend the range, of curricular diversity. Whether this is to take place 'within the walls' of state institutions or not depends on the willingness of the state system to resist the present pressure towards centralisation and to develop, instead, facilities for more ambitious variations in curricula than have been seen even in the period of relative 'teacher autonomy' during the late sixties and early seventies. Examples of alternative 'whole school' schemes will be found in Woollcombe (1978) and ACE (1979) but, of course, many other degrees of variation are possible.

Behind the currently fashionable idea of a 'national framework' for curriculum lie some years of pressure from, in particular, two lobbies: those who claim to speak for industrial Britain, and those who claim to have identified the philosophical basis for a universal education.

But pressures do not become policies unless they coincide with concrete interests, in this case the interests of centralised administration. The Conservative government which came to power in 1979 published several policy documents within its first year of office indicating an intention to effect greater central control over curricula – while at the same time imposing further cuts on an education service already severely reduced from its zenith of about 1973. The first of these documents (DES 1979d) emphasised the need for 'a national framework for curriculum' based on 'areas of special concern', none of which were innovatory.

Educational theory tends to elevate abstract idealism into the dominant principle of curricular deliberations. This pursuit of the abstract ('the whole man', 'the balanced personality') distracts us from the fact that schools need to be areas of broad negotiation, letting in as much light from as many different departments of life as possible *without* attempting to reconcile them. The 'aim of education' may be to produce 'the educated man'. But the aim of Catfield Comprehensive School is to facilitate 122 aims within a single institution. Nothing will be less helpful in the execution of this responsibility than the attempt to reconcile all these aims theoretically. A school where all the aims were known to be compatible would be a good preparation only for life in a totalitarian society.

It is the institution of schooling which lends an appearance of unity or coherence to educational theory. The theory is really the theory of an institution. There is no theory of educational *content* for that is simply the theory of each subject, which belongs separately to each subject.

What theories of education actually do is to arbitrate between the claims of various subjects and activities to institutional promotion. There can be no absolute rationality in this process. The limits of time, energy, finance, tradition and talent which in practice determine the limitations of curricula have no intrinsic connection with the content of the disciplines. The content of the disciplines is infinite.

The move towards greater centralisation in Britain has been plainly visible since the accession of Mrs Williams to the Department of Education and Science under the Labour administration of 1974. The change in climate was, however, prepared by trends reaching much further back. The call for accountability can be detected at least ten years earlier in curriculum evaluation literature – usually with an American accent. And the main thrust of the Black Paper campaign which built up over this period – its own hidden curriculum, so to speak – was precisely the move to greater central control.

It was the impulse to centralise control rather than mere hostility to progressive educational practices which united the various Black Paper contributors. Their substantive arguments, as many commentators pointed out, were often conflicting on particular educational issues.

If the real aim of the Black Paper lobby had been that schools should equip the nation with a more effective workforce there would have been some analysis of what work the nation actually does, and some attempt to derive new curriculum principles from this. The first thing that would have been discovered is that half the national adult work is done in the home and immediate community, and that this half requires skills of intellect, management and personality at least as complex as those demanded in most paid work (Equal Pay and Opportunities Campaign, 1978, 1979). In fact there was only a determination to fall back on precedent – that is, to freeze educational practice into the form that is most amenable to centralised control.

The legitimacy of greater central control has also been an implication of much educational research and the mental testing movement that underlies it. Research and testing, though supposedly neutral as to policy, assists the impetus towards central control by reflecting and lending authority to the viewpoint of administrators, who frame the research questions, rather than that of teachers, pupils or parents (Chanan, 1976).

It should not be thought that a drive to centralisation in the name of standards or national needs will necessarily lead to any closer fit between education and the real needs of adult life. Centralisation of policy begets generalisation in argument. Hence the usefulness of abstract aims to an interventionist administration. It has been a common weakness of curriculum theories to omit contemporary predicament from the basic criteria governing the organisation of knowledge. References to the contemporary world come in at various points but usually only with the status of illustrations.

One major exception, however, is another DES document of 1979, *A Basis for Choice* compiled by the Further Education Curriculum Review Unit. This document does take its bearings primarily from the anticipated adult predicament of students, and should be considered in a wider context than the short intensive post-school courses for which it was primarily intended. It seems absurd that pupils of high academic ability should be thought *not* to need help from the education system in learning about relationships, money management, the world of industrial work, and contemporary world affairs.

A more characteristic general formula is the one by T.W. Moore (1974): any worthwhile theory of education, Moore says, must include three elements or rest on three sets of assumptions: assumptions about the nature of man, assumptions about educational ends, and assumptions about knowledge. Predicament does not figure. It is true that the three categories are vague enough to be regarded as including the contemporary predicament, if you choose so to regard them, but little educational discussion takes its primary bearings from any concrete examination of the life-tasks that the pupil can be expected to face in a given time and place.

I cannot aspire, in this brief speculative discussion, to supply the deficiency. But it is not difficult to point to major areas of contemporary life which will affect all people now going through school but which do not figure explicitly in the traditional school curriculum to which administrators and even philosophers seem to revert whenever they start talking about 'fundamentals', 'basics', or 'forms of knowledge'. No curriculum scheme should be taken seriously which does not have something to say about such areas as psychology, philosophy, world history and trade, health, child care, law, sociology, technology, politics, economics and community affairs. It may say that for some reason they are not important or should not be taught in schools, but if so, one would want those reasons spelled out, since the fact that they are not now taught in schools is merely a result of historical accident, and I cannot see that any amount of theorising could render them less 'fundamental' than say, French or geography.

Or it may be said that it is impossible to draw up a core curriculum or national framework which is so inclusive. In that case, however, the logical next step would not be to resign oneself to a dangerously narrow common core but to question whether prescriptions on common core or national framework are justified at all. Would we not benefit far more by fostering a good deal of diversity, even as between arguably fundamental subjects, so that even if there truly are too many fundamentals to be included in everyone's diet, at least each fundamental will be mastered by some sizeable proportion of the population and will be present as a living force in society?

There should be provision for experimental variations in the curricular package, and not just in the peripheral options. Universal secondary education in Britain goes back only 30-odd years, to the 1944 Education Act. The discussion on common curriculum is really very young. Unlegislated consensus and the effects of both the examination system and the system of teacher education ensure a broad degree of common practice. It is sensible to try to clarify this common ground but it must be an essential corollary that we also promote experiment and variation lest we lose the possibility of comparison between different practices and hence the basis for development. Experiment should be sanctioned and supported where it demonstrates independent vigour and a degree of local acceptance. School governing bodies show signs of becoming more active than they have traditionally been, and more representative of the full constituency of parents, teachers and pupils. If such reinvigorated bodies are prepared to sanction major curricular variation, that should be regarded as adequate grounds for support by the relevant education authority. There should also be support at earlier stages to enable groups with innovatory ideas to have the chance to pilot them and put proposals to local constituencies.

There is a continual temptation to conduct 'common core' and 'national framework' discussion only in terms of the oldest-established and most widely practised curriculum areas. It is said that there is always room left for other options and innovations, that there is not going to be any centralised prescription for the entire curriculum. But where certain things are seen as central and others as peripheral, it is the peripheral things which suffer when it comes to provision and implementation. This alone ensures an unadventurous package, for the question of whether, say, ecology, community studies, child care or politics are more fundamental to a late twentieth century education than French or RE simply doesn't come on to the agenda. Ecology, community, childcare and politics are assumed to be taken care of somewhere within a general 'civics' or 'humanities' area – which, in its entirety, can hope for about as much in the way of time and resources as the learning of a foreign language or religion or a single science; possibly considerably less.

What is missing from the curriculum debate is a sense that in educating the next generation, we are educating a community of complementary people, not a mass of interchangeable individuals. Most discussion is predicated on the assumption that one can sensibly work out a curriculum by thinking first of an individual pupil and what it would be good for him to know, and then generalising to all pupils from that. This bias is clear in the writings both of educational philosophers and of administrators. They speak of providing 'a balanced curriculum' for a single mythical archetypical pupil – who is usually male, to boot. It seems to be almost impossible, even for philosophers, to hold in mind the fact that education has to cater for a vast variety of actual people, situations, needs and types of contribution to society. It seems to be assumed, somewhere below the level of explicit theorising, that people can only understand one another and hold society together by having more or less the same knowledge in their heads. The idea of *reciprocity* within the tremendous variety of a single language and culture has been little developed. But in education as in life generally, reciprocity is really more fundamental than common ground.

A debate on national common core or national framework is severely inadequate if it concentrates only on the uniform or unifying area. It should address half its energies to a national framework for *options*. Centralising minds are not sufficiently concerned that the individual pupil entering a particular school in a particular locality should, as well as having the same basics as everyone else, have the same opportunities when it comes to choosing his particular line of development. The range of those opportunities is evidently going to be left to individual schools to make the best of within whatever time and resources are left after the grand common ground has been defined. But if it is a national responsibility to see that everyone has adequate basic grounding in common areas, it is equally a national responsibility to ensure that everyone has an equal choice of the other areas too.

This is not merely a matter of equal opportunity. It is a matter of national resources, just as much as the basic grounding is. For if we concentrate only on the basic grounding and say nothing of the range of options, that range is bound to suffer. If schools are obliged to put their main resources into a defined proportion of common ground, the resources left for the options will undoubtedly be affected. This means that whereas we will all be able to understand one another in a general way the nation will be in danger of losing many of the particular talents and skills which it needs.

If we are talking of 'common core' it should be clear at any point whether we are talking about the whole curriculum, including practical, social and recreational activities, or only about the know-ledge curriculum; if only about the knowledge curriculum, it is not enough merely to make a ritual nod in the direction of other functions of the school, for these are easily forgotten where the assumption is that they are 'extra' or marginal. In particular it is made more difficult to introduce the idea of some essential relation between them and the 'basic' subjects; for example between community activities and intellectual work.

This particular point has been much obscured by the determination of educational philosophers to keep the term 'education', which is colloquially associated with all kinds of developmental activity, practical, social and intellectual, only for intellectual matters. Thus learning how to type, how to comfort someone in distress, or how to address a public meeting would be forms of 'training' rather than education. The philosophers concede that these are useful things to learn but in 'pure' educational schemes they are always seen as incidental. The drawback of this 'pure' view is that it constantly draws us away from looking at education in relation to the needs of adult life as a whole. An institutional distinction is maintained between 'intrinsic' and 'practical' educational outcomes, disguising the fact that all successful learning produces both intrinsic satisfaction and practical benefit. It is not considered that intellect may achieve its highest expression in its engagement on practical tasks; and that practical needs are one of the major stimuli to intellectual work.

But neither is it adequate to speak of intellectual and practical life if we cannot integrate our approach with a serious view of pupils' emotional life. There is a general invisibility of emotional life in educational debate. The distinction between 'cognitive' and 'affective' life of pupils, consolidated in hundreds of curriculum schemes on the model of Bloom's *A Taxonomy of Educational Objectives* (1956), has been objected to by a number of theorists on the grounds that it artifici-ally separates thought and feeling into two massive monolithic areas, which is indeed disturbing enough. These objections have not prevented the continuing spread of this model. An even more fundamental point, however, is that even the 'affective' area does not in fact correspond to emotional life. It is to do principally with *attitudes*.

No doubt attitudes are in part the result of emotions but it is stretching an assessment convenience beyond sense to assume that by measuring or evaluating attitudes one has actually evaluated emotions. In Bloom and hundreds of subsequent studies (whose assumptions reflect assumptions much more widely held than just among researchers) it is assumed that the 'affective' life can be assessed in the same disintegrated way as intellectual life.

It may well be that knowledge has to be broken down into small parts in order to be seen. Though reality is arguably a 'seamless cloak' we can only find our way about in it by differentiating it into constituent parts. But the invention, by testers and others, of an 'affective' life which is similarly differentiated by objects in the outside world ('attitude towards learning French', 'attitude to teachers') is a huge misrepresentation. The principal fact about emotional life is that, being within the individual, it is an integrated and integrating faculty. To bring it closer to the centre of the educational enterprise will require much better recognition of its intrinsic connections with both practical and intellectual disposition.

There are plenty of indications of the kinds of emotional predicament that today's pupils will face as adults, if they are not doing so already: the incidence of mental breakdown, depression, anorexia, agoraphobia on the one hand – the internalised forms of stress if you like, perhaps most frequent among women; and the externalised forms of stress, perhaps most visible in men – aggression, pornography, compulsive competitiveness.

Alarmingly, these stresses and aggressions appear to be compatible with a general bemused submissiveness to impersonal authority. Milgram (1974) showed by a series of ingenious experiments with fake shock treatment that a startlingly high proportion of people of all classes will suspend their own moral judgement and humanitarian norms in a situation where they believe themselves to be under the direction of a scientific authority. The idea of a surfeit of obedience superficially contradicts the widespread contemporary observation that there has been a marked increase in violence and breakdown of moral norms over the past 15 years. The alarming point, however, is that these two phenomena, passive obedience in 'official' situations, and irrational violence in 'unofficial' situations, appear to go together. I know of no writer in Britain who has gone into these questions in as much depth as Hannah Arendt (1961), whose work was one of the starting points for Milgram's experiments.

The question of relations between men and women, and between the 'male' and 'female' sides of personality in general – autonomy and resignation, authority and submission – are at the centre of these problems. They are also at the centre of cultural life – the subject matter par excellence of the serious arts, and indeed of high quality popular entertainment. For too long we have treated the great traditions of literature, art and music merely as the products of exceptional human skill. Far more important is their capacity to touch the deep structure of modern emotional life. Despite the regular obeisance made to them in principle, they are, as *experiences*, much under-used in education.

How, then, are we to decide what children should be taught? Surely there are necessary and valid universals?

There is no difficulty in agreeing that the earliest things which should be taught are those that will open up the most pathways later on. Literacy and numeracy are accepted by most people as the *sine qua non* of further learning. The difficulty arises with the attempt to extend the principle of 'maximum access' beyond this fundamental level – the attempt to find a limited number of universally valid 'forms of knowledge' which underlie all further specialisation and so have a fundamental claim on educational time. There are many writers in this tradition. Paul Hirst is perhaps the most often quoted, but, among recent books, J.P. White's (1973) takes the argument most explicitly into the field of national policy.

The basic idea of the forms-of-knowledge argument is that there are a limited number of fundamental ways of knowing, and that the best way to give every pupil some access to our whole culture is to identify those fundamental forms and then initiate all pupils into them. From that point onwards it is possible for pupils to choose individual directions to develop in, since they are now 'on the inside' of the basic forms. The same idea in less sophisticated presentation, underlies most recent government documents on national educational policy.

The emphasis on knowing, rather than an equal attention to knowing, doing and experiencing, prejudices the argument in favour of an unduly limited curriculum. The critical question for curriculum design, however, is what relationship is to be promoted between intellectual and practical life: how do you marshal facts about public expenditure? How do you persuade someone in the depths of depression that there is another way to look at his existence? How do you work out whether or not to support a certain political position? How do you work out the best way to deal with a child who is distressed and aggressive? These kinds of perfectly ordinary, common and inescapable adult problems demand the highest mental resources. Wide knowledge and effective thinking are a resource for living, though fuller reflection can perhaps only take place when the immediate urgency has receded. The intrinsic satisfaction to be derived from mental reflection is a phase in a cycle of practical life-tasks.

If intellectual life does have practical importance, if literature and art actually help us in our relationships, if maths and science help us in managing the technical world, there is no essential difference between intrinsic and practical education. Everything that is valuable has the dual value of enlightenment and profit. Educators are the last people who could assert from their own occupation and social position any purely intrinsic value to knowledge.

The emphasis on forms of knowledge also obscures the immense possible variations in selection and treatment of content within any one form, which may in real terms be greater than the difference between including or excluding a certain form or field of knowledge from a core curriculum or a range of options.

The claim that 'forms of knowledge' should be used as the central structuring element in school curricula is based on two plausible but actually very dubious notions: firstly, that mastering the structure of the basic forms of knowledge will give the pupil a balanced outlook on life; secondly that being brought onto 'the inside' of the fundamental forms brings the pupil to a point where he can freely choose what aspects of life and culture to concentrate on thereafter.

Where does the sense of balance come from in those who aspire to devise balanced curricula? Are we not all, ourselves, unbalanced people, both occupationally and in personality? How many of those of us who seek to establish a 'balanced' curriculum have any personal idea of what it is like to be trying to balance one's mind between all the important fundamental areas of modern life?

There is an echo here of the pernicious perfectionism of the eugenics movement which, from the middle of the nineteenth century to the late 1930s, justified its curricular schemes and progressively stratified testing procedures on the ground of attempting to perfect humanity. Presumably it was accepted that humanity, as represented even by the eugenicists themselves, was not yet perfect. So an imperfect creature was attempting to design a perfect one. No wonder the result was abysmal. An imperfect creature's idea of perfection is bound to be grotesque. Now we have the same aspirations regarding 'balance'. We cannot claim to be balanced in our knowledge or experience – far from it – yet here we are prescribing what the next generation need to know and experience in order to be so.

The move from R.S. Peters' gentlemanly model of 'the educated man' (singular and male) to J.P. White's (1973) 'compulsory curriculum' has been rapid and all too logical. It is complemented at the popular or propagandist level by a great deal of talk about standards. But while the talk is about standards, the policy plans are all about standardisation. And if there is one product which, for the health and prosperity of the nation, should not be standardised, it is people's minds. Standardisation is madness when one looks at the actual variety of things to be done in society. It is as if we should try to produce multiples of a single perfectly balanced person who could turn his or her hand to anything whatsoever. It is as if Renaissance man could suddenly be reinvented 400 years after his demise. But who are we to talk about educating the whole person? Are we whole people ourselves? If we are not, what sort of vision of wholeness can we project?

It is utopian to imagine that pupils can be brought to a position of free, rational and individual choice from a range of possibilities representing access to every major department of contemporary life. Pupils are constrained by such 'irrelevant' factors as what their best friend does, what their parents are interested in, which teacher personalities they take to, what their big brother or sister does, what happens to have some accidental connection with something they have heard about before, what happened to be well taught in their primary school or what they have heard discussed on television.

It may be held that the purpose of the curricular scheme is precisely to make sure that pupils come into contact with other possibilities than those that arise accidentally. But the 'accidental' reasons for interest in a thing are the *operative* reasons. They are irreplaceable, and should be respected, encouraged, built upon. They are not something to be left behind – they are an essential link in the continuity of cultural cues which enables people to attach a personal meaning to knowledge. Schools should always have scope to exploit all such promising accidents at the expense of some purely theoretical balance in the individual's learning. Interest should be encouraged to extend from these points, but we should not imagine that the pupil can ever attain a balanced comprehensive view of possibilities before choosing what to specialise in. No-one who asks himself how he came to be interested in what he is interested in will find this to be true of his own development.

Instead of regretting the haphazardness of the process by which people become interested in one thing rather than another, by comparison with our abstract model of free choice, we should recognise that this haphazardness is actually the very texture of cultural cohesion. Our model of the educated person must be subordinate to a model of an educated *community*. The ability to fit one's own strengths and weaknesses into a network of people with other strengths and weaknesses – the ability to benefit from other people's abilities *without* understanding what these abilities are or how they work, is far more important than the aim of having a bit of all abilities in yourself. In other words *being able to take part in reciprocal relationships in a problem-solving situation* is far more realistic and important than the aspiration to personal possession of balanced knowledge.

It is important that as full as possible a range of worthwhile activities is vigorously present in the school community as a whole, not in the curriculum of each individual. At the same time the school should become a real problem-solving community by participation in the affairs of its wider community. If we impose a mandatory uniform 'breadth' on all pupils, we will reduce the school's ability to include real breadth in its options.

If we put this aim – reciprocity – at the centre of our curriculum approach, if reciprocity were to be accepted as the necessary common element, we might arrive at some very different curricular schemes from those now being sharpened up in the corridors of administration. One cannot anticipate all the differences, and acceptance of not being able to anticipate them is a crucial point: we must not cut off our options or saddle ourselves with monolithic constraints, particularly at this time when the nature of work and social life in our society is even more volatile than usual. 'The needs of the world of work' are frequently invoked to justify the new curricular centralisation. But the world of work is in at least as much turmoil as the world of education, and it is, again, only in administrative abstractions that those needs seem so stunningly obvious. 'Work' has been traditionally used as the ultimate reality of adult life by which school is to be judged. But that is a mere totem. When industry itself is being discussed nationally, we are all aware that it is in a state of turmoil. But when education is being discussed, 'work' suddenly assumes a statuesque solidity as the unchanging reality with unquestionable needs which education must service.

If we were serious about orienting the school curriculum to the needs of adult life, we would use our limited educational research funds to find out what the typical predicaments of adult life are, and how they relate, or could relate, to available knowledge. We would follow samples of people from different walks of life through ordinary days. We would record what skills the person used to get through his day, and what situations presented themselves as problems. I am sure we would get some surprises. I think we would find that the ability to do a particular paid job was by no means the largest part of the daily problem. In or out of the job, we would surely find that the ability to mesh in with the activities of others, to place one's own skill or experience in a positive relation to other people's, the ability to benefit by other people's abilities and experiences were all crucial. I believe we would find that some of the hardest work being done did not come under job descriptions but in the field of family and community activities, individual and collective self-help.

We would find that facing real tasks in adult life, whether in or out of the paid work situation, draws on all forms of experience in various combinations. Even confining our thoughts initially to paid work situations, there must be very few where merely knowing, or even knowing and understanding, suffice to get a particular task done. In most work situations, whether on the factory floor, in management, in an office, in a shop, in journalism, defence, medicine, nursing, teaching or even in theorising, the tasks actually confronting you demand a combination of knowing, understanding, practical making, creativity, physical health and personal relations.

We would find, I believe, that when things went wrong or did not get done, it was not so much because of lack of ability as because of not seeing the *possibility* or the *point* of doing them – lack of imagination or motivation, reflecting an education weak in attention to emotion and the arts, an education which has failed to get across to people the fact that society is a human creation that can be further changed by further human creativity. No national framework is going to be able to remedy this – only a renewal of the drive to make schools themselves into centres of creative curriculum development.

13
Community Based Education

John Watts

If we look at the attempts to relate education to local community in the first half of this century, two distinct styles, with contrasted motivation, become apparent. There was the approach which sought to regenerate community life by the introduction of fresh ideas, action and 'high culture'. This required capital, planning and salesmanship. It was innovatory in the sense that it entailed persuading those involved to alter attitudes and practice, to start doing things that they had not done before. And there was another, quite different approach, quieter, much less publicised, which sought not so much to bring new life to a moribund culture as to offer new opportunities for developing the activities of an existing way of life. In horticultural terms, the former was akin to grafting while the latter was more like layering. Each has merit in its own lights.

It is worth considering these two strands in our tradition of popular education because, with the close of the century in sight, their contrasting implications are still being worked out.

The 'grafting' tradition became manifest during the economic decline of the 1920s. It was both romantic, in that it drew upon an idealised past and offered a utopian vision of the future, and patrician, in that it conferred its blessings upon the benighted from on high. Appropriately, its operation was in rural districts, though urban decline at the time was quite as much in evidence. The most broadly based endeavour of its kind was that of Leonard Elmhirst at Dartington. He and his wife, a wealthy American, had purchased Dartington Hall in 1925, not as a country retreat but as a centre for community development. With a blend of the creative, artistic vision that they shared with Tagore, and the capitalist 'know-how' that they brought from the world of successful business enterprise, the Elmhirsts used their money to make things work and pay dividends. They put the forestry of the estate onto an economic footing, they opened a pottery and a textiles mill. Local crafts were revived. But Dartington's greatest distinction lay in the home it provided for progressive education and the numerous artists who flourished there, people like Laban and Imogen Holst. No doubt the local native Devonians enjoyed a richer life, in all senses, but it is unlikely that their own traditions ever crossed paths with those of Laban's dancers, or that many of them ever had their children educated under Bill Curry at Dartington Hall School. The water of sound business and the oil of fine art remained essentially separate. Dartington may have been a crucible for ideas and artistic creation, but in itself it provided no educational solutions to the community problems of our times.

At exactly the same time as the Elmhirsts were enlivening South Devon, Henry Morris was moving mountains to prepare for the first of his village colleges. Lacking an inheritance of capital, or indeed any but the barest essentials from the Cambridgeshire County Council, he turned himself into what Leonard Elmhirst called 'the most expert of beggars', cajoling supplementary funds from any possible source, not excluding the benefactors of Dartington themselves. Morris shared with the Elmhirsts not only a small portion of their capital, but a desire to stem the depopulation of rural England, 'to keep the boys and girls of the villages in the country, instead of sending them into the towns', as one county councillor put it bluntly. More than that, they wanted those young people to enjoy a life that had coherence and meaning, not just a life based on a stable economy.

Morris hoped to achieve this through the system of maintained popular education, but both he and the Elmhirsts saw the task as one of importing culture and learning. Morris, however, was more insistent that this initiative was the means to eventual community autonomy. In 1926 he wrote: 'The welfare of communities, and the vigour and prosperity of their social life depend on the extent to which centres of unfettered initiative can be developed within them. The great task of education is to convert society into a series of cultural communities . . .'. And the instrument of realising this dream was to be 'the organic provision of education for the whole adult community'.

Undoubtedly, Morris's emphasis was on *adult* education, a limitation to be raised again later. Perhaps his greatest pioneering achievement was to plant the notion of 'abolishing the barriers which separate education from all those activities which make up adult living'. Sawston, the first village college, opened in 1930. After 50 years, we could well reappraise the implications for our own times of that prophetic idea. Certainly Sawston did not in itself present a seamless garment of community and education, but at least, unlike Dartington, it was a milestone along the road of popular education. For all Morris's paternalism, he opened the eyes of R.A. Butler when he was framing the Act of 1944, and he left us ideas in incubation for much later hatching. In particular, he left us the challenge of determining what are 'the activities that make up adult living' and how to relate them to education.

I want to draw attention also to that less well-funded tradition of community education, taking two men as illustrations, one from Lancashire and one from New Zealand. What unites the two men, Terry O'Neill and Crawford Somerset, is their recognition of the culture that their pupils brought into school with them from their home background, however humble. Of course each brought to his teaching not just facilitating skills but a passion for discovery, for learning, for making, for shared enjoyment of life, its simplest offerings and its great achievements. They were teachers who had studied in books, in nature and in their fellow men and women. They made their own insights accessible. But they wanted those they taught to look and learn for themselves as well. For both of them, education was essentially about the meeting of minds, the cross-fertilisation of one set of experiences with another, starting at the point of contact, here and now.

Terry O'Neill grew up in impoverished Salford, trained as a teacher before the First World War and devoted his whole life until retirement in 1963 to school teaching in Lancashire. For 55 years he was headmaster of one school, Prestolee. The story of his early trials and triumph is told by Gerard Holmes in *The Idiot Teacher*. The triumph consisted principally in convincing the down-to-earth people of Lancashire (during the same period of the 1920s that found Morris and Elmhirst going their very different ways into community education) that school for ordinary children could simultaneously entail love and learning, that achievement could arise from interests that linked home and school, that parents and teachers could work in partnership and indeed share in educational activities themselves. In the face of initial hostility, particularly from those who did not send their children to his school, but who had a lot to say about how to educate other people's children, O'Neill introduced much that even today is still the subject of furious debate. He individualised study, he mixed the 'abilities', he trusted and respected his children, and he broke down the barriers between school and non-school.

In 1924, without seeking permission from his Managers, O'Neill started reopening his school after tea. As his biographer, Gerard Holmes explains:

At first only schoolchildren returned. Then came some older boys who had left school and were now at work. Then parents. Their children failing to return home because they were so engrossed in work of all kinds, the parents began to turn up and look for them, and these, after a while, came earlier and got into the habit of staying and watching the children at work and play. The habit spread with the older people and the school became for some an alternative relaxation to the local pubs. . . . An increasing number of people moved about, talked, sang, sewed, sawed, read books, made pictures.

There was trouble of course. But then Henry Morris would never have allowed this kind of hurly-burly. The village colleges kept their school curriculum carefully distinct from adult education. Morris was not at all happy in practice to mix the ages across that date-line of the school leaver. In fact he was more than faintly embarrassed by children. The distinguishing feature of that picture of O'Neill's community in the school is the fact that 'people moved about'. It would be absurd to imply that in the village colleges people were not encouraged to move about: there was always an extensive interchange going on in them, but at Prestolee one has the distinct impression that all this activity was based essentially on what the children were doing in extension of their school work. And Henry Morris would have winced to have it suggested that what he was offering was an *alternative* to the pubs. But then Terry O'Neill would have winced to have it suggested that Prestolee was a 'college'. Salford and Cambridge. Where people are and where they might be. How to reconcile the 'is' with the 'ought'?

At the same time, but as far away as it is possible to be, in the South Island of New Zealand, Crawford Somerset, like Terry O'Neill, was given charge after the First World War of a small town school and expected to conform to a curriculum, with its inbuilt style of relationships, that he found stultifyingly divorced from living. In his study *Littledene: Patterns of Change*, Somerset describes how his knowledge of the local community, its values and interdependent occupations, grew to the point of challenging the validity of what he was giving to the children enclosed within the walls of his school. Steadily he transformed his teaching.

When Terry O'Neill opened his doors, the community came in: when Crawford Somerset opened his, the pupils and teachers went out into the community. The relative climates of Lancashire and Canterbury may have had something to do with it, though more likely the difference was more a reflection on the one hand of life in mill towns and on the other of colonial farming and trading. Somerset began to locate the basic studies where things that were in the mainstream of his pupils' lives took place. He gained the co-operation of farmers to allow pupils to measure land, calculate costs, plan construction projects. They wrote about animal husbandry as they learnt about it from observation and enquiry. They discussed the politics of local decision-making as they learnt crafts from the local craftsmen, by talking about it and by imitation.

But Somerset was no early de-schooler. Far from dissolving his school, he used it in part as the place where all this community learning was co-ordinated, worked into coherence, and in part as the location for his own contribution. He was, for example, a lover of drama, and drew a large following to his productions of Shakespeare. The point was, that Somerset, as much as O'Neill, was relating his curriculum and his style of teaching and learning to the real and *serious* occupations of the community. Where the New Zealander had an undeniable advantage was in the much more unified life-style of a community where work was hard but what people lived for, whereas O'Neill was facing the problem, unfortunately far more common, where work was employment in occupations unrelated to the rest of living, and leisure was unrelated to gainful production.

The strength of Morris's development lay not in having at one stroke answered the problem of popular cultural decline but in its establishing a maintained and institutionalised programme. He provided a chance for continuity and propagation. The extraordinary thing is that in spite of the protracted period of incubation, the village college was an egg that eventually hatched. The delay may in part be attributed to Morris's own personality, which left as many opponents behind him, resolved to resist the spread of a new orthodoxy, as it left disciples ready to take the next steps when their time came to exercise power. In the end perhaps, the strength of the idea had to grow detached from the memory of the man. As it was, it needed the period of the expanding 1960s to see the seed bear fruit outside Cambridge, with the exception of one early germination.

There is an interesting study yet to be made of the men and women who, fired with Henry Morris's ideals, set out from Cambridgeshire, taking only their sandals and a staff, but foremost among them must be Stewart Mason. Mason became Director of Education for Leicestershire in 1947. Unlike Morris, who tended to sweep forward in pursuit of his goal, taking opposition head-on, Mason trod with delicacy through the minefields of a Tory county, achieving his aims by good administration and stealth. As well as developing the three-tier system of comprehensive schooling, well known as the Mason–Pedley Line (the partner in ideas being Robin Pedley, then of the Leicester University School of Education), he began to extend his schools, at their secondary levels, into community colleges.

The first Leicestershire community college, opened at Ivanhoe, Ashby, in 1954. In conception it was not far in advance of the village colleges – a school with added accommodation and staffing for youth and community activities, the whole provision co-ordinated by a headmaster or warden. However, over the period up to his retirement in 1971, Mason wrought organic changes that culminated in 1970 with the opening of Countesthorpe. In the architecture of Countesthorpe, Mason had synthesised the different elements of provision, removing the last traces of Morris's prestige Adult Rooms, looking ahead to the raising of the school-leaving age to 16 and, in the 14–18 Upper School that was incorporated, a continuity of pre-adult and adult activity in the college's community. For all Mason's diplomacy, and partly because it had been his final fling, Countesthorpe had to prove itself in the teeth of intense opposition. (That story has been told elsewhere.) However, there was no going back. The community colleges that followed, first Wreake Valley, then Hind Leys, Groby and Earl Shilton, all adopted the integrated provision.

One of Mason's main innovations, alongside the integration of school and community provision, had been a constitutional arrangement that gave considerable powers of decision to the user-members of a community college. The idea of a Community Council, a democratic representative body, determining policy with the warden, goes right back to the early days of Morris's village colleges. Mason's departure dating from 1969, was to give each college's Council the power to handle its own finances. In essence, this scheme required of a council that it return to the Education Committee a certain proportion of the cost of tutoring fees, after which it was free to fix its own fee-structure, plan either to break even or to raise a surplus and use it as it wished for the general benefit.

This represented a considerable breakthrough. Hitherto Education Committees had always acted paternalistically in determining what was good for 'Adult Education'. I discovered this to my cost when opening Les Quennevais School as a community college for Jersey in 1965. But the Jersey Education Committee were not unusual in their view of how public money should be spent in improving the public itself. Their view was rooted in the idea of the industrious apprentice studying in night school, and had nothing to do with needs identified by the local community itself. My classic example was the refusal of the Committee to agree to my organising classes in dog-handling in response to anxieties on the neighbouring estate about roaming strays. This, I was told, was not education.

There are, of course, safeguards, but the users of a Leicestershire community college are virtually empowered to promote their own programmes, inside and outside the premises, according to their own perceived needs. After that, as Andrew Fairbairn, Mason's number two, who succeeded him in 1971, is quoted as saying, 'All we can do is to foster the local climate and adopt the role of a permissive father', the father-figure, he hoped, gradually fading away. If they want a dog-handling class, they have one.

Let me now select from this pioneering tradition five threads that seem to be significant in any attempt to relate to the future of community education. They are

1   the attempt to revive decaying rural culture,

2   the introduction of 'high culture' into mass education,

3   the opening of school to admit the community so as to relate schoolwork to local adult activities,

4 the physical extension of the school curriculum out into the life of the community, in an attempt to make it reality-based,

5 the democratic determination by users of locally maintained provision.

The question now arises as to how far these antecedents adequately meet the needs of the present and, as far as we can foresee them, the needs of the rest of the century. A taxonomy of the needs of society and of the individual would be voluminous. Any selection from it would in turn make certain assumptions about models of community education and which models were considered the most viable. An added consideration is that our tradition of community education is rooted in rural life.

In the late 1950s, after Morris's retirement, it was commonly said that his ideas would not translate into the urban setting. If this had been true, the village college might have remained a minority curiosity. After all, 60 per cent of our population is housed in the 150 biggest towns. However, the evidence of a successful transfer of the community school to urban and suburban districts began to accumulate. In the 1960s Cyril Poster developed the Lawrence Weston School in an estate area of Bristol. Wyndham School was designed to fit into the shopping centre of Egremont in Cumberland, and Les Quennevais was sited on a suburban estate in Jersey. In the 1970s the practice was developed further. The Abraham Moss Centre in Manchester was designed as an interchange of shops and other community provision with the school, while in Nottinghamshire, Henry Swain, the county architect, conceived of the Sutton Centre as a community provision, including the school, built around an ice-rink right in the town's shopping precinct. The concept of the school set among green fields had been finally abandoned. Coventry was able to develop a whole city network of community schools, typified by the Sidney Stringer School, but by no means overshadowed by it.

But does the 'community school' adequately offer the optimum basis for community education? Boyd (1977) has usefully related three models of community development identified by Ashcroft (1973) to forms of community education, and made a case for a school curriculum that develops individual awareness and directs that in turn towards community responsibility. Boyd points fairly to weaknesses in a 'mainstream' model that focuses upon the deprived in society, and in a 'radical' model that repudiates institutionalised 'safe' forms of community education in favour of alternatives. The former is condemned in caricature as 'downtown curriculum for downtown children', while the latter hardly meets what most parents and teachers see as the legitimate business of the school. The way forward would seem best to lie in a model which bases its curriculum in what may be identified as an emerging common culture, 'taking notice', as Boyd puts it, 'of local differences which would require schools and education authorities to reinterpret the core and to plan curriculum content according to perceived educational needs'.

This is helpful, but it stops short of specifying 'perceived needs'. It may then be worth considering ten identifiable needs that have emerged during work in this field. That selection may then serve as a basis for strategies designed to meet the needs and thereby give some prognostication of the coming shape of community education.

1   Most obviously, there is a need for opportunities to resume education in some form, part-time or full-time, after compulsory schooling is concluded. This is not a new need. It is just more pressing as the rate of change accelerates. The explosion of knowledge, the growth of technology, the creation of new skilled occupations, the disappearance of others, all contribute to the obsolescence of curricula. People find a need for a refit or for taking a new chance where the first one was lost. To a great extent, the training and re-training schemes of employment are geared to these needs, but of course they only deal with those in their employment and can hardly be expected to cope with those who are unemployed or seeking a change of employment.

There are also many people who find after some years of reflection that the image of themselves given to them by their schooling is unacceptable and wish to replace it, within the same terms of the educational system. Our school system has up to now, through its obsessional preoccupation with Pass and Fail gradings, managed consistently to leave a high proportion of school leavers with a marked sense of inadequacy. Far from having let standards fall, we have set a certain scale of academic expectation which few of our population have reached, and in many respects, particularly in job-requirements, have had no need to reach, and then we condemn them for failing. In particular, we have required evidence, by the arbitrary age of 11, of certain conceptual skills, failing which we have classified children as lacking capacity for academic education. This persists in spite of the growth of comprehensive schooling: the categorisation into sheep and goats has continued. Even were it to stop now and teachers in comprehensive schools really tried to develop each child to the full of his or her potential, we should still have for the rest of this century a population most of whom were told at school, if not in so many words then even more emphatically by the structure, that they were intellectual duds. Any who now wish to modify that classification need every help in doing so.

2   The large-scale injustice of branding adolescents, politely as non-academic, less politely with a battery of epithets ranging from 'thicks'

to 'dregs', resulting primarily in denying them the opportunity to handle abstract concepts. The 'non-academics' were always thought to be in need of more practical subjects, more woodwork, more home-craft, or the practical aspects of citizenship, like filling in forms correctly. Repeatedly in talking to adults who, in their own words, were 'no good at school', I find what they have most come to want, as a conscious need, is opportunity to form and use abstract concepts. Since their school days, they have begun to conceptualise in ways often suppressed in their youth. They have begun to realise that their so-called non-academic brains *could* grasp an understanding of ideas like Political Power, or Energy, or Law, or Design, and not just their particular concrete manifestations. Of course, opportunities arise for using and exchanging ideas both at home and at work, but in neither place is the setting designed for that activity, whereas an educational setting should be and can be.

3 Everyone needs to create, to make something new and unique. It is a basic human need. We either create or we destroy. What we create may be a work of art, or a plum-pudding or a brick wall. The source of creative satisfaction will have been the element of choice that we had to do it our way rather than in someone else's way. Even repetitive work may give some satisfaction if it is what we have chosen to do.

4 Related to the need to create, is the need to find work that makes demands on the individual and therefore makes sense to him. Those who find their work boring are not likely to be too unintelligent to carry out more demanding work, but are more likely to be capable of more complex and varied tasks than are being made available. Parker (1971) has concluded that 'those who find work more demanding are more likely to be socially or intellectually active in their spare time than those who find work less demanding'.

5 Professor Entwistle has drawn attention to Parker's findings, and thrown considerable light on the problem of the dichotomy of work and leisure. He has ably exposed the inadequacy of the common slogan of adult education – Learning for Leisure. There is a place in any community programme for games, crafts, Spanish for tourists and so on, but as leisure, especially enforced leisure, increases, it reveals the need that people feel for more satisfying work. Indeed, as Entwistle has stated elsewhere (1978), 'It is most fruitful to conceive of leisure, not as a residue which remains when economic obligations have been fulfilled, but rather as a way of life, indeed, as life itself.' In the era of the micro-chip, the challenge to community education may well be less that of providing variety in recreational activity than of how to equip the individual with the skills and insights that will enable him to choose when, how and where to work, whether remunerated or not.

6   The 1980s have opened with a rise in unemployment and a decline in living standards. Both conditions tend to breed tension in a multi-cultural society. And yet there are grounds for looking forward to a peaceful, and indeed an enriched future for a polyglot community. In the past, Britain has absorbed foreign invasions by gradual assimilation. This is not so likely to be the future solution, if only because our own population is more mobile than ever before, and because communications enable cultural minorities both to retain contact with their place of origin and to relate more coherently with their members here. The need facing community education therefore is one of cultural exchange, the need for common ground on which the differences may be explored with reduced threat, and where familiarity may breed tolerance.

7   There is a growing need for individuals and groups to know how to exploit the media of communication instead of merely being exploited by them. At a time when we hear frequent grumbles that shop-assistants cannot add up and subtract as they used to, it is a sad fact that so few of the grumblers find anything remarkable in the general level of competence among the same humble, and usually young shop-assistants in their dexterous use of calculators. Almost unnoticed, a new wave of clerical workers is emerging to take in its stride the use of micro-processors and electronic systems of information retrieval. We continue to emphasise the importance of literacy, yet in most forms of first employment there is little demand for reading compared with the increased need for skills of data retrieval. There is consequently a life-long need for the individual to keep abreast not only with the advancing techniques of miniaturised electronics but with the social implications. People need to know where they have become vulnerable, where their privacy may have been invaded or even lost, and where their protections may be found or built.

8   Visitors from Europe, raised perhaps in more turbulent settings, unsheltered by seaboard boundaries, often shake their heads at the Briton's political naivety. With little fluctuation we still tend to cling to party loyalties of family or place. Even with the increased social mobility of our time, voters tend to fall in line with their neighbours. Because schooling has tended to play the conservative role of preserving the status quo, education in politics has always been suspect, as if it were somehow better that they didn't know too much about it in case they start asking awkward questions. That is already changing in schools, but that provides no immediate answer to the wider community need that already exists.

9   All these needs so far point to one other gap left by our traditional curricula. Increased mobility, social and geographical, increased

demands for the servicing industries and decline of employment in production, has led to increased person-to-person contact involving some kind of negotiation. People are having to come to terms, often in one-off relationships, with many more and much more diverse kinds of other people than ever before. The interpersonal skills of the family, the restricted neighbourhood, the life-long place of work, are proving inadequate. Rapid change entails either negotiation or conflict. Indeed, conflict may often be unavoidable and then we need the skills of resolving it, unless violence is to ensue. The violence may be physical, or moral in the sense that the smarter party outwits the slower. In my own recent involvement in planning in-service programmes I found that heads referred more frequently than to anything else, to the need, in face of reduced expenditure, falling rolls and slower rates of mobility, for training in interpersonal skills, among their staffs and for themselves. Instead of taking and giving orders, it was felt, teachers need to learn more about such matters as non-verbal signalling, mutual assessment, and group decision-making. I suspect that these needs in school can be extrapolated.

10 'Needs' implies 'needy', and that suggests deprivation and discontent. Perhaps the very act of engaging in attempts to meet perceived needs is itself satisfying, so that relish may be found in 'doing something about it' as much as in coming up with an answer. Even so, a challenge exists for community education to meet the need of people to have fun. One pitfall in the common approach to Education for Leisure (quite apart from the graver defect pointed out in 5 above) has been the solemnity with which programmes have often been presented. The traditional festivals have by and large become meaningless at a popular level. One cannot create instant tradition, but there are those trained and experienced in providing forms for spontaneous group activity that has no other purpose than to get people to make fun together. It is a sad fact that over such a short span as 20 years, adolescents have lost much of the knowledge of mutual amusement and a generation has emerged robbed by the mass-entertainment industries of the resources for *making* fun. The possibilities of participatory amusement are enormous and often inexpensive. In a consumer society we need positive initiatives to reinstate the ludic and the festive.

Needs such as these ten, and the list is not exhaustive, have implications for education. Some of them I have sketched in in passing, but there are others. If we return to my opening distinction between the two styles in our tradition of community education, we may posit the question of where we should start to meet these community needs. My own conviction is that it must begin in school and not wait to form part of a separate adult provision. In particular, our target should be that span of compulsory schooling, 14–16, which has come into existence during my own lifetime. Without a clear and respected element of community education in their curriculum, this age group, not so long ago accorded a degree of adult status, a place in the economic community through employment, will be condemned to prolonged childhood and political impotence. This is degrading for them and dangerous for everyone.

This does not imply only that the adolescent needs to be given opportunities to handle abstractions, to take pleasure in creativity, to understand communications systems, engage in cross-cultural exchanges and to study politics. It means all those, but it also means that the traditional structures and relationships that still prevail in school must undergo radical change. If school students are to discuss moral and political issues, the teacher, though still needing to be an authority, cannot afford to be authoritarian. He must be seen to be subject to universals equally with the students. He will be seen to be fallible. He will be in a position of negotiating with his students, negotiating over practical arrangements and negotiating knowledge rather than just dispensing it.

This will impose heavy demands upon the teacher. Nevertheless, if he will only meet those demands and work for the reshaping of his school in accordance with them, he will create a new place of learning in which age will no longer be a barrier. He will create a setting in which the adolescent and the adult may sit together because they wish to solve a common problem.

In turn, the adult may find a setting which no longer offers the threat of humiliation and failure that most associate with school. Parents still too often regard 'coming up to the school' as synonymous with trouble: grown men falter and drop their gaze when confronted by the head teacher on his or her own territory. If the school becomes a 'community college' in some form or other, it must above all create an atmosphere in which the public is free and welcome to pass in and out of its doors. It will for a start need to *look* less like a museum and more like a shopping centre. The task of the professional, and of the initiated non-professional, is to use this ease of entry as the opportunity for setting up the dialogue. How else, other than in a relaxed social setting, can someone begin to articulate the abstract idea that they feel a need to rectify their earlier failure to handle abstractions at all? So the professional needs to be a skilled counsellor, able not only to diagnose needs but to advise on courses of action.

All this will weaken the boundary between school and non-school. If we continue and combine the traditions in which Terry O'Neill and Crawford Somerset respectively worked, the community will flow through the school, and the school students will move about the community. Does this not mean that the school will lose its identity? Not if it is clear about aims and as long as those aims add up to its being a place for learning: learning in the fullest sense, not just a market place for inert ideas, where teachers issue prepared information for their students to memorise and later to be tested on their ability to reformulate it and hand it back. If the school is concerned to help its students, of whatever age, to make coherent sense of experience, to learn the forms of the creative arts, to learn the skills of collaboration, it will achieve identity.

The identity of the 'learning centre' will not be weakened if at the same time it is the co-ordinating agency for outreach work in the community. There are already in existence many such agencies, not all based in 'learning centres'. The advantage of establishing them alongside the adolescent in compulsory schooling, is twofold. The adolescent may provide resources for community service, thereby standing to learn things of value, and at the same time become familiar with the network of local supports against the time shortly ahead when they may be of use to him.

Education cannot itself do anything to resolve the unemployment that has become structural in society. What it can do is prepare and then assist the growing number of people who, while technically unemployed, are spending more working hours than many of the employed in what might be called unremunerated occupation. While drawing social security benefits they may be working unpaid as unofficial play-leaders, home-helps, or advisers. There are graduates in social sciences who act as non-charging agencies assisting anyone confused by bureaucracy to find their way through the mazes of claims and appeals. Others, with no qualifications, may be giving their time to community arts groups. Clearly they are deriving satisfaction from work, often uncomfortable work, but drawing their income from a totally different and public source. Perhaps more should be done to relate these currently grey areas to school and the adolescent, though to do so there would be many prejudices to overcome regarding the respectability of paid employment.

There is one final consideration. A recurrent stumbling block in any discussion of community and education is the uncertainty surrounding the very term 'community'. The Seebohm Committee defined it thus: 'The notion of a community implies the existence of a network of reciprocal social relationships, which among other things ensure mutual aid and give those who experience it a sense of well-being.' This is helpful, but more often than not those of us working in the field may, by that definition, be serving several distinct communities, some of them with conflicting interests. This should not necessarily bedevil us. Education cannot itself unaided create community where none exists. What it can do however, is to help make networks more effective and to help reconcile separate networks. In his recent book, *India: A Wounded Civilisation*, V.S. Naipaul accuses the Indian press of retaining a caste vision, of saying 'what is remote from me is remote from me', instead of seeking 'to put India in touch with itself'. That insight might serve as a goal for community education, the attempt to put a locality in touch with itself as a means to its becoming more of a community.

And if, in conclusion, we are looking for the central activity that will put a neighbourhood in touch with itself, I cannot end better than with John Berger's honouring of *gossip*. In *Pig Earth*, he writes:

> the function of this *gossip* which, in fact, is close, oral, daily history, is to allow the whole village to define itself . . . What distinguishes the life of the village is that it is also *a living portrait of itself*: a communal portrait, in that everybody is portrayed and everybody portrays. . . . Without such a portrait – and the *gossip* which is its raw material – the village would have been forced to doubt its own existence. Every story, and every comment on the story – which is a proof that the story has been *witnessed* – contributes to the portrait and confirms the existence of the village.

The definition of a community might well be a network of people continuously engaged in telling each other stories about themselves. And a worthwhile goal for community education, whatever its form, might be to facilitate the availability to its public of the resources, including technological ones, for the richest continuous redefinition of its identity, its membership and its values. In an age of increased contacts but thinned relationships, we all stand in need of confirmation of our existence and identity, individually and communally. We must all go on telling stories.

14
The Media and Education *

Kim Taylor

Idleness, we are told, accounts for the debasement of language. The tongue's preference for easy forms melts sharp sounds in a word; the mind's reluctance to strike a new coin blurs original meaning. The drift in the shape of a word follows well-established linguistic rules; the drift in meaning reflects social change, leaving traces which historians value. No matter how often purists insist that there are many mediums through which humans communicate their thoughts and feelings, 'the media' has come more and more to mean 'broadcasting', often simply 'television'. This corrupt and limited use of 'the media' best suits the dimensions of this essay; and its use here is the more justified by current technical development. The television screen can already be employed not only for broadcasting but for video-recordings, as a monitor of remote events, as the terminal for access to computer stores of print and picture information and for creative interactions with them. The place of the 'box in the corner' is set to increase in our lives. But even in terms of broadcasting alone, the potentialities of so pervasive a medium for education merit reflection. We shall be able to squint into the future a little more confidently if we note where we stand now in educational broadcasting and consider how we got here. What comes next will not just reflect a range of technical possibilities but the projection of the tensions and pressures that have brought educational broadcasting to its present equivocal position.

Was there ever a medium which promised so much for education and delivered so little? All those resources of cash and talent, that power to penetrate into every household and school in the land – and yet we count television as peripheral, if not inimical, to education. Reports about how the provision of school or adult education might be improved seldom devote more than a paragraph or two to broadcasting. The customary reference to the media's *potential* serves both to

---

* The views expressed in this chapter are the author's own, and not necessarily those of the Independent Broadcasting Authority.

show that the writer or committee is up to date, and to underline the media's actual irrelevance. Vigorous and extensive writing about television generally deals with its anti-educational not its educational role, its encouragement to passivity, materialism, envy, disrespect, violence, prurience, and the rest of the Media's Deadly Sins, rather than with its contribution to the pursuit of sweetness and light.

If we attempt to consider what educational broadcasting has and has not done, as a step towards understanding what it can and cannot do, we had best focus on its contribution to the education of people at home. For viewing in school or other institutions is a very special case. Schools' television closely reflects the requirement of teachers. From reports and through meetings, teachers' opinions are mediated to broadcasting's administrators and producers. Committees made up largely of teachers, and of ex-teachers turned administrators, professors, inspector's and the like, help to plan and monitor what is done. One may say, then, of schools' broadcasts in relation to the classroom what Hugh Kingsmill said of those military exercises held at the start of the War: 'as close an approximation to the real thing as was consistent with the absence of the enemy and the presence of a general'. There are serious problems to do with the utilisation of the substantial output for schools, and question marks against the future effect of video-recordings and other technical developments on current patterns of transmission, but in general schools broadcasting has assumed settled forms which tell us more about the expectations dominant in schools than about the possibilities inherent in broadcasting.

And yet the school, or at any rate the college, has left a strong mark on that large portion of educational television intended for home consumption. The transference of a word can bring unfortunate accompaniments. Suppose we try that technique from psychoanalysis fashionable in the twenties and thirties – free association. What springs to our minds in response to the word 'education'? For most of us, impressed by early experience, the corresponding image is of someone teaching some matter to a group or class – briefly, 'school' or, by simple extension, some similar institutional setting for the education of adults. The formal organisation of learning has come to monopolise the many possible images the word 'education' might legitimately evoke. When adult education took to the air, the dominant living model was transplanted to the broadcast. Thereby a measure of educational authenticity was bestowed upon the suspect medium. As early motor cars were carriages without horses, so early adult educational broadcasts were lectures without halls; and the imitation extended to both subject and style.

Thus, the early choice of subject matter on ITV was notably academic. The very first series was *Midnight Oil*, a set of lectures by university dons. It was followed by other academic offerings – a City and Guilds Farming Course, 'O' level Physics, instruction in French and the like. There were occasional series on hobbies and domestic interests, but the intention was less to satisfy popular taste than to elevate it. Just as Lord Reith required his news-readers on radio to wear dinner jackets, so educationists sought to add dignity to the new enterprise by insisting on Sunday-best subject matter. Besides, it was the dominant belief of the time, to which Reith gave firm expression, that the difference between popular taste and cultivated taste was to be accounted for not by any difference in capacity or settled inclination but by opportunity. What had been planted in the few could now be broadcast to the many; and they would prove a fertile soil. Response would be ardent, for all of us 'needs must love the highest when we see it'.

Alas, for all but a few of the romantic intelligentsia, time has dimmed that generous illusion. It belonged to a period in which, although a more geniune democracy had been politically embraced, a strong sense of hierarchy persisted. Certain manifestations of culture, like certain patterns of behaviour, were thought so obviously superior that everyone would wish to pursue them. Such – for reasons we shall later examine – is still the accepted view among our continental neighbours, especially where the Roman and Byzantine traditions have been stronger than the Germanic. In such countries they teach 'high culture' in the schools and promote it in daily life with a confidence that astonishes an Anglo-Saxon. For with us, democratic criteria reign. What Michael Young has called 'the social basis for different subjects' has become so unclear that a once hierarchical pyramid has been eroded into a rubble of individual choice. The consensus about what constitutes a worthwhile education has long since fragmented. Many of our universities now profess disciplines until quite recently thought basely practical or laughed at as trans-atlantic; and in colleges of further education and the like, wherever a dozen people can be gathered together under a banner, almost any banner, there (the current state of finances permitting) a course can begin.

It is no wonder that such changing perceptions about the subject matter appropriate for education, shifting always in the direction of being broader and more popular, have found a ready response in a medium accustomed to count its audiences by the million. Let's try an examination question about some television programmes, the subject matter of which their titles, or some brief description, will sufficiently indicate. Which of the following recent series were 'educational': from the BBC, *Life on Earth*, *Darwin and the voyage of the Beagle*, the complete cycle of Shakespeare's plays; from ITV, a three-hour study of the making of the new ballet *Mayerling*; *Nuts and Bolts of the British*

Economy; the season's offerings from Glyndebourne; *The Mighty Micro* – about the silicon chip? As happens sometimes in exams, there's a trick in the question. The answer is none: none of these is officially educational. None, that is, were processed by educational committees and 'validated' as educational, nor made by an educational department. On the other hand, ITV's *educational* offerings in a recent season included series on soccer skills, astronomy, sex roles, toy making, basic numeracy, self-sufficiency, the evolution of plant life, motorcycle maintenance and safety, self-help health care . . . the educational broadcasters plainly have no prerogative over what Parkinson would call 'the OK subjects'. To the contrary, they have abandoned their once separate pool of subjects for the open sea, and now seek the same popular and palatable fish as any other of the more 'serious' sorts of broadcaster.

Same fish perhaps: but surely, when served, cooked differently. Should we search for the distinctive quality of educational broadcasting not in its subject matter but in its style? In some contexts the answer must be a resounding 'yes'. There's something about the tone of voice, the austerity of effects, a certain rather dour directness, that tells us when we've switched on to an Open University broadcast. There are brilliant exceptions, of course, but the dominant style in OU broadcasts is economically designed – in pedagogy as well as in resources – to meet the requirements of committed students. School broadcasts were once similarly distinctive. And the manners of the lecture hall and the classroom have certainly left marks on adult education broadcasting directed to viewers at home. We expect educational broadcasts to be in their tone sober, in their intent improving, and in their character expository – that is, they consist of verbal explanations, just as does most lecturing or teaching. They emphasise sense rather than sensibility, education of a rational rather than an experiential kind, fit for the cool and formal environment of learning in public. But despite such basic similarities in expectation, broadcast education has begun more and more to stray from being a two-dimensional reflection of institutional education in the flesh. Many schools series could now be mistaken in the style they adopt for general output broadcasts. It is the more necessary to avoid any obtrusive characteristics in the case of educational broadcasts designed to attract adults at leisure. After all, in an institution a teacher can insist that his students attend – well, outwardly at least. His hand, not theirs, is on the switch. How different in the home. Minds wander – no questions are asked; feet wander – other things can be done. A flick, a prod, even now a touch made without moving from an easy chair and there's something more alluring to look at, or the balm of a blank screen. Small wonder, then, that adult education broadcasters find themselves using the same techniques as their general output colleagues quickly to catch and then firmly to hold the viewer's attention. David Bellamy's *Botanic Man* on ITV was an educational series where David Attenborough's *Life on Earth* on BBC was not. It needs acute perception indeed to see some style in the one and not the other that establishes its claim to a distinctive educational identity.

Besides being expository, educational broadcasting runs to long series. Why *series*? Teaching in schools and colleges is also done that way, of course. Tuesday, 11.30 Maths, Friday 2.15 Science double period, or whatever, week after week. There's good reason in the arrangement. On the one hand there's need for variety; on the other, in education we deal with things in depth. We aim at something beyond journalism, which tends to be shallow, and beyond casual speculation and reading, which remains superficial. We probe, we dissect; and it all takes time. In parallel, educational programmes on television are generally arranged in extended series – normally in six or seven or 13 half-hour parts. Half an hour is the standard module of our schedule. Any mystery in the number of parts is explained by 13 weeks making up the quarters into which the broadcasters divide the year.

Educationists will wonder if even 13 parts is deep enough: broadcasters have begun to ask if six is too deep by half. This doubt has been stimulated by a bombshell of a book. Its unexciting title is *The Television Audience: patterns of viewing* (Goodhardt, Ehrenburg and Collins 1975). These researchers traced a pattern in the viewing of series (usually weekly) so consistent that you could almost call it a law. It runs like this: of the people who see programme one of the series, some 55 per cent will watch programme two; of these, about 55 per cent will see programme three; and so on. By programme seven, therefore, only three or four per cent will have stayed throughout the course. Deceptively, the viewing figures for each separate programme remain much the same. The viewing habits of the individuals comprising successive audiences are a great deal more volatile than the consistency of the totals suggests. Viewers in large numbers it seems cheerfully drop in and out. And this is true for *all* series, educational as well as entertainment.

At first impact, this viewing 'law' astonishes to the point of disbelief. Other artefacts of a serial character do not suffer a comparable fickleness. For example, those who publish newspapers, magazines and part-works count on a high consistency in the behaviour of consumers. What evening class could run if its members indulged such casualness? Besides, addiction to each instalment of a televised soap opera is legendary. And from our own experience we recall our devotion to, say, *Edward and Mrs Simpson*; we would not have missed it for the world. Old friends turning down our dinner invitation confessed an immovable date with *The Forsyte Saga*. Indeed, like all the best 'laws', the one for series-viewing embraces a normal range of deviations from the average it represents, and certain special exceptions. Sometimes, of course, viewers find a series exceptionally significant or compelling and, especially if the competition is weak, exhibit a rare persistence. Some series gather a small but more committed audience. ITV's programme on basic numeracy, *Make It Count*, was watched through all its 13 parts by some 25 per cent of its viewers who clearly valued help with a severe disability (Stringer 1979). Similarly, Open University television programmes are watched (though radio programmes are not listened to) with quite a high degree of regularity by a fairly high proportion of enrolled students (Grundin 1978). These rare exceptions noted, the law, carefully researched and independently checked, provides a remarkably sound basis for forecasting viewers' behaviour.

Upon reflection we should not perhaps be so surprised by it. ITV recently broadcast a 13 part series called *Make Your Own Boat*. Goodhardt, Ehrenburg and Collins (1975), taken *au pied de la lettre*, conjure up a vision of millions of homes cluttered with boats in various stages of incompleteness. More plausibly, what their law implies is that normal television viewing is an activity unlike, for example, buying a publication, taking a course, or setting out to construct a boat. All these activities involve a degree of deliberate commitment which switching on the telly does not. Those who pursue them constitute a relatively stable, self-selecting group, whereas the viewing masses, far larger in number, are more random in behaviour. We have to pay for each specific publication we choose; it costs nothing to switch about on the television set. To enrol for a course (still more to pursue it) involves an investment of intention and effort; watching television implies no more than the capacity to resist sleep. 'Selecting' programmes often means no more than pushing the most familiar of the buttons, or choosing the least of available evils. Friends drop in, we're invited to dinner, we get talking and forget the time, we go to the cinema, some other programme attracts us more . . . for a thousand and one reasons we miss parts in a series. Among the millions who happen to have watched any one programme in a series, then, we should not be surprised that only a modest percentage have watched a majority of them, that a very small percentage indeed have watched the lot, and that the longer the series the smaller those percentages become.

This realisation poses a considerable problem for those who hope to educate by broadcasts to the home. Recollections of our own behaviour as viewers may make us yet more uneasy. Even when the programme counts as 'being watched' by the researchers, we recall how people in the room chat, how 'phones ring and visitors come to the door; how we sometimes wander off to get a drink or listen vaguely while glancing at the evening paper . . . it is as well, perhaps, that Goodhardt, Ehrenburg and Collins have got no further than counting whether a set is switched on. The situation is wholly different when programmes are watched in an institution, or as part of a course. Teachers and examiners can question; missing a programme, even a lapse of attention, may carry a penalty. Different too is the case with print where flickering concentration can be remedied by re-reading. Print sits faithfully waiting our bidding like Old Dog Tray; a television series goes scampering on, out of sight, out of mind. Educational broadcasters, then, must come to terms with the transience of their broadcasts and with the viewers' ability to dismiss or ignore them. Their special mode – exposition in longish series – is particularly vulnerable. It is likely to hold the viewers' attention best when richly elaborated as in, say, Kenneth Clark's *Civilisation*; and to fail when, as is usually the case for officially educational programmes, the resources stretch to producing only the poorest of relations to that patrician model. So that it will not matter too much if parts are missed, educational producers have begun to loosen the 'educational' structure of some series, that is the degree to which one part is a development of another part, the whole constituting a coherent exploration of a subject. Many series have begun to look more and more like a collection of discontinuous items around a particular theme – scarcely more than a magazine or miscellany. There are in practice some good reasons, educational as well as audience-building and economic, for retaining the form of a series, but we should no longer retain the customary justification for series that a television producer deals for the millions, as the class-teacher deals for the few, with a subject in depth. That is a delusion, however plausible. 'Depth' may characterise an educational series as planned by the broadcaster; it does not characterise educational broadcasts as seen in the home, by the overwhelming majority of viewers.

Besides this technical 'pattern of viewing' reason, there is a social reason for educational broadcasting in Britain taking on, more and more, the colour of general broadcasting. Recently I spent five years living in Paris and working in Mediterranean countries. Each autumn the railway stations all over France blossom with posters put out by the nationalised railway company. The SNCF invites would-be signal-men, engine-drivers, firemen, and various *petits fonctionnaires*, to enter the railway service – by sitting a competitive written examination. Our predilection runs counter. It lies with learning by practice not theory, by experience not books. We doubt the value of paper qualifications, putting our trust in character and commonsense. Such an emphasis is most celebrated in the context of the public schools, of course, but is far more widespread. Its prevalence has been traced by Paul Willis in the less academic classes of comprehensive schools, among boys expecting to work in factories, and he adds: 'the adult working class world: the air of practicality which prevails on the English shopfloor, and the distrust of theory there, considerably strengthen this kind of perspective' (Willis 1977).

And then I remember going, one Wednesday at lunch time, to see an exhibition of Millet's paintings, notoriously crowded at the weekends, only to find long queues outside the Grand Palais and crowds within – young children with their mothers (Wednesday being a primary school free day), and teenagers in school groups – all astoundingly docile and serious. What they made of it I do not know; but no child I saw protested in words or demeanour, nor did any adult to which I expressed amazement doubt the propriety of imposing such cultural rituals. Such would not be questioned by many parents in other Latin countries, still less among Slavs and other 'Byzantines'. Our own emphasis is very different. We care less about the formal transmission of high culture through classrooms, galleries or other means than that the recipients should actively respond, participate, positively enjoy. A strong inclination toward equality, reinforced over many generations by Protestantism, leads us to worry not only about whether in some uncertain final sense a thing is good, but whether the individual finds it so. Not mere assent but conviction or enthusiasm is the aim. Hence, in contemporary education, the emphasis on 'relevance' – a term which embraces, *inter alia*, what is appropriate to a particular learner at a particular time, the only convincing test being in practice whether he takes to it fairly readily, or chooses it among various options. We have lost our stomach for academic and cultural enforcement. The absence of a nationally required curriculum never ceases to amaze continental educationalists. To them, justification by personal choice would seem as marginally relevant as would 'Justification by Faith' to Catholic or Orthodox theologians.

This reluctance to attend to what experts and teachers declare to be best (and of experts and teachers to assert it), this brash predilection for giving pride of place to our untutored reactions, Matthew Arnold in *Culture and Anarchy* called 'philistinism'. He drew his contrast chiefly between England and France. It has not lessened with the passage of time. How shall we account for it? Many Europeans, perplexed by English peculiarities, attribute them to our climate. The islanders' notorious difficulty with logic, their resistance to the dictates of reason, their inability to accept classical canons of taste and style, are visible signs of minds etiolated by a lack of clear sunlight, clouded by mist, soggy with rain. At this same level of amiable generalisation, we may speculate upon the chicken-and-egg connection between a country's history and its educational style. Our emphasis on character can be seen as part cause, part effect of success, during the first Industrial Revolution, in creating the simpler sorts of machinery and making them work; and our wish to make education relevant to the individual has to do with an ancient disposition to democracy, a belief that the declared wishes and opinions of individuals should be taken seriously, even those now of the young.

The persisting belief in standards which merit respect beyond the individual's own appreciation of them leads, on the continent, to an un-English status for the 'priesthood' of experts and teachers, even in some countries – as the English note with amusement – to the incorporation of academic titles as a form of respectful address. Such attitudes have left a mark on continental broadcasting, which strikes an Englishman as curiously didactic. We need not doubt that the French, for example, like being entertained as much as we do; but they seem to accept that exposure to high culture, like actually going to church, is a necessary constituent of a life properly conducted. We more confidently dismiss any such afflictions. On radio we did once make a brave attempt to establish a channel for broadcasting of a sustained, consistently cultural and 'serious' kind. The Third Programme has long since been reduced to tattered remnants of what it was. France, to the contrary, still boldly labels an extensive radio service 'France Culture'. On television, BBC2 in its early days took the cultural high road: now with lots of sport, assorted comedians, jazz musicians and the like, it strives to win that accolade of public ratings which even a licence-based public broadcasting system seems to regard as an indispensable justification. Such a preoccupation (all too visible at times) does not rule French television. Academia colonises the most unlikely places. I recall once, in early innocent days, switching on at the scheduled time to watch the *Lives of a Bengal Lancer*, only to find it dressed fore and aft with long explanations of its socio-political and artistic significance which would surely have amazed MGM and Clark Gable. Almost any film that is foreign or rather old or vaguely experimental is likely to be dubbed a *dossier d'écran*, towards which viewers will be instructed in the proper response. Music is minutely dissected and analysed. Everyday events disappear under elaborations of serious comment, like a bone or hank of hair in a jewelled reliquary. To an Englishman, it all seems intrusive, pretentious and, worst sin of all, generally boring. French television, closely controlled by the State, still works on the Reithian principle that 'if you can't get what you like, you like what you get'. No longer is it so with us. In France – still more in Eastern Europe – the style of popular television is strongly educative: in Britain the style of educational broadcasting is increasingly popular. The public's low tolerance for being 'improved' or 'instructed' or 'got at', leads producers to reckon that anything visibly educational is a turn-off. Consequently both BBC and ITV have adopted a policy of 'education by stealth', and educational programmes for home consumption creep forward unannounced, without any labels or mannerisms that might identify them.

Worse by far than that wearing of masks, which television has forced upon educationalists, has been the crisis of identity inflicted upon them by local radio. For local radio, like television and national radio, is also required by Act of Parliament to provide education as well as information and entertainment; and this applies to the independent stations as well as to those of the BBC. We normally use television for a succession of set pieces each lasting, with rare exceptions, somewhere between a half-hour and an hour. Into that scheme of things, programmes of a length similar to the traditional lesson or lecture can be mounted in succession to comprise an educational series. But local radio has not adopted any such scheduling practice. Long stretches of time are treated as a continuum of music and chat. It is a sort of stream of consciousness – or, some unkindly suggest, of unconsciousness. How do you fit education into that? Goodhardt, Ehrenburg and Collins (1975) have told us that viewers do not, for the most part, attend throughout a televised series as though they were enrolled in a class; all the same, they *could* do so. A certain plausibility remains, therefore, in building educational television around more-or-less structured series. Not so with local radio. Then again, we talk of people being glued to the box, but no-one imagines them being glued to the transistor. They listen and half listen while getting on with other things – housework, or factory work or shop work – and while thinking or talking about this and that. Local radio is above all a friendly, easy-going companion, altogether less demanding than television. Can we accommodate the primary expectation of education – serious attention to what is being taught – to so amiable a medium?

Within this unpromising context, local radio broadcasters have displayed invention and ingenuity. Their educational offerings are chiefly contained in a succession of interviews and discussions, interwoven with music; in phone-ins, quizzes and questions, and music; notification of what's on, what to read, what to see, and music; access programmes, information about groups to join, and music; brief comments by experts on news or current affairs or viewers' problems, and music. Sometimes an interview or a discussion or phone-in grows into a sizeable item, but the general pattern is of an archipelago of small islands of speech in a sea of music. The broadcasters know that the majority of local radio listeners, even if they wanted to do so, cannot stop everything to listen to a sustained and closely reasoned argument or piece of instruction. Instead, they have tried to offer a scatter of items which in themselves provide some interest for the majority, and which may stimulate a minority to some further thought or conversation or reading. Some items are followed by details of local activities – club and society meetings, forthcoming plays and concerts – or invitations to write for various pamphlets, or information about related articles in magazines and the like. Sometimes an item or programme is linked to an appeal by an organisation for volunteers to help with some particular local need. One can quite often trace, then, an encouragement to individuals to put themselves in the way of an experience which may prove broadly educational. But an occasional encouragement to some educational activity off air, which only a small minority will undertake, is scarcely a reasonable discharge of the duty to disseminate education. The phone-ins and chats and short inter-views and jaunty bits and pieces need justification as educational *in their own right* if the Act is to be fulfilled. We have seen how home education on television has moved from education by declared intent to 'education by stealth'; on local radio we seem to have arrived at 'education on the wing'. Can anything so fragmentary properly be called education at all?

We can approach the problem through another medium than broadcasting. A book on horticulture and a popular gardening magazine: which of them is educational? Perhaps both are. They belong to differently conceived ways of learning which, to confuse us, readily interweave. In the one, the things we learn have been economically organised to help us achieve a defined objective – mastery of a skill or body of knowledge at a determined level, often checked by an exam. In the other, there is no clearly defined objective, no fixed level of achievement, and seldom much organisation. Most of us, as parents, teachers or friends, have known children who display obdurate stupidity in learning something quite simple taught in class, and extraordinary facility with some elaborate 'trivia' of their own choosing. Acquiring a few grammatical structures or dates or required facts or foreign words defeats them; yet they learn intimate details about pop stars, or recite ancient cricket scores, or identify passing aeroplanes, or build complex models. They are not taught such things; they 'pick them up'. In much the same way, adults speak of learning 'by experience'. A man decides to start growing vegetables. He reads a bit, digs and plants, and observes how his plants progress. He runs into a difficulty, takes out a book from the library, talks with an expert neighbour, consults the man who runs the gardening shop. He buys what he needs, reads the label and accompanying leaflet and applies what it says. He gets gardening magazines, watches programmes on television and tries out some of the tips. He joins the local gardening club, visits the trial gardens at Wisley, chats with an allotment holder. He reads some more, practises, observes, enquires . . . three or four years of this and he is likely to find, to his surprise, that people ask him questions and that he often knows the answers. As a way of learning, it is slow, messy, individual, patchy, disorganised, incoherent, uneven and uninstitutionalised. Its achievements pass unmeasured. But it is how we learn, to the level we actually require, most of what we use or enjoy in our daily lives.

Educationists call this 'informal education' – and concentrate on the formal sort. It happens any old way and defies professional organis-ation. Only in the kindergarten and the early years of primary education have teachers tried to exploit it. There the emphasis has been laid on providing an environment for informal learning rather than a structure for formal teaching. As a method it is sometimes called 'child-centred', for in informal learning, the teacher is not centre stage. The learner invokes the teacher's help when he needs it: the conventional image of teaching puts the initiative the other way round. Informal learning looks chaotic because it depends, critically, on the interest of particular learners at particular moments. In the formal sort, order reigns because one person – the teacher – shapes what is to be learnt, when it is to be learnt, responding to more settled imperatives than individual interest. He carves, from the gross and formless matrix of the possible, a course which responds to some requirement of time or structural economy. This he tries to convey in coherent and uniform sequence to a whole, disparate group of learners. None the less, despite the teacher's best efforts, and often to his despair, individuals 'select' fragments from the whole, noting the trivial and overlooking the essential, in a manner so idiosyncratic that it can seem wanton. For unless constrained, we obstinately and naturally learn by the accretion of those fragments which interest us or seem to us significant. In the early stages these can seem random pieces in a formless mosaic: in time, a high degree of comprehensiveness and coherence may emerge. Insecure and uncertain, we often have difficulty in recognising the fact. Unless we have some check with what some external authority establishes – a teacher, an examiner, a course, a book by a recognised expert – we're not sure what we do know, still less whether it 'counts' as knowledge. Impressed by early experience of formal instruction, we don't perceive our knowledge for what it is unless and until it is officially defined and labelled – the 'myths' of 'packaging values' and of the 'measurement of values' which Illich has so vividly attacked (Illich 1970). Between formal and informal ways of learning there need be no contradiction: at best they powerfully combine. But we who have been taught in schools and universities, and those who have taught us, suffer a myopia like that of the well-disciplined British armies faced with American revolutionaries: we have difficulty in recognising, still more of taking seriously, something that can't drill to order and doesn't wear a scarlet coat.

We have suggested that British homes provide for television educationists a terrain better suited to skirmishing than to formal manoeuvres. So far we have examined, as reasons, problems arising from patterns of serial viewing and from an insular scepticism towards the pronouncements of the cultural and academic establishment. There are, in addition, certain 'technical' shortcomings in television (used within Western norms) as a medium for conveying ideas or skills or knowledge of the complexity we normally connect with education. In examining these we must distinguish sharply between television used institutionally and television beamed at uncommitted viewers at leisure in their homes. Jonathan Miller has described television as 'a hole you can push anything through'. True. Educationists however are concerned with *learning*; which is to say less with the pushing through than the picking up. Institutional television is set in the context of a variety of learning activities, whether arranged by the teacher for a class or by the designers of a distance-learning 'package' for committed learners. Suppose there were no such context: no pressure from a future requirement – neither verbal questioning, nor written exercise, nor discussion, nor exam. And then suppose there was no record of what the teacher said – no notes taken by the listener, nor parallel text for every learner. In such circumstances, we might be entertained, or stimulated; we might pick up the odd bit of information, be stirred by an intriguing idea, be motivated to find out something more elsewhere . . . but how much, except in this very diffuse, informal, hit-and-miss sense, would we expect to learn from the ephemeral words of the teacher? 'No impression without expression' ran the saw once regularly used in the training of teachers. Secure learning is an active, participant process. Television enters the great majority of homes without any prospect of subsequent activity, and offers small prospect of accurate assimilation or retention. No wonder it disappoints those whose expectations derive from formal education.

Even those obvious advantages which educators on television enjoy over their room-bound colleagues sometimes prove, on closer examination, two-edged. The physical process of watching television – that is, gazing in a subdued light at a small, flickering screen – has been described by a recent critic as 'living within a nationwide sense-deprivation tank' (Mander 1979 Chapter 8). It is a condition in which we would normally become quickly bored. Producers are trained in a variety of compensatory expedients. Anxious to keep viewers' attention, television has a bias continually towards the heightened, the dramatic and the richly varied. Conflict makes 'better television' than harmony, strong emotions than reasonableness, a high frequency of incident than the normal diffuseness of everyday experience, personalities than generalities, Many heads are more interesting than one; in any discussion, then, best to multiply the number of participants, even if each is thereby forced to pare complex issues to the bare bones. Indeed, words should be kept to a minimum. Whenever possible a picture should be used. 'Do not qualify', a producer told Milton Shulman in the studio, 'you are here to speak captions to pictures' (Shulman 1973 p. 81). So visual a medium reduced ideas to headlines. All the words spoken by BBC national newsreaders in a day, it is reckoned, would comfortably fit on the front page of *The Times*. Moreover, the sort of visual sequences that make 'good television' are often too over-charged, too distractingly suggestive, too swift-changing to suit a didactic purpose. When an educational producer subdues the visual element to give prominence to words, or trims the images of redundancies, accidental juxtapositions, half-seen details and all the confused richness of the real world, what remains provides a diet too Spartan for the 'ravenous eye' to enjoy. In short, the biases in domestic television (though these may occasionally be triumphantly overcome) are ill-suited to teaching purpose. When educationists seize upon television to enhance one element – the visual – they need to be aware that they may thereby seriously diminish the others.

None of this is to deny, of course, that television can be used effectively as direct teaching (a commonplace in a number of countries – see Mackenzie, Postgate and Scupham 1975) or as a valuable ancillary component where the burden of the essential teaching lies elsewhere (the more familiar mode with us). However, if our essential model is derived from the elaborated learning context of formal education, then the appropriate programmes, whether designed didactically or as 'enrichment', will only fortuitously and occasionally appeal to those outside the circle of organised and committed learners. If we try to appeal to a more general audience, without the supportive and varied learning context, we shall find ourselves making compromises which may well induce us to dismiss television as corrosive to our high purposes, gimmicky, shallow and so on. To the contrary, if our model of education is informal, then television's usual modes and manners will suit us well enough, and we shall find no shortage of willing viewers. Television documentaries and features, long-running magazines and miscellanies (*World in Action, Horizon, Man Alive, The South Bank Show, Gardener's World* and the rest) appeal to the taste of many people, just as do their equivalents in print. British reading habits, by comparison with those on the continent, are characterised by a taste for newspapers, journals, and an unparalleled variety of specialist and hobby magazines. It is the other side of that disregard for the more organised, official and formal sort of education, a manifestation of the predilection for idiosyncratic ways, which we earlier suggested as an attitude particularly widespread in Britain.

Yet no one would want to suggest that the television equivalent of fluttering from article to article, or from paragraph to paragraph, is the only way to learn, or the best way for someone whose appetite has been whetted. Informal education on television need not end with adding fragments to coalesce with what we already know, inserting ideas which set us questioning our previous thoughts and attitudes, or – in the faint praise of the Annan Report – 'helping some people to understand something about a topic which they would otherwise have never encountered' (Annan 1977 p. 305). To such self-contained, immediate, mental acts can be added motivation to subsequent activities, of various kinds. We noted earlier that the only teachers so far to exploit informal modes (what might be called *natural* modes) of learning have been those concerned with small children; it should be no surprise that a clear expression of broadcasting's value as informal education has come from Monica Sims, for many years the producer of the BBC's series for young children, *Playschool*. Here, following an interview, are her reported comments on the celebrated American series *Sesame Street*.

> If Monica Sims has a particular conviction on how children's programmes should be made, 'active participation' would probably be the right word. She experienced a feeling of success if one of her programmes prompted a child to turn away from the screen and do something the programme had suggested. What shocked Ms Sims about *Sesame Street* was that the producers of the programme wanted to keep the child's eyes glued to the screen – although she admitted it was an excellent entertainment series. To quote Ms Sims: 'what would make me happiest would be if they went away; if we could stimulate them enough to go away and do something creative themselves'. To find out, make, build, watch, enquire, listen and help . . . to wonder, think, imagine.

Sesame Street, here dismissively described as 'an excellent entertainment series', is in fact designed to teach basic literacy to children *directly off the screen*. When the BBC mounted a series to help with the basic literacy of adults it adopted a wholly different strategy. The series' chief aim was to lead illiterates to the one-to-one tuition provided by thousands of volunteer supporters (Hargreaves 1980). It is fairly common for educational broadcasts to be linked to some related learning activity, conceived as an ancillary, an extension to the broadcast itself. The curiosity of *On the Move* lay in the explicit rejection of any attempt to teach or to explore a topic in depth – such educational dimensions being exclusively catered for off-screen. Such a shift presupposes that resources have been found for the prepared activities (funded in the case of adult literacy by the government). Even so, establishing and sustaining the three-way connection between broadcasters, viewers and agencies on the ground is complex, and provides numerous opportunities for recrimination. Despite the difficulties, we may expect an increasing proportion of educational broadcasting for the home-viewer to shift from the mode of *Sesame Street* to that of *Playschool*, to aim less at *providing* education than *promoting* it.

Although television as leisure viewing may be ill-adapted to dealing with a matter in depth and complexity, none (least of all the advertisers) doubt its power to stimulate viewer response. The serialisation of a book may require crass simplification; it may be followed through every part by only a minority of viewers; but the bookshops and libraries experience a surge of interest in it such as no other medium evokes. The percentage of viewers prompted to respond is certain to be very small, but the number, by the standards of any other force of attraction, will be large. For the reach of television is unparalleled. The great majority of the audience that watches at least one part of a popular serialisation – say, conservatively, some 30 million viewers – will see the programme as a substitute for reading the book (IBA 1980): but if one per cent of the viewers bought the book, the publisher would have a best-seller on his hands, if one per cent of one per cent, a sound investment. In parallel, the percentage of viewers induced by television to embark on a course of study may be minuscule, and yet the actual number large by the standards of adult education institutions or distance-learning colleges. Taken over, say, a year, such small percentages but sizeable numbers, arising cumulatively from a succession of television programmes, would mean that a great many adults had been brought to some active, and perhaps unfamiliar, experience of learning. Some of the immediate effects would be measurable (the purchase of books, enrolment in courses and the like) but the possible continuation thereafter into a variety of informal ways of learning are likely to remain unmeasured and unknown. And we should remember that this sort of broadcast stimulus may be provided as readily by a single programme as by a long series: in such a perspective, the argument for running a series becomes less a matter of the depth that a series allows than the succession of separate chances it provides to connect individuals with the available opportunities. And not merely single programmes but programmes of many kinds – not just planned educational series – may act as an appropriate trigger to subsequent learning.

For we have noted that educational series, in order to gain admittance to British homes, have had to don a disguise which allows them to be mistaken for 'information', or even 'entertainment' programmes of the more sober sort: reciprocally, such programmes can be mistaken for education. Some general output programmes (like *Civilisation* or *Life on Earth*) are in any case indistinguishable in character from specifically educational broadcasts: but the range of possibilities is much wider. In 1977 a modest educational experiment was carried out in the Yorkshire Television transmission area with a four-part popular drama series. Intended for viewing at 'peak' evening hours, this dealt entertainingly with Disraeli the man – his rise to fame, his relations with his remarkable wife, his ambivalent place in the glittering public world of his day. Educationally significant elements – political events, social conditions, economic developments, changing attitudes, artistic and scientific achievements and the rest – were referred to only in passing. Amongst the viewers, however, there was a minority whose interest in such matters was stimulated by the *un*educational programme. They were invited to write in for a package of materials. This included brief essays on Victorian themes, quotations from Disraeli and his contemporaries, an annotated bibliography, a special feature about Victorian Yorkshire, a list of relevant exhibits in local museums, suggestions for Sunday afternoon drives to places of Victorian interest, details of related courses in further education colleges and education institutes, and so on. Local newspapers, local radio and libraries joined in the exercise. The public response was unexpectedly strong and – as a subsequent questionnaire revealed – came from individuals in a wide span of socio-economic classes. In this way a programme designed as entertainment – utilising skills, a budget and a viewing time seldom available to education broadcasting – was suborned to serve an educational purpose. As General Booth once said, 'Why should the devil have all the best tunes?'

Contemplating principal 'types' of educational broadcasting, then, we may distinguish these: first, the *institutional/instructional* – a service to organised and/or committed viewers, whether in itself the main exposition or a planned portion of a course; second, the *informal* – a contribution to the flux of items from which individuals select those elements they find interesting, useful or enriching; third, the *oblique* – an encouragement and a lead to learning opportunities off-screen. We might characterise these three types of educational broadcasting fishily, as feeding the inhabitants of an aquarium, casting bread upon the waters, and using bait on a hook and line.

If we try to discern the future which current technology sketches, we shall be reinforced in wanting to use educational broadcasting informally and obliquely rather than instructionally. Video cassettes and video discs will soon make carefully constructed audio-visual courses of the formal sort generally accessible. Looking a bit further ahead, the use of the home television screen as the visual display for items held in a computer will make stores of print and pictures available on request. Such resources – differentiated, permanent, repeatable, allowing selection and learner control – will serve the instructional element in 'learning' better by far than broadcasting can. Further, the home computer will be able to supply detailed information on demand (for which purpose, Ceefax, Oracle and Prestel are precursors). It should become easier than at present, therefore, to provide details of the learning materials and of the local learning opportunities which a broadcast may stimulate a viewer to pursue.

As this essay is being written, preparations have begun for the Fourth Channel. There has been the predictable demand that the time promised for education should be used for 'respectable', educational purposes – the dreaming spires of television education or at least a concrete-and-tile equivalent. Such visions have marked education by broadcasting from its earliest days and still haunt it. They explain how, in a recent public lecture, the then chairman of the BBC Governors, Sir Michael Swann, could describe education on broadcasting as 'a minority interest'. Images from formal education, like a will o' the wisp, have led broadcasters into the mire of inapt attempts at 'depth' and series of unwarrantable length. Similar notions have resulted in a frustrating and inadequate conception of 'educational copyright'. In Britain, relaxation of copyright is confined to certified educational broadcasts: in several continental countries, it is not some spurious distinctiveness in the type or origin of the broadcast, but the place and context of use which defines the exemption of any broadcast. An educational broadcast is simply a broadcast used educationally. Of the three obligations laid upon broadcasters – the 'dissemination of information, education and entertainment' – only education has attempted to establish a distinct signature, a particular style, a recognisable genre. Those concerned with the dissemination of 'information' or 'entertainment' accept that many departments – news, current affairs, documentary, features, drama, music, arts, sport, comedy, children's and the rest – can contribute to their wide purposes. 'Education' alone has been set into an identifiable education department, making a separate sort of programme with which, exclusively, educationists are supposed to be concerned.

We might now do well, if we could, to disregard the misleading form of words 'educational broadcasting' altogether. It has no merit other than brevity and is an example of the perils of reification. Rather, we need to think of 'education through broadcasting' (of many kinds and origins) and, as a sub-set of that, 'educationists' broadcasting', which is to say a portion of time and resources set aside for purposes which educationists can help decide. Similarly, in broadcasting (which respects no age barriers) the *significant* difference is not – as it is in educational institutions – between 'schools' and 'adult education' but between 'formal' and 'informal/oblique'. 'Educational broadcasting' has built a wall around itself, much as schools and universities have built walls between themselves and the disorganised learning nature of the surrounding community. If you build a wall, however, it's as well to be sure that what you keep in serves your purposes better than what you keep out, and in the case of education on television we may doubt that such has proved to be the case.

Now to extend the wall to enclose another small patch of orthodox education would be to persist in a self-defeating separateness. Education deals continually with excellence which exceeds, and with standards which often controvert, our immediate preferences. It harps upon considerations we would rather forget, and values we would rather ignore. It nags us to view the particular in relation to the general, the present as 'the latest moment of the past and the first moment of the future'. It is not a boundaried sector of activity (though professional institutionalisation has made it look so) but a pervading perspective. Education on broadcasting is not properly a thing apart from 'information' and 'entertainment'. It has to do with the more illuminating sort of information, as the means of promoting understanding; and the richer sort of entertainment, as the source of deep and lasting pleasure. Those broadcasters – whether officially 'educational' or not – who try to project long perspectives into their instant, hectic, transient, impressionistic medium have no easy task. That it has become an important one few would doubt: the time adults spend with television is greater in Britain than in any other European country, and at an average of four and a half hours a day exceeds time spent with all other media combined. In the eighties, educationists will certainly continue to serve the important if small minorities whose disposition or sharply-felt needs makes them willing to submit to somewhat austere, established rituals. But there are millions who prefer easier forms, which educationists can turn to account, as did the early Christian Fathers the pagan festivals. Still more than in the past, educationists in broadcasting will want to leave off their habit, to act as 'ordinaries' rather than 'peculiars', and to work with their many natural allies, beyond 'education' in broadcasting, and beyond the broadcast itself.

Bibliography

ACLAND, H. (1973) *The Social Determinants of Educational Achievement: An evaluation and criticism of research* Unpublished D.Phil thesis, Oxford University

ADVISORY CENTRE FOR EDUCATION (1979) *A Case for Alternative Schools within the Maintained System* London: Advisory Centre for Education

AINSWORTH, M. and BATTEN, E. (1974) *The Effects of Environmental Factors on Secondary Educational Attainment in Manchester: a Plowden follow-up* London: Macmillan

AMERICAN EDUCATIONAL RESEARCH ASSOCIATION (1935) *The Application of Research Findings to Current Educational Practice* Washington: National Education Association

ANNAN, N. (1977) (Chairman) *Report of the Committee on the Future of Broadcasting* London: HMSO

ANWEILER, O. (1969) *Bildungsreformen in Osteuropa* Kohlhammer

ARENDT, H. (1961) *Between Past and Future – Six Exercises in Political Thought* London: Faber and Faber

ARNOLD, M. (2nd ed. 1874) *High Schools and Universities in Germany* London: Macmillan

ASHCROFT, R. (1973) 'The school as a base for community development' in CERI, *School and Community* OECD

AULD REPORT, THE (1976) Report of inquiry into William Tyndale Junior and Infants Schools London: ILEA

BACON, W. (1978) *Public Accountability and the Schooling System* London: Harper and Row

BAIN, A. (1855) *The Senses and the Intellect* London: J.W. Parker & Son

BAIN, A. (1859) *The Emotions and the Will* London: J.W. Parker & Son

BAIN, A. (1868) *Mental and Moral Science* London: Longman

BAIN, A. (1879) *Education as a Science* London: Kegan Paul

BALL, C. and M. (1973) *Education for a Change* Harmondsworth: Penguin Books

BANKS, O. (1955) *Parity and Prestige in English Education* London: Routledge and Kegan Paul

BARNARD, H.C. (1969) *A History of English Education from 1760* London: University of London Press

BARNES, J. (1975a) *Educational Priority: 3* London: HMSO

BARNES, J. (ed.) (1975b) *Curriculum Innovation in London EPAs: 3* London: HMSO

BARNES, J. and LUCAS, H. (1975) 'Positive discrimination in education:

individuals, groups and institutions' in Barnes, J. (ed.) *Curriculum Innovation in London EPAs: 3*   London: HMSO

BARON, G. and HOWELL, D.A.   (1974)   *The Government and Management of Schools*   London: Athlone Press

BEATTIE, N.   (1978)   'Formalised parent participation in Europe: a comparative perspective'   *Comparative Education* 14 1

BEC, P.   (1963)   *La langue occitane*   Paris: Presses Universitaires de France

BECHER, A., ERAUT, M. and KNIGHT, J.   (1981)   *Policies for Educational Accountability*   London: Heinemann (in press)

BEECHER, A. and MACLURE, S.   (eds)   (1978)   *Accountability in Education*   Windsor: NFER Publishing Co.

BELL, R. and GRANT, N.   (1977)   *Patterns of Education in the British Isles*   London: Allen and Unwin

BERGER, J.   (1979)   *Pig Earth*   London: Writers and Readers Publishing Cooperative

BLOOM, B.S. *et al*   (1956)   *A Taxonomy of Educational Objectives I: The Cognitive Domain*   London: Longman

BLOOM, B.S. *et al*   (1964)   *A Taxonomy of Educational Objectives II: The Affective Domain*   London: Longman

BLOOM, B.S.   (1966)   'Twenty-five years of educational research'   *American Journal of Educational Research* 3

BOBBITT, F.   (1918)   *The Curriculum*   Austen: Houghton Mifflin

BOBBITT, F.   (1924)   *How to Make a Curriculum*   Austen: Houghton Mifflin

BOGDANOV, V.   (1979)   'Power and participation' *Oxford Review of Education*, 5 (2)

BOUDON, R.   (1974)   *Education, Opportunity and Social Inequality*   London: Wiley

BOURDIEU, P. and PASSERON, J.C.   (1977)   *Reproduction in Education, Society and Culture*   London: Sage

BOWLES, S. and GINTIS, H.   (1976)   *Schooling in Capitalist America*   London: Routledge

BOWMAN, M.J.   (1975)   'Education and opportunity: some economic perspectives'   *Oxford Review of Education*, I

BOYD, J.   (1977)   *Community Education and Urban Schools*   London: Longman

BRAVERMAN, H.   (1974)   *Labour and Monopoly Capital*   London: Monthly Review Press

BRIAULT, E. and SMITH, F.   (1980)   *Falling Rolls in Secondary Schools*   Windsor: NFER Publishing Co.

BRIDGES, D.   (1978)   'Participation and political education'   *Cambridge Journal of Education*, 8, 2 and 3

BRIDGES, D.   (1979)   *Education, Democracy and Discussion*   Windsor: NFER Publishing Co.

BRITTAIN, E.   (1976)   'Multi-racial education: teachers' opinions on aspects of school life, Part 2, *Educational Research*, 18

BROOKS, D. and SINGH, K.   (1978)   *Aspirations Versus Opportunities*   London: Community Relations Commission

BROUDY, H.S., SMITH, B.O. and BURNETT, J.R.   (1964)   *Democracy and Excellence in American Secondary Education*   Chicago: Rand McNally

BROWNE, S.J. (1979) 'A school for education' University of Exeter

BRUNER, J.S. (1972) *The Relevance of Education* London: Allen and Unwin

BURT, C. (1921) *Mental and Scholastic Tests* London: Staples Press

BURT, C. (1950) 'Testing intelligence' *The Listener*, 16 November

BUXTON, R.J. (1970) *Local Government* Harmondsworth: Penguin Books

BYRNE, E.M. (1974) *Planning and Educational Inequality* Windsor: NFER Publishing Co.

CHANAN, G. (1976) 'Levels of debate and levels of control – research and the Black Papers' *Forum for the Discussion of New Trends in Education* 19, 1

CHANAN, G. (1977) 'The curricular transaction: prescription and autonomy' in Edmund King (ed.) *Reorganizing Education: Management and participation for Change* London: Sage

CLIFFORD, G.J. (1973) 'A history of the impact of research on teaching' in Travers, R.M.W. *Second Handbook of Research on Teaching* Chicago: Rand McNally

COLEMAN, J.S. *et al* (1966) *Equality of Educational Opportunity* US Government Printing Office

COLEMAN, J.S. (1975) 'Methods and results in the IEA studies of effects of school on learning' *Review of Educational Research*, 45

COMMUNITY RELATIONS COMMISSION (1974) *The Response to the Select Committee on Race Relations and Immigration* London: CRC

COMMUNITY RELATIONS COMMISSION (1975) *Participation of Ethnic Minorities in the General Election, October 1974* London: CRC

COMMUNITY RELATIONS COMMISSION (1976a) *Urban Deprivation, Racial Inequality and Social Policy* London: HMSO

COMMUNITY RELATIONS COMMISION (1976b) *Funding Multi-racial Education: a national strategy* London: CRC

Compare (1978) 'Linguistic Minorities and National Unity' Special Number 8, 1

CORKERY, D. (1968) *The Fortunes of the Irish Language* Cork: Mercier

COUNCIL FOR EDUCATIONAL TECHNOLOGY (1978) *Micro-electronics: their Implications for Education and Training:* A statement by the Council London: CET

CROCKER, A.C. (1974) *Predicting Teaching Success* Windsor: NFER Publishing Co.

CRONBACH, L.J. and SUPPES, P. (eds) (1969) *Research for Tomorrow's Schools: a disciplined inquiry for teaching* London: Macmillan

CROWTHER REPORT, THE (1959) 15–18 London: HMSO

CUÍV, B.Ó. (1969) *A View of the Irish Language* Dublin: Stationery Office

DAHRENDORF, R. (1975) *The New Liberty* London: Routledge and Kegan Paul

DALIN, P. (1976) *Guidelines for Case Studies* (mimeograph) Norway: University of Oslo

DAVID, A.A. (1932) *Life and the Public Schools* Edinburgh: Maclehose

DEALE, R.N. (1979) 'The shadow over the sixth form' *Education* 8 June

DEAN, J. *et al* (1979) *The Sixth Form and its Alternatives* Windsor: NFER Publishing Co.

DEARLOVE, J. (1973) *The Politics of Policy in Local Government*

Cambridge: Cambridge University Press

DEPARTMENT OF EDUCATION AND SCIENCE (1977) *Circular 14/17* London: DES

DEPARTMENT OF EDUCATION AND SCIENCE (1977) *Education in Schools: A Consultative Document* (Green Paper), Cmnd. 6869, London: HMSO

DEPARTMENT OF EDUCATION AND SCIENCE (1978) *Higher Education into the 1990s: A Discussion Document* London: HMSO

DEPARTMENT OF EDUCATION AND SCIENCE (1979a) *Report on Education 96* London: DES

DEPARTMENT OF EDUCATION AND SCIENCE (1979b) *Statutes of Education 1976* London: HMSO

DEPARTMENT OF EDUCATION AND SCIENCE (1979c) *Aspects of Secondary Education in England* (A Survey by HMI) London: HMSO

DEPARTMENT OF EDUCATION AND SCIENCE (1979d) *Local Authority Arrangements for the Curriculum* London: HMSO

DEPARTMENT OF EDUCATION AND SCIENCE (1973) *A Basis for Choice* London: Further Education Curriculum Review and Development Unit

DEPARTMENT OF EDUCATION AND SCIENCE (1980) *A View of the Curriculum* London: HMSO

DEPARTMENT OF EDUCATION AND SCIENCE AND WELSH OFFICE (January 1980) *A Framework for the School Curriculum* London: DES

DIEZ, M., MORALES, F. and SABIN, A. (1977) *Las Lenguas de Espana* Madrid

DIVORKY, D. (1979) 'Burden of the '70s: the management of decline' *Phi Delta Kappa* October

DODGSON, C.J., PRICE, E. and WILLIAMS, I.T. (1968) *Towards Bilingualism: Welsh Studies in Education Vol. 1* Cardiff: University of Wales Press

DOE, V. (1978) 'Big fall in adviser numbers' *Times Educational Supplement* 3 November

DORE, R. (1976) *The Diploma Disease* London: Allen and Unwin

DRIVER, G. and BALLARD, R. (1979) 'Comparing performance in multiracial schools' *New Community* 11, 2

DUCKWORTH, E. (1979) 'Either we're too early and they can't learn it or we're too late and they know it already: The dilemma of "applying Piaget"' *Harvard Educational Review* 49, 3

DUNLOP, F. (1979) 'On the democratic organisation of schools' *Cambridge Journal of Education* 9, 1

EASTON, D. (1965) *A Systems Analysis of Political Life* New York: Wiley

EEC (1957) (a) & (b) Treaty Establishing the European Economic Community (Rome), 27 March, Article 57(a), Article 48(b)

EINSTEIN, A. (1947) Quoted in Suppes P (ed.) *Impact of Research on Education: Some Case Studies* Washington: National Academy of Education

EISNER, E.W. (1969) 'Instructional and expressive educational objectives: their formulation and use in curriculum 11–18' in Popham, Eisner, Sullivan and Tylor (1969) *Instructional Objectives* AERA Monograph Series on Curriculum Evaluation 3, Chicago: Rand, McNally

ELLIOT, J. (1980) 'Educational accountability and the evaluation of teaching' in A. Lewy (ed.) *Evaluation Roles* London: Gordon and Breach

ELLIS, T. et al (1977) *William Tyndale: The Teachers' Story* London: Readers and Writers Publishing Cooperative

ENTWISTLE, H. (1970) *Education, Work and Leisure* London: Routledge and Kegan Paul

ENTWISTLE, H. (1978) *Class, Culture and Education* London: Methuen

EQUAL PAY AND OPPORTUNITIES CAMPAIGN (1978) *Work and the Family* London: EPOC (159 Canonbury Park N1)

EQUAL PAY AND OPPORTUNITIES CAMPAIGN (1979) *Work and Parenthood* London: EPOC

ERAUT, M. (1981) 'Accountability at school level – some options and their implications' in Becher, Eraut and Knight *Policies for Educational Accountability* London: Heinemann

FAIRBAIRN, A.N. (1979) *The Leicestershire Community Colleges and Centres* University of Nottingham

FARMER, C. (1978) 'Falling rolls' letter in *Education* 22, September

FELKIN, H.M. and E. (1895) *An Introduction to Herbart's Science and Practice of Education* London: Routledge

FISKE, D.F. (1977) 'Secondary organisation in an Area' Paper circulated in connection with a conference on comprehensive education, December

FITCH, J. (1898 edn) *Lectures on Teaching* Cambridge: Cambridge University Press

FLETCHER, A.E. (ed) (2nd edn 1889) *Cyclopaedia of Education* Swan Sonnenschein

FORD, J. (1969) *Social Class and the Comprehensive School* London: Routledge and Kegan Paul

FORSYTH, J.P. and DOCKRELL, W.B. (1979) 'A case study of reaction to the Munn and Dunning Reports' Edinburgh: *Scottish Council for Research in Education*

FOWLER, G. (1976) Article in *The Guardian,* November

FRAGNIERE, G. (1976) *Education without Frontiers* London: Duckworth

FRAGNIERE, G. (1979) 'Is it too early for a European educational policy?' *European Journal of Education* 14, 4

FREEMAN, C. (1978) *Government Policies for Industrial Innovation* J.D. Bernal Memorial Lecture, Birkbeck College, London

FREEMAN, C. (1980) 'Government policy' in Pavitt, K. (ed.) *Technical Innovation and British Economic Performance* London: Macmillan

FROEBEL, F. (1912 edn) *The Education of Man* New York and London: Appleton

GALBRAITH, J.K. (1972) *The New Industrial State* London: Hamish Hamilton

GALTON, M., SIMON, B. and CROLL, P. (1980) *Inside the Primary Classroom* London: Routledge and Kegan Paul

GARLICK, A.H. (1896) *A New Manual of Method* London: Longmans Green

GLASS, G.V. and SMITH, M.L. (1978) 'The technology and politics of standards' *Educational Technology* 18, 5

GLAZER, N. (1975) *Affirmative Discrimination: Ethnic Inequality and Social Policy* New York: Basic Books

GOODHARDT, G.J., EHRENBURG, A.S.C. and COLLINS, M.A. (1975) *The Televi-*

sion Audience, Patterns of Viewing   London: Saxon House

GORDON, P. and LAWTON, D.   (1978)   *Curriculum Change in the Nineteenth and Twentieth Centuries*   London: Hodder and Stoughton

GORDON, P. and WHITE, J.   (1979)   *Philosophers as Educational Reformers*   London: Routledge and Kegan Paul

GORZ, A.   (1978)   'Technology, technicians and the class struggle' in Gorz, A. (ed.) *The Division of Labour*   London: Harvester Press

GOSDEN, P.H.J.H. and SHARP, P.R.   (1978)   *The Development of an Education Service, The West Riding 1889–1974*   Oxford: Martin Robertson

GRANT, N.   (1969)   *Society, Schools and Progress in Eastern Europe*   Oxford: Pergamon

GRANT, N. and MAIN, A.   (1976)   *Scottish Universities: the case for devolution*   Edinburgh: EUSPB

GRANT, N.   (1977)   'Educational policy and cultural pluralism: a task for comparative education'   *Comparative Education* 13, 2

GRANT, N.   (1979)   *Soviet Education*   Harmondsworth: Penguin Books

GRAY, J.   (1979a)   'The statistics of accountability'   *Education Policy Bulletin* 7, 1

GRAY, J.   (1979b)   'Reading progress in English infant schools: some problems emerging for a study of teacher effectiveness'   *British Educational Research Journal* 5, 2

GRAY, J.L. and MOSHINSKY, P.   (1938)   'Ability and opportunity in English education' in Hogben, L. (ed.) *Political Arithmetic*   London: Allen and Unwin

GRETTON, J. and JACKSON, M.   (1976)   *William Tyndale: Collapse of a School or a System?*   Times Educational Supplement/Allen and Unwin

GRUNDIN, P.   (1978)   *Open University Broadcasting: Results of the 1978 Survey and Overviews of Survey Results*   Milton Keynes: Open University Press

HALDANE, R.B.   (1923)   'An organized civil service'   *Journal of Public Administration* 1

HALL, P. et al   (1975)   *Change, Choice and Conflict in Social Policy*   London: Heinemann

HALLS, W.D.   (1974)   'Towards a European educational system?'   *Comparative Education* 10, 3

HALSEY, A.H.   (1972)   *Educational Priority I*   London: HMSO

HALSEY, A.H., HEATH, A.F., and RIDGE, J.M.   (1980)   *Origins and Destinations: family, class and education in modern Britain*   Oxford: Clarendon Press

HARGREAVES, D.   (1980)   *Adult Literacy and Broadcasting: the BBC's experience*   London: Frances Pinter

HARLEY, J.K. (ed.)   (1978)   'Other languages'   *McGill Journal of Education* Spring 13, 2

HENCKE, D.   (1978)   *Colleges in Crisis*   Harmondsworth: Penguin Books

HILL, D.M.   (1974)   *Democratic Theory and Local Government*   London: Allen and Unwin

HMI   (1977)   *Curriculum 11–16*   London: Department of Education and Science

HMI   (1979)   *Aspects of Secondary Education in England*   London: HMSO

HOLMES, G.   (1952)   *The Idiot Teacher*   London: Faber (reprinted, with

Preface by John Watts, Spokesman 1977)

HOLT, M. (1980) 'Catch a falling roll' *Times Educational Supplement* 25 May

HOLTERMANN, S. (1975) 'Areas of urban deprivation in Great Britain: an analysis of the 1971 census' *Social Trends* 6

HOME OFFICE (1974) *Educational Disadvantage and the Educational Needs of Immigrants* Cmnd. 5720 London: HMSO

HOME OFFICE (1975) *Racial Discrimination* Cmnd. 6234 London: HMSO

HONEY, J.R. de S. (1977) *Tom Brown's Universe* London: Millington

HOUGHTON, V. (1974) 'Recurrent education' in Houghton V, and Richardson, K. (eds) *Recurrent Education* London: Ward Lock Educational

HOUSE OF COMMONS DEBATES 906 (1976) March

HOUSE OF COMMONS DEBATES 912 (1976) May

HOUSE OF COMMONS DEBATES 964 (1979) March

HOUSE OF COMMONS DEBATES 1027 (1979) March

HOUSE, E.R. (1978) 'An American view of British accountability' in Becher, A. and Maclure, S. (eds) *Accountability in Education* Windsor: NFER Publishing Co

HOWELL, D.A. (1976) 'The government and management of schools reconsidered' *Research in Education* 16, Autumn

HURN, C.J. (1978) *Limits and Possibilities of Schooling* Boston: Allyn and Bacon

HUSSAIN, A. (1977) 'Crises and tendencies of capitalism' *Economy and Society* 6 4

HUTCHINSON, D. and MCPHERSON, A.F. (1976) 'Competing inequalities: the sex and social class structure of the first year Scottish university student population 1962–72' *Sociology* 10, 1

ILLICH, I.D. (1970) *Deschooling Society* London: Calder and Boyars

INDEPENDENT BROADCASTING AUTHORITY (1980) *Fiction and Depiction* (Audience Research Report) London: IBA

INTERNATIONAL REVIEW OF EDUCATION (1978) *Languages of Instruction in a Multi-Cultural Setting* (Special Number 24, 3) Hamburg: UNESCO

ISAACS, S. (1932) *The Children We Teach: 7 to 11 years* University of London Press

ISAACS, S. (1963 edn) *The Psychological Aspects of Child Development* London: Evans

JENCKS, C. (1973) *Inequality: A reassessment of the effect of family and schooling in America* London: Allen Lane

JENNINGS, R.E. (1977) *Education and Politics – policy making in LEAs* London: Batsford

JOHNSON, T. (1972) *Professions and Power* London: Macmillan

JONES, W.R. (1966) *Bilingualism in Welsh Education* Cardiff: University of Wales Press

KALTON, G. (1966) *The Public Schools: a factual survey* London: Longman

KANDEL, I. (1950) 'Educational research' *School and Society* University of Chicago Press

KAY, B.W. (1975) 'Monitoring pupils' performance' *Trends in Education* 2

KEDDIE, N. (1971) 'Classroom knowledge' in Young, M.F.D. (ed.) *Know-*

ledge and Control London: Collier Macmillan

KOGAN, M. (1978) *The Politics of Educational Change* London: Fontana

KUHN, T.S. (1962) *The Structure of Scientific Revolutions* University of Chicago Press

LAMKE, T. (1955) 'Introduction' *Review of Educational Research* June

LANDON, J. (1894) *The Principles and Practice of Teaching and Class Management* Oxford: Holden Press

LAWTON, D. (1973) *Social Change, Educational Theory and Curriculum Planning* London: Hodder and Stoughton

LAWTON, D. (1975) *Class, Culture and the Curriculum* London: Routledge and Kegan Paul

LEGGATT, T. (1970) 'Teaching as a profession' in Jackson, J.A. (ed.) *Professions and Professionalisation* Cambridge: Cambridge University Press

LEGGE, J.G. (1929) *The Rising Tide* Oxford: Blackwell

LEVIN, H.M. (1974) 'A conceptual framework for accountability in education' *School Review 82*

LILLEY, S. (1957) *Automation and Social Progress* London: Lawrence and Wishart

LINKLATER, E. (1971) *Orkney and Shetland* London: Robert Hale

LITTLE, A. and WESTERGAARD, J. (1964) 'Trends of class differentials in educational opportunity in England and Wales' *British Journal of Sociology*

LITTLE, A.N. (1975) 'Performance of children from ethnic minority backgrounds in primary schools' *Oxford Review of Education* I, 2

LOCKE, M. (1974) *Power and Politics in the School System* London: Routledge and Kegan Paul

LORTIE, D.C. (1975) *Schoolteacher: a sociological study* University of Chicago Press

LUKES, S. (1974) *Power: A Radical View* London: Macmillan

LURIA, A.R. (1962) *Voprosy Psikhologii* 1962, 4

LYNCH, J. (1979) *The Reform of Teacher Education in the United Kingdom* Guildford: Society for Research into Higher Education

MACDONALD, B. (1978) 'Accountability standards and the process of schooling' in Becher, A. and Maclure, S. (eds) *Accountability in Education* Windsor: NFER Publishing Co.

MACDONALD, B. (1979) 'Hard times: educational accountability in England' *Educational Analysis* I, I

MACKENZIE, N., POSTGATE, R. and SCUPHAM, J. (1975) *Open Learning* UNESCO Press

MACLURE, S. (1978) 'Background to the accountability debate' in Becher, A. and Maclure, S. *Accountability in Education* Windsor: NFER Publishing Co.

MCKINNON, K. (1974) *The Lion's Tongue* Inverness: Club Leabhar

MCKINNON, K. (1977) *Language, Education and Social Processes in a Gaelic Community* London: Routledge and Kegan Paul

MCCLURE, J.D., AITKEN, A.J. and LOW, J.T. (1980) The *Scots Language: planning for modern usage* Edinburgh: Ramsey Head

MABEY, C. (1974) 'Social and ethnic mix in schools and the relationship with attainment of children aged 8 and 11' *Centre for Environmental Studies*, Research Paper 9, London: CES

MANDER, J. (1980) *Four Arguments for the Elimination of Television* Brighton: Harvester Press

MARKS, C.T. (1976) 'Policy and attitudes towards the teaching of standard dialect in Great Britain, France, West Germany' *Comparative Education* 12, 3

MASON, S. (ed.) (1970) *In Our Experience* London: Longman

MIDWINTER, E. (1973) *Patterns of Community Education* London: Ward Lock Educational

MILGRAM, S. (1974) *Obedience to Authority* London: Tavistock

MILNER, D. (1975) *Education and Race* Harmondsworth: Penguin Education

MINISTRY OF EDUCATION (1950) *Report and Statistics for 1950* London: HMSO

MITTER, W. (1979) *Secondary School Graduation: University entrance qualifications in socialist countries* Oxford: Pergamon

MOORE, T.W. (1974) *Educational Theory, an Introduction* London: Routledge and Kegan Paul

MORGAN, C. (1980) 'Common core curriculum: the main issue for government' *Educational Research*: 22, 3

MURPHY, G. (1938) *Historical Introduction to Modern Psychology* New York: Harcourt, Brace

NAIPAUL, V.S. (1977) *India: A Wounded Civilisation* London: Deutsch

NASH, R., WILLIAMS, H. and EVANS, M. (1976) 'The one-teacher school' *British Journal of Educational Studies* XXIV, 1

NASH, R. (1978) 'Perceptions of the village school' in Williams, C. (ed.) *Social and Cultural Change in Contemporary Wales* London: Routledge and Kegan Paul

NATIONAL COUNCIL FOR EDUCATIONAL RESEARCH (1978) *4th Annual Report* Washington: National Institute of Education

NATIONAL SOCIETY FOR THE STUDY OF EDUCATION (1938) *The Scientific Movement in Education* 37th Yearbook Bloomington: Public Schools Publishing Co.

NEWSAM, P. (1978) 'To plan or not to plan' *Times Educational Supplement* 20 January

NEWSOM REPORT, THE (1963) *Half our Future* London: HMSO

NEWSOME, D. (1961) *Godliness and Good Learning* London: Murray

NISBET, J. and BROADFOOT, P. (1980) *The Impact of Research on Policy and Practice in Education* Aberdeen: University of Aberdeen Press

OFFICE OF POPULATION CENSUS AND SURVEYS (1977) *Monitor* No. 1

O'KEEFE, D.J. (1979) 'Capitalism and correspondence: a critique of Marxist analyses of education' *Higher Education Review* Autumn

OPEN UNIVERSITY, THE (1977) *Education, Equity and Income Distribution* (Block V of Open University Course ED322) Milton Keynes: The Open University Press

O'TOOLE, J. (1975) 'Work and the quality of life' in Dyckman, W.V. (ed.) *Life-long Learners: A New Clientele for Adult Education* London: Jossey-Bass

OWEN, J. (1978) 'A new partnership for our schools: The Taylor Report, *Oxford Review of Education* 4, 1

PARKER, S. (1971) *The Future of Work and Leisure* London: Paladin Books

PARKIN, F. (1979) *Marxism and Class Theory: a Bourgeois Critique* London: Tavistock

PATEMAN, C. (1970) *Participation and Democratic Theory* Cambridge: Cambridge University Press

PATTON, M.Q. (1980) *Utilization – Focussed Evaluation* London: Sage

PAVITT, K. (ed.) (1980) *Technical Innovation and British Economic Performance* London: Macmillan

PEAKER, G.F. (1967) 'The regression analysis of the National Survey' Plowden Report 2, Appendix 4

PEAKER, G.F. (1971) *The Plowden Children Four Years Later* Windsor: NFER Publishing Co.

PETERSON, A.D.C. (1977) 'Applied comparative education: The International Baccalaureate *Comparative Education* 13, 2

PICKERING, D.M. (1973) 'Education in the Channel Islands' in Bell, R.E., Fowler, J. and Little, K. (eds) *Education in Great Britain and Ireland* London: Open University Press/Routledge and Kegan Paul

PILE, W. (1976) *Decision Making in DES* (10th Report of the Expenditure Committee, House of Commons) London: HMSO

PLOWDEN REPORT, THE (1967) *Children and their Primary Schools* London: HMSO

POLLAK, M. (1972) *Today's Three-year Olds in London* London: Heinemann

POPHAM, W.J. (1978) 'Practical criterion-referenced measures for intrastate evaluation' *Educational Technology* 18, 5 May

PSACHAROPOULOS, G. (1977) 'Family Background, Education and Achievement' *British Journal of Sociology* 28:3

QUICK, R.H. (1869) *Essays on Educational Reformers* London: Longmans Green

RAY, D. and LAMONTAGNE, J. (eds) (1977) *Cultural Diversity and Political Unity* Montreal: World Council for Comparative Education Societies

RAY, D. (1978) 'Cultural pluralism and the reorientation of educational policy in Canada' *Comparative Education* 14, 1

REDBRIDGE COMMUNITY RELATIONS COUNCIL (1978) 'Cause for concern: West Indian pupils in Redbridge', Black Peoples' Professional Association

REE, H. (1973) *Educator Extraordinary, The Life and Achievement of Henry Morris* London: Longman

REID, M.I. (1979) 'Common core curriculum: reflections on the current debate' *Educational Research* 20, 2

RICHARDSON, E. (1973) *The Teacher, the School and the Task of Management* London: Heinemann

RINEHART, J.W. (1975) *The Tyranny of Work* Longman of Canada

ROBBINS REPORT, THE (1963) Committee on Higher Education London: HMSO

ROSENSHINE, B. and MCGAW, B. (1972) 'Assessing teachers in public education' *Phi Delta Kappa* 44, 10

ROSS, J.M. *et al* (1972) *A Critical Appraisal of Comprehensive Education* Windsor: NFER Publishing Co.

ROTHSCHILD REPORT, THE (1971) *A Framework for Government Research and Development* London: HMSO

RUSSELL, M. and PRATT J. (1979) 'Numerical changes in the Colleges of Higher Education' *Higher Education Review* 12, 1, Autumn

RUTTER, M.L. *et al* (1974) 'Children of West Indian Immigrants I: Rates of behavioural deviance and of psychiatric disorder' *Journal of Child Psychology and Psychiatry* 15

RUTTER, M.L. *et al* (1975) 'Children of West Indian Immigrants III: Home circumstances and family patterns' *Journal of Child Psychology and Psychiatry* 16

RUTTER, M.L. *et al* (1979) *Fifteen Thousand Hours: Secondary Schools and their Effects on Children* London: Open Books

SAHLINS, M. (1976) *Culture and Practical Reason* University of Chicago Press

SALLIS, J. (1977) *School Managers and Governors – Taylor and After* London: Ward Lock

SALMON, D. (1898) *The Art of Teaching* London: Longmans

SCHON, D.A. (1971) *Beyond the Stable State* New York: Norton

SCHUMPETER, J.A. (1943) *Capitalism, Socialism and Democracy* London: Allen and Unwin

SCOTTISH COUNCIL FOR RESEARCH IN EDUCATION (1975) *47th Annual Report* Edinburgh: SCRE

SCRIMSHAW, P. (1975) 'Should schools be participatory democracies?' in Bridges, D. and Scrimshaw, P. (eds) *Values and Authority in Schools* London: Hodder and Stoughton

SECONDARY HEADS ASSOCIATION (1979a) 'How will my school be affected?' *Working Party on Falling Rolls Paper II* London: SHA

SECONDARY HEADS ASSOCIATION (1979b) *Big is Beautiful* London: SHA

SELECT COMMITTEE ON RACE RELATIONS AND IMMIGRATION (1973) *Education*

SELECT COMMITTEE ON RACE RELATIONS AND IMMIGRATION (1976–1977) *The West Indian Community*

SÉRANT, P. (1965) *La France des Minorités* Paris: Laffont

SHARP, L.M. and FRANKEL, J. (1979) 'Organisations that perform educational R & D: a first look at the universe' *Educational Researcher* 8, 11

SCHULMAN, M. (1973) *The Ravenous Eye: the impact of the fifth factor* London: Cassell

SILVER, H. (1973) *Equal Opportunity in Education: a reader in social class and educational opportunity* London: Methuen

SIMON, B. (1965) *Education and the Labour Movement, 1870–1920* London: Lawrence and Wishart

SIMON, B. and BRADLEY, I. (eds) (1975) *The Victorian Public School* Dublin: Gill and Macmillan

SKILBECK, M. and HARRIS, A. (1976) *Culture, Ideology and Knowledge* (Units 3 and 4 of Open University Course E203(Milton Keynes: The Open University Press

SKILBECK, M. (1980) *A Core Curriculum for Australian Schools* Canberra:

Curriculum Development Centre

SMITH, G. and JAMES, T. (1975) 'Effects of pre-school education' *Oxford Review of Education* 1, 3

SMITH, B.O., STANLEY, W.O. and SHORES, J.H. (1957) *Fundamentals of Curriculum Development* New York: Harcourt Brace and World

SOCKETT, H. (1976) *Designing the Curriculum* London: Open Books

SOCKETT, H. (ed.) (1980) *Accountability in the English Education System* London: Hodder and Stoughton

SOMERSET, C. (1938) *Littledene: Patterns of Change* New Zealand Department of Education

SPEARMAN, C. (1927) *The Nature of 'Intelligence' and the Principles of Cognition* London: Macmillan

SPENCER, D. (1980) 'Primary goes to High Court over closure' *Times Educational Supplement* 18 January

SPOONER, R. (1979) 'The end of the ladder' *Education* 4 May

STAKE, R.E. (1973) 'Measuring what learners learn' in House, E.R. (ed.) *School Evaluation, the Politics and Progress* Berkeley: McCutchen

STANYER, J. (1976) *Understanding Local Government* Part II London: Fontana

STEEDMAN, H. (1979) 'The education of migrant workers' children in EEC countries: from assimilation to cultural pluralism?' *Comparative Education* 15, 3, October

STEEDMAN, J. (1980) *Progress in Secondary Schooling: Findings from the National Child Development Study* London: National Childrens Bureau

STENHOUSE, L. (1975) *An Introduction to Curriculum Research and Development* London: Heinemann

STEPHENS, M. (1976) *Linguistic Minorities in Western Europe* Llandysul (Dyfed) Gomer Press

STONES, E. (1979) *Psychopedagogy: Psychological Theory and the Practice of Teaching* London: Methuen

STORR, F. (ed.) (1889) *Life and Remains of the Rev. R.H. Quick* Cambridge: Cambridge University Press

STRADLING, R. (1977) *The Political Awareness of the School Leaver* London: Hansard Society

STRINGER, D. (1979) *Make it Count* London: Independent Broadcasting Authority

TAYLOR REPORT, THE (1977) *A New Partnership for our Schools* London: HMSO

TAYLOR, B. (1978) 'Week by week' *Education* 6 October

TAYLOR, J.H. (1976) *The Halfway Generation* Windsor: NFER Publishing Co.

TAYLOR, W. (1963) *The Secondary Modern School* London: Faber and Faber

TAYLOR, W. (1973) *Research Perspectives in Education* London: Routledge and Kegan Paul

TAYLOR, W. (1978a) *Research and reform in Teacher Education* Windsor: NFER Publishing Co.

TAYLOR, W. (1978b) 'Values and accountability' in Becher, A. and Maclure, S. *Accountability in Education* Windsor: NFER Publishing Co.

THOMAS, R. (1978) *The British Philosophy of Administration* London: Longman

THOMSON, D. (1978) *Gaelic in Scotland* Glasgow: Gairm

TIZARD, B. (1974) *Pre-School Education in Britain* Social Science Research Council

TOWN, S.W. (1974) in Morrison, C.M. (ed.) *Educational Priority 5: EPA – a Scottish study* Edinburgh: HMSO

TOWNSEND, H.E.R. (1971) *Immigrant Pupils in England: The LEA Response* Windsor: NFER Publishing Co.

TOWNSEND, H.E.R. and BRITTAIN, E.M. (1972) *Organisation in Multi-racial Schools* Windsor: NFER Publishing Co.

TRAVERS, R.M.W. (1978) *An Introduction to Educational Research* 4th edition London: Macmillan

TUCK, M.G. (1974) 'The effect of different factors on the level of academic achievement in England and Wales' *Social Science Research* 3

TYLER, R. (1949) *Basic Principles of Curriculum and Instruction* Chicago: University of Chicago Press

URBAN DEPRIVATION, RACIAL INEQUALITY AND SOCIAL POLICY – a Report (1976) London: HMSO

VARLAAM, A. (1974) 'Educational attainment and behaviour at school' *Greater London Intelligence Quarterly* 29, December

VIGOTSKI, L.S. (1962) *Thought and Language* London: Wiley

VIGOTSKI, L.S. (1963) 'Learning and mental development at school age' in Simon, B. and Simon, J. (eds) *Educational Psychology in the USSR* London: Routledge and Kegan Paul

VIGOTSKI, L.S. (1967) Vigotskian Memorial Issue of *Soviet Psychology and Psychiatry* 5, 3

VILLEMARQUE, H. de la (1977) *Aux origines du nationalisme breton* (2) Paris: Union Générale d'Editions

WARD, J. (1926) *Psychology Applied to Education* Cambridge: Cambridge University Press

WARING, M. (1979) *Social Pressures and Curriculum Innovation* London: Methuen

WATTS, J.F. (ed) (1977) *The Countesthorpe Experience* London: Allen and Unwin

WATTS, J.F. (ed.) (1980) *Towards an Open School* London: Longman

WEBB, D. (1979) 'Home and school: parental views' *Education 3–13* 7, 2

WEISS, C.H. (ed.) (1977) *Using Social Research in Public Policy Making* Lexington: Heath

WESTERGAARD, J. and RESLER, H. (1975) *Class in a Capitalist Society: A Study of Contemporary Britain* London: Heinemann

WESTMAN, J.C., ARTHUR, B. and SCHLEIDLER, E.P. (1965) 'Reading retardation: an overview' *American Journal of Disadvantaged Children*

WHITE, J.P. (1973) *Towards a Compulsory Curriculum* London: Routledge and Kegan Paul

WHITE, J.P. (1976) 'Teacher accountability and school autonomy' *Proceedings of the Philosophy of Education Society of Great Britain* 10

WHITE, P. (1977) 'Political education in a democracy: the implications for teacher education' *Journal of Further and Higher Education* 1, 3

WHITE, P. (1979) 'Work-place democracy and political education' *Journal of Philosophy of Education* 13

WHITEHORNE, J. (1977) 'Temporary promotion: a substitute for mobility' *Times Higher Education Supplement* 25 March

WILLIAMS, I.T. (1968) *Towards Bilingualism* Welsh Studies in Education I Cardiff: University of Wales Press

WILLIAMS, R. (1958) *Culture and Society* Harmondsworth: Penguin Books

WILLIAMS, R. (1961) *The Long Revolution* Harmondsworth: Penguin Books

WILLIS, P. (1977) *Learning to Labour: how working-class kids get working-class jobs* London: Saxon House

WILSON, B. (1975) Introduction to Wilson, B. (ed.) *Education, Equality and Society* London: Allen and Unwin

WISE, A.E. (1977) 'Why education policies often fail: the hyperrationalization hypothesis' *Journal of Curriculum Studies*

WOODS, P. (1979) *The Divided School* London: Routledge and Kegan Paul

WOOLLCOMBE, D.R. (1978) *Tvind, Subsistence Education* London: David Woollcombe

WORSLEY, T.C. (1967) *Flannelled Fools* London: Alan Ross

WRIGHT, N. (1977) *Progress in Education* London: Croom Helm

Index